Internationaler Designpreis
Baden-Württemberg

Baden-Württemberg
International Design Award

Design Center
Stuttgart

avedition

Ernst Pfister	04	**Ernst Pfister**
Focus Open 2010		Focus Open 2010
Gutes Design ebnet den Weg		Good design pav...
zu wirtschaftlichem Erfolg		business succes...

Ernst Pfister — 04
Focus Open 2010
Gutes Design ebnet den Weg
zu wirtschaftlichem Erfolg

Johannes Schmalzl und Sabine Lenk — 06
Der Wettbewerb
Herausragendes Design prämieren,
echte Innovationen präsentieren und
Trends aufspüren

Juroren Statements — 08 – 19
Einblicke – Ausblicke
Ralf Christoffer — 08
Roland de Fries — 10
Matthias Held — 12
Iris Laubstein — 14
Christophe Marchand — 16
Karin Schmidt-Ruhland — 18

Ernst Pfister
Focus Open 2010
Good design pav...
business succes...

Johannes Schma...
The competition
Honouring excell...
presenting true i...
identifying trend...

Judges' stateme...
Insights – outloo...
Ralf Christoffer
Roland de Fries
Matthias Held
Iris Laubstein
Christophe Marc...
Karin Schmidt-R...

Andrea Scholtz	20 – 207
Wettbewerbsergebnisse	
Produktion, Montage, Logistik	20
Kommunikation, Audio / Video, Optik	42
Medizin, Rehabilitation, Geriatrie	50
Bad, Sanitär, Wellness	60
Küche, Haushalt	66
Tisch- und Küchenkultur	82
Wohnen	96
Objekt	120
Ambiente, Lifestyle	138
Beleuchtung	158
Freizeit, Outdoor	168
Sport	180
Kids, Familie	184
Architektur	188
Public Design	198
Transport, Verkehr	200

Wolfgang Berger	208 – 222
Mia Seeger Preis 2010	

Appendix	223 – 236
Adressen	224
Hersteller,	
Designer	
und Vertriebe	
Namenregister	232
Fotonachweis	234
Impressum	236

Andrea Scholtz	20 – 207
Results of the competition	
Production, assembly, logistics	20
Communication, audio / video, optical equipment	42
Medicine, rehabilitation, geriatric medicine	50
Bathrooms, sanitary installations, wellness	60
Kitchen, household	66
Tableware and kitchenware	82
Living	96
Contract furniture	120
Ambience, lifestyle	138
Lighting	158
Leisure, outdoor	168
Sport	180
Children, family	184
Architecture	188
Public design	198
Transport, traffic	200

Wolfgang Berger	208 – 222
Mia Seeger Prize 2010	

Appendix	223 – 236
Addresses	224
Manufacturers,	
designers	
and distributors	
Index of names	232
Photographs (acknowledgements)	234
Publishing details	236

Ernst Pfister MdL Wirtschaftsminister des Landes Baden-Württemberg

Gutes Design ebnet den Weg zu wirtschaftlichem Erfolg. Dies hat mehrere Gründe: Kunden verlangen heute beim Kauf eines neuen Produktes nach einer professionellen Gestaltung. Das Produktdesign gibt dem Kunden eine erste Auskunft über die Wertigkeit eines Gegenstandes. Gleichzeitig wird über die Gestaltung eine bestimmte Zielgruppe angesprochen. Nicht zuletzt kann sich ein Produkt durch eine prägnante Gestaltung aber auch von Wettbewerbsangeboten absetzen.

Kompetentes Design trägt dazu bei, den Wert eines Produktes zu steigern. Denn gutes Design erhöht den Gebrauchswert, etwa dadurch, dass das Produkt intuitiv zu benutzen ist und Fehlbedienungen vermieden werden. Professionelle Gestaltung muss den Kunden beim Gebrauch überzeugen. Hierzu muss das Produkt optimal auf den Anwender abgestimmt sein.

Ein schlüssiges Designkonzept beinhaltet viele Bereiche, angefangen beim Produktdesign, der Verpackungsgestaltung, dem Interfacedesign bis zum Kommunikationsdesign. Design – will es erfolgreich sein - muss als Entwicklungsprozess vom Anfang bis zum Ende verstanden werden.

Innovation und Kreativität sind der Nährboden für nachhaltiges Wachstum und Beschäftigung. Baden-Württemberg weiß dies längst, ist doch unsere Region, ohne nennenswerte Bodenschätze, das Land der »Tüftler und Denker«. Unsere Unternehmen haben es verstanden, kreative Strategien mit gut fundierten Geschäftsmodellen zu verknüpfen.

Vielen Unternehmen aus Baden-Württemberg gelang es erfolgreich, eine Marke zu schaffen. Marken kann man als Mythen des Alltags betrachten. Verbraucher benutzen Produkte als Vermittler von Botschaften. Dieser Mehrwert von Design stellt einen emotionalen Nutzen in der Gefühlswelt seines Besitzers dar. Vielen fallen hier sicherlich zuerst Beispiele aus der Automobilbranche sowie dem Maschinenbau ein, aber Baden-Württemberg ist auch in anderen Bereichen wie der Medizintechnik oder der Optik stark aufgestellt.

Der Schnelleinsatzkran »81 K« besitzt ein innovatives Konstruktionsprinzip, das eine enorme Anpassungsfähigkeit an unterschiedliche Baustellensituationen und Anforderungen bietet.

So lässt er sich im zusammengeklappten Transportzustand durch ein modulares Achssystem bequem und sicher auch auf schwer zugängliche Baustellen transportieren. Dank einem ausgeklügelten Aufstellmechanismus kann er auf geringstem Raum aufgebaut werden. Der teleskopierbare Turm erlaubt ganz nach Bedarf Arbeitshöhen zwischen 25 und 55 Metern und eine Auslegerreichweite von 31 bis 45 Metern.

Bei der Neuentwicklung wurden zum einen die funktionalen Aspekte des Krans in die Gestaltung integriert und zum anderen markante Corporate Merkmale entwickelt, die »81 K« von nah und fern als Liebherr Kran definieren. So wurde für die Statikstruktur der Drehbühne eine dynamische Linienführung entworfen und als stabile und optisch tragende Plattform ausgebildet.

Die Schaltschränke sind in die Gestaltung eingebunden und unterstützen die kraftvolle Basis des Krans. Deren schräge Farbtrennung greift als dynamisches Element die Linien der Drehbühne wieder auf, gibt so dem Kran eine Richtung und schafft als markantes Gestaltungselement ein hohes Wiedererkennungsmerkmal. Die Schaltschranktüren lassen sich nach oben öffnen. Das ermöglicht nicht nur optimale Zugänglichkeit und Bedienbarkeit sondern dient zugleich als Wetterschutz.

Die großflächigen Scheiben der Kabine garantieren eine optimale Rundumsicht. Ihre Tönung verringert das Erhitzen der Kabine und bietet Blendschutz. Durch den markanten Scheibenzuschnitt wird der Kran auch von ferne als Liebherr Kran erkennbar.

Jury

Dieser Kran verkörpert deutlich das Schnelle, Mobile, Leichte, Transparente. Bei ihm wurde zum einen die gute Komprimierbarkeit und Transportabilität und der schnelle Aufbau optimiert. Zum anderen wurde das Corporate Design so weiterentwickelt, dass der Kran schon von weitem als Liebherr-Kran erkannt werden kann, was durch verschiedene gestalterische Maßnahmen überzeugend umgesetzt wurde. Ein hochinnovatives Produkt.

The »81K« fast-erecting crane is based on an innovative design principle that makes it extremely adaptable to different construction site topographies and requirements.

When knocked down for transport it can conveniently and safely be transported to poorly accessible construction sites, thanks to its modular axle system. A sophisticated erecting mechanism allows it to be set up in the smallest of spaces. Its telescopic tower allows working heights of between 25 and 55 metres, and a maximum radius of between 31 and 45 metres.

In this new development, the functional features of the crane have been integrated in the design. At the same time, striking corporate characteristics have been created that identify the »81 K« as a Liebherr crane from close up and far away. When designing the statics of the support base, for example, a dynamic layout was chosen that gives the load-bearing platform a stable appearance.

The switch panels are integrated in the design, and add to the idea of the crane's powerful base. The oblique line separating different blocks of colour is a dynamic element that repeats the lines of the turning platform, giving a direction to the crane. As a striking design element, it creates a highly recognizable feature. The hoods covering the switch panels open upwards. This not only allows optimum access and ease of operation, but also gives protection from the elements.

The large panes of the cabin ensure the best possible all-round vision. They are tinted to prevent over-heating and to protect against glare. The distinctive shape of the panes means that the crane is identifiable from a distance as a Liebherr crane.

Judges panel

The crane embodies speed, mobility, lightness and transparency. A crane that has been optimized in terms of its transport volume and transportability, as well as speed of erection. Moreover, corporate design has been developed further to create a crane that is recognizable from a distance as a Liebherr product. The various design elements used to achieve this work very well. An extremely innovative product.

Rontron-RJ-Edelstahl Befehlsgeräte
Produktion, Montage, Logistik **Silber**

Control units
Production, assem

Befehlsgeräte sind die »Visitenkarte« einer Maschine. Die neuen Tasten der Baureihe »Rontron-RJ-Edelstahl« werden in Bedientableaus von Maschinen und Geräten eingesetzt und stehen damit an der Schnittstelle Mensch-Maschine. Sie verbinden Bedienerfreundlichkeit mit technischer Funktionalität und zeichnen sich durch ihre Ergonomie, ihre exzellente Qualität und ihr innovatives Design aus.

Zudem sind sie robust, sodass sie auch rauen Einsatzorten standhalten. Die sehr flachen Betätiger – sie sind gerade mal zwei Millimeter hoch – bestechen durch ihr elegantes Erscheinungsbild, das durch ihre runde Form und ihre hochwertige Edelstahloberfläche noch unterstrichen wird. Neben den laserbeschriftbaren Betätigern mit Ringbeleuchtung, den beleuchtbaren Wahl- und den Schlüsseltasten sind auch beschrift- und beleuchtbare Folientasten mit Edelstahlfrontring erhältlich. Bei der Ringbeleuchtung kann zusätzlich die LED-Farbe gewählt und damit den individuellen Bedürfnissen angepasst werden.

Mit diesem modularen Baukastensystem hat der Anwender beim Einrichten von anspruchsvollen Bedienoberflächen zahlreiche Gestaltungsmöglichkeiten.

Jury

Hochwertige Bedienelemente, die nahezu formschlüssig in die Fläche integriert sind. Schöne grafische Bearbeitung. Sehr gelungen finden wir auch die Farbkodierung. Die Tasten bekommen vor allen Dingen durch ihre Hinterleuchtung ein sehr markantes und signifikantes Erscheinungsbild.

Control units are a machine's »calling card«. The new pushbuttons in the »Rontron-RJ-Edelstahl« series are used in the control panels of machines and appliances, and are thus positioned at the human-machine interface. They combine user-friendliness and technical functionality, and stand out by virtue of their ergonomics, excellent quality and innovative design.

They are also robust, and suitable for use in tough environments. The extremely flat actuators – they are just two millimetres high – are strikingly elegant, and this elegance is further underscored by their round shape and high-quality stainless-steel surface. The series includes laser-printable pushbuttons with ring-shaped illumination, illuminable selector switches and key-operated buttons, as well as printable and illuminable touch keys with a stainless steel bezel. There is also a choice of colours for the ring-shaped LED illumination, allowing the pushbuttons to be adapted to customers' requirements.

This modular kit system allows the user to select from a wide range of design options when designing upmarket user interfaces.

Judges panel

High-quality operating elements that are integrated almost flush into the panel surface. Elegant graphic adaptation. We also think the colour-coding is very well done. With their backlighting especially, the pushbuttons have been given a very striking and meaningful appearance.

VMT6000 Serie   Terminal
                         Produktion, Montage, Logistik   **Silber**

Terminal
Production, assen

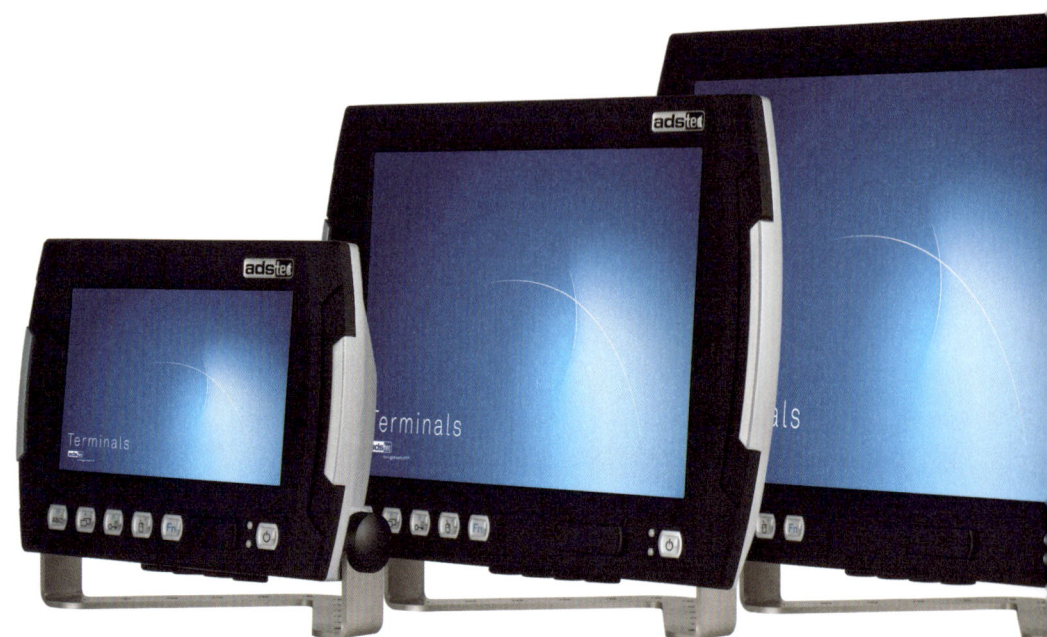

Schön, schlank und robust sind die PC-kompatiblen Terminals der »VMT6000 Serie«. Sie wurden eigens für die rauen Umgebungsbedingungen des industriellen Alltags geschaffen. Durch die sehr kompakte Bauweise des All-In-One-Gerätes sind sie sehr vielseitig einsetzbar. Sie leisten zuverlässig ihre Arbeit in der Logistik als Stapler- und Buchungsterminal, als Visualisierungs- und Bedieneinheit in der Automation, auf Fahrzeugen, als stationäres und mobiles Mess- und Diagnosegerät sowie im Healthcare Bereich.

So müssen sie hart im Nehmen sein. Dafür sorgt der vibrationsunkritische Aufbau sowie das stabile Aluminium Druckgussgehäuse mit einer Frontblende aus glasfaserverstärktem lackiertem Kunststoff. Die WLAN-Antennen sind zur Vermeidung von Zerstörung und Diebstahl in der Frontblende integriert. Zudem bieten sie einen per Software deaktivierbaren Front-USB und integrierte Lautsprecher. Die Schnittstellen sind unter einer Abdeckung gut geschützt. Die sehr stabilen und lüfterlosen Terminals sind für einen erweiterten Temperaturbereich tauglich – von minus 20 bis plus 55 Grad Celsius.

Sie bestechen aber auch durch ihre klare, übersichtliche und attraktive Gestaltung sowie durch ihre Nutzerfreundlichkeit – sie lassen sich über fünf Fronttasten komfortabel bedienen. Das Terminal ist in drei Bildschirmgrößen erhältlich: 8, 12 und 15 Zoll. Für die Montage an unterschiedlichen Einsatzorten sind verschiedene Halterungen verfügbar, die alle aus stabilem Edelstahl verschleißfest gearbeitet sind.

Jury

Das ist eine Serie von sehr robust ausgeführten Terminals, die auch in der Anmutung die Aussage wiederholen, für den Einsatz im Heavy-Duty-Bereich, also wo es rau zugeht und mitunter das Terminal auch mit Stößen ramponiert wird. Die Gestaltung gibt darauf sehr gute und überzeugende Antworten sowohl von der funktionalen als auch von der ästhetischen Seite her.

The PC-compatible terminals in the »VMT6000« series are elegant, slim and sturdy. They have been created especially for the tough conditions of everyday industrial operation. The extremely compact design of these all-in-one devices makes them very versatile. They are a reliable helper in logistics as a terminal for stacking and booking, in automation as a visualizing and operating unit, in vehicles as a stationary and mobile diagnostic device, and in healthcare.

They have to be tough. This toughness is provided by their vibration-resistant construction and by their sturdy die-cast aluminium housing with a front panel made of glass fibre-reinforced and varnished plastic. To prevent damage and theft, the WLAN antennas are integrated in the front panel. There is also a front USB, which can be deactivated by software, and integrated loudspeakers. The interfaces are well protected beneath a cover. The very sturdy, fanless terminals are designed to work in a wide temperature range – from minus 20 to plus 55 degrees Celsius.

They stand out by virtue of their clear and attractive design and of their user-friendliness – they are easy to operate, using five keys in the front panel. The terminal is available in three different screen sizes: 8", 12" and 15". Various brackets are available for mounting them in different places of use. All brackets are made of hard-wearing stainless steel.

Judges panel

This is a series of very sturdily designed terminals, whose appearance also underscores the message that they are made for use in the heavy-duty world, where conditions are tough and the terminal will be banged about occasionally. The design provides excellent, convincing answers to this challenge, both functionally and aesthetically.

Gallus ECS 340 Etikettendruckmaschine Label printer
Produktion, Montage, Logistik **Silber** Production, assem

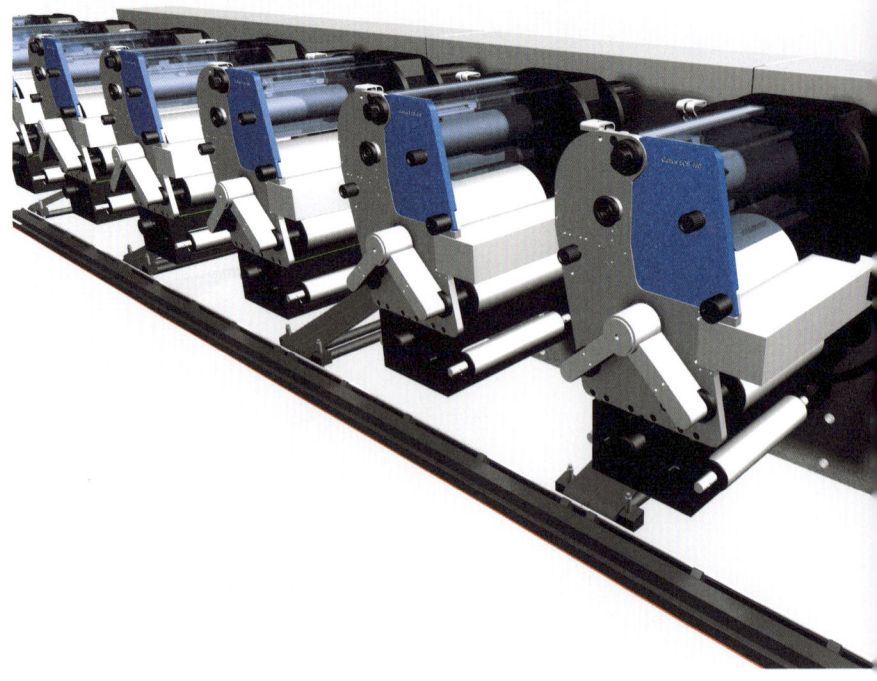

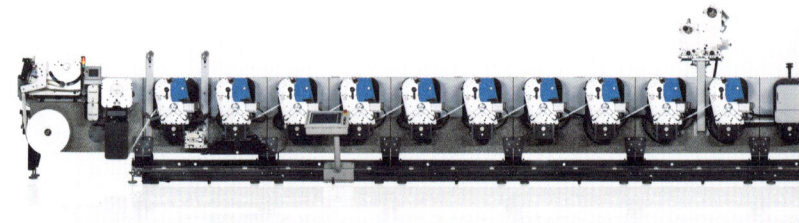

Die »Gallus ECS 340« begründet eine neue Ära bei der besonders wirtschaftlichen Produktion der Commodity-Etiketten. Bei der Entwicklung dieser Maschine konzentrierte man sich auf das Wesentliche, um bei geringsten Kosten höchste Druckqualität zu erreichen, verbunden mit Effizienz und Komfort.

So reduziert ihr extrem kurzer Bahnlauf von gerade mal ein Meter zehn von Druckwerk zu Druckwerk die Makulatur drastisch. Außerdem ist sie die erste Druckmaschine aus Granit. Ihre Basis bildet ein robuster Kern aus technischem Granit. Das macht sie besonders langlebig und sorgt für eine bisher unerreichte Laufruhe in dieser Maschinenklasse. Durch den Einsatz des Materials wurde es möglich die »Gallus ECS 340« sehr bedienerfreundlich zu konstruieren. Die Druckwerke ruhen auf direkt am Granit montierten Konsolen, das bietet dem Bediener einen sehr guten Zugang zu den Funktionen.

Granit als natürlicher Rohstoff beeinflusst die CO_2 Bilanz der Druckmaschine sehr positiv und leistet damit einen wichtigen Beitrag zum Umweltschutz. Auch schont ihre abluftfreie, wassergekühlte UV-Trocknung die Umwelt und durch die geringe Geräuschentwicklung das Gehör.

Die »Gallus ECS 340« besticht nicht nur durch ihre selbsterklärende Bedienbarkeit dank Touchscreen Technologie sondern auch durch ihre klare und durchgängige Gestaltung sowie ihre schlichte und hochwertige Grafik. Für Flächen wurde Weißaluminium verwendet – dunkelgrau für tragende Strukturen und zur Akzentuierung besonderer Funktionen und Bereiche sparsam das Gallus Blau.

Jury

Die Reihung der einzelnen Druckelemente auf dem Granit ergibt zum einen eine wunderschöne Gesamtskulptur. In der minimalistischen Ausführung der Gestaltung, den Proportionen, Farbe und Form-Einsatz dieser sehr durch die Technik bestimmten Bauelemente hat das Gerät eine hohe ästhetische Qualität. Das eingesetzte Material ist wirklich etwas sehr Innovatives und zudem nachhaltig. Es handelt sich um einen technischen Granit und insofern auch um eine CO_2-Entlastung. In dieser Form haben wir das bisher noch nicht gesehen.

The »Gallus ECS 340« heralds a new era of extremely cost-efficient commodity label manufacture. When developing this press, the essential features were focused on in order to maximize print quality while minimizing cost, and combining this with efficiency and convenience.

The machine's extremely short web path of just 1.1 metres between printing units cuts waste significantly. Moreover, this is the first printer to be made of granite. Its base is a robust core of technical granite. As a result, the press has a particularly long service life and is quieter than any other machine in this class. The way the material is used allowed »Gallus ECS 340« to be designed in a very user-friendly way. The printing units rest on consoles that are attached directly to the granite, which gives the operator excellent access to the various functions.

The use of the natural material granite has a very positive impact on the printer's carbon footprint, and is a significant contribution to environmental protection. The water-cooled UV drying generates no exhaust air and is easy on the environment as well as on the ear.

Further striking features of the »Gallus ECS 340« are its self-explanatory operation, thanks to touch-screen technology, its clear and coherent styling and its unassuming and high-quality graphics. For larger surfaces, white aluminium has been used. Supporting structures are coloured dark grey, while Gallus blue has been used sparingly to highlight special functions and areas.

Judges panel

The arrangement of the individual printing elements on the granite results in a beautiful sculptural effect. The machine's aesthetic quality is outstanding – with its minimalistic design, its proportions, its use of form and colour, and its components that are greatly influenced by the technology. The material used is really an innovative feature, it's sustainable, too. This is technical granite, and as such it also reduces carbon footprint. We have never seen it in this form before.

Merlin SEM Elektronenmikroskop Electron microsco
Produktion, Montage, Logistik **Silber** Production, assem

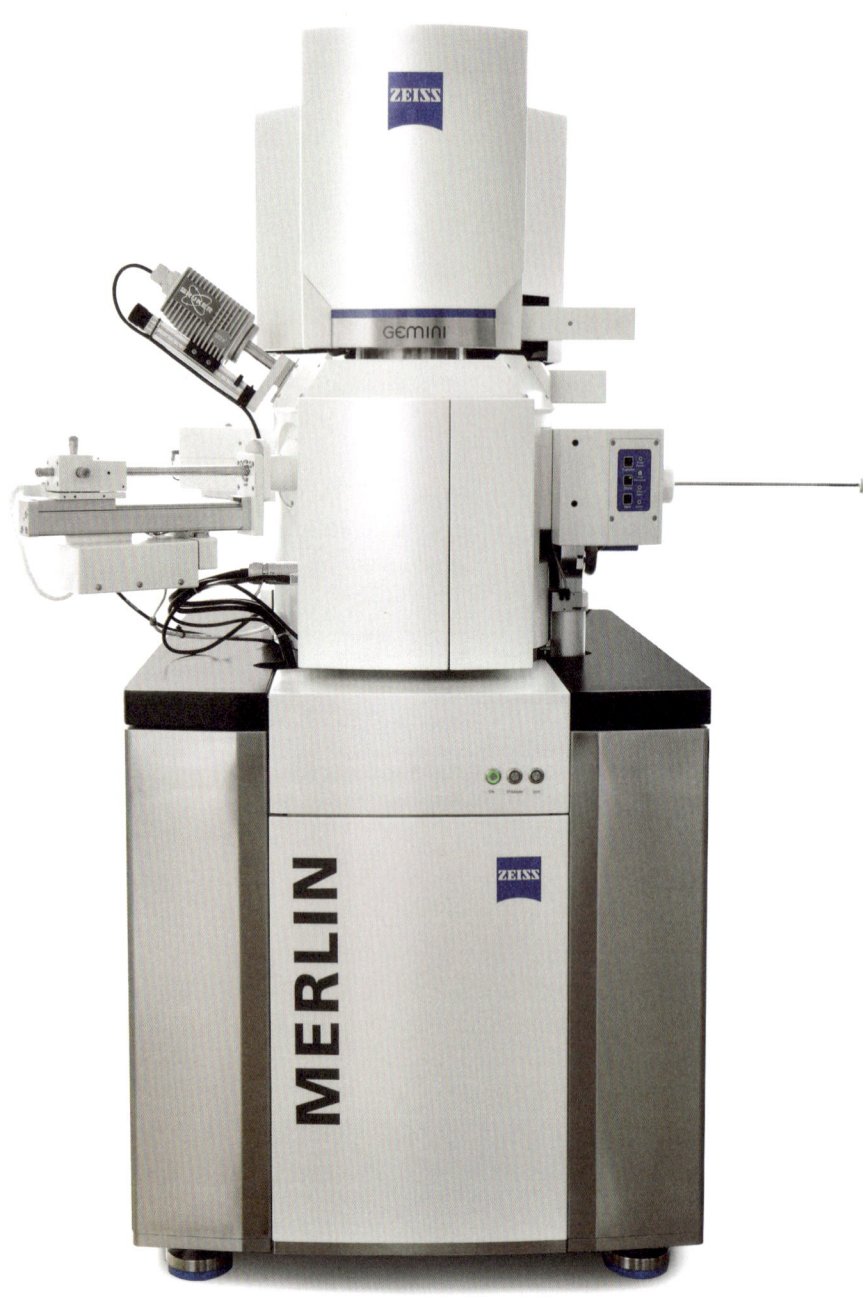

»Merlin SEM« ist ein wissenschaftliches Werkzeug mit neuer Dimension – ein Entwicklungssprung in Forschung und Fertigung. Das Elektronenmikroskop wird eingesetzt in der Halbleiterindustrie, Life Science, Nano-Forschung, Wissenschaft und industrieller Fertigung.

Durch seine innovative Technologie wird es zum ersten Mal möglich, Materialproben in ihren spezifischen Eigenschaften darzustellen. Bisher musste beim Anpassen der Elektronenstrahlspannung die Blende nachgeregelt werden, wodurch sich Bildschärfe und Auflösung verschlechterten. Das wird nun durch einen neuen Aufbau überwunden.

Durch ein geschicktes Teilekonzept wurde das Gerät auch sehr wartungsfreundlich. Die neue Elektronik erlaubt eine flexible Konfiguration der Instrumente. Zusätzliche Detektoren können schnell und einfach ergänzt und das System den Anforderungen entsprechend angepasst werden. Es bildet mit der bestimmenden, sichtbaren Gestaltungsgeometrie eine Synergie.

Das Design wird durch die gelungene Mischung aus Authentizität eines wissenschaftlichen Laboraufbaus und einer geordneten Architektur mit deutlich erkennbarer Struktur bestimmt, die den Einfluss von variablen Detektoren und komplexen Einbauteilen geschickt integriert. Dadurch wird nicht nur ein skulptural überzeugender Ausdruck, Kompetenz und Wissenschaftlichkeit, sondern auch Verlässlichkeit, Modernität sowie Wertigkeit vermittelt.

Die Materialkombination Edelstahl-Weiss symbolisiert Reinheit und Präzision sowie Leichtigkeit in der Beherrschung der wissenschaftlichen Materie. Das wird durch die klare übersichtliche und bedienerfreundliche Gestaltung noch unterstrichen.

Jury
Eine innovative Form die Verbauung der sehr komplexen elektronischen Bauteile, die zentrisch um die eigentliche Untersuchungsstelle angeordnet sind. Dies vermittelt das Gefühl, dass wirklich in diesem Zentrum auch alles bearbeitet wird. Aufgrund der Maschinenverbauung ergibt sich trotzdem eine schlanke, sympathische Form als Gesamterscheinung.

»Merlin SEM« opens up a new dimension in scientific tools – a development leap in research and manufacturing. This electron microscope is used in the semiconductor industry, nano-research, science and industrial production.

Its innovative technology makes it possible to show the specific properties of materials samples. In the past, the aperture had to be reset when adjusting the voltage of the electron beam, and this adversely affected definition and resolution. A new column solves this problem.

A clever parts concept means that the apparatus is extremely easy to maintain. The new electronics allows the instruments to be configured flexibly. Supplementary detectors can be added quickly and easily, so that the system can be adapted to requirements. The geometry of its layout harmonizes with the elements of the system.

The design is a well executed combination of the authenticity of a scientific laboratory with an orderly architecture that has a clearly recognizable structure. It cleverly integrates the influence of variable detectors and complex fitted components. The result is a sculpturally convincing design that expresses both competence and a scientific air, as well as reliability, modernity and high quality.

The combination of stainless steel and white surfaces symbolizes cleanliness and precision, as well as an easy command of the scientific subject matter. This is underscored by the clearly arranged and user-friendly layout.

Judges panel
An innovative way of installing very complex electronic components. The examination function forms the centre around which the other components are arranged. This creates the impression that everything is being processed at the heart of the apparatus. Nonetheless, the way the machine is designed means that the overall impression is slim and appealing.

Garant 46 7010   Wasserwaage mit zuschaltbarem Magnet   Spirit level with se
Produktion, Montage, Logistik   **Silber**   Production, assem

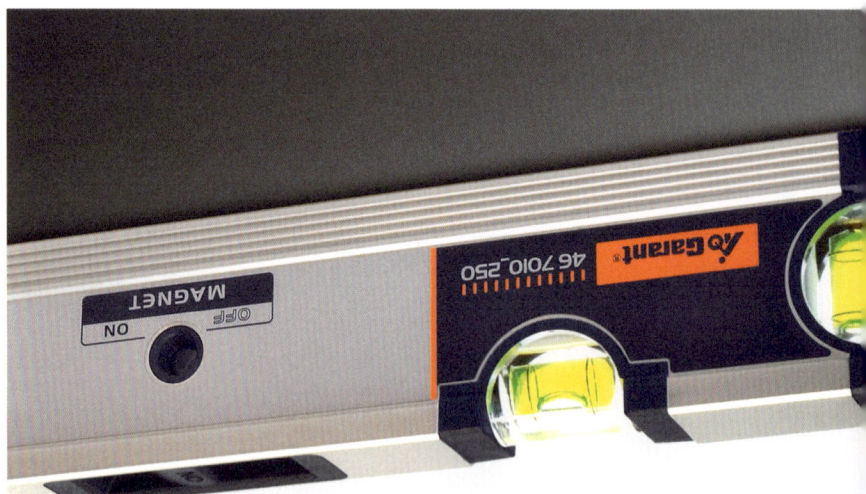

Bei manch kniffligen Montagearbeiten, bei denen der Handwerker an die Grenzen seiner Koordinationsfähigkeit stößt, bräuchte er drei Hände. »Garant 46 7010« bietet dem Metallbauer sozusagen eine dritte Hand; denn ein integrierter Magnet in der innovativen Wasserwaage nimmt ihm die Halte-Arbeit ab.

Sicher am Werkstück haftend, ermöglicht ihm die Magnetwasserwaage sich ganz aufs Anzeichnen oder Montieren konzentrieren zu können. Wird die hohe Haltekraft des Magneten in manchen Situationen nicht gewünscht, kann über einen integrierten Mechanismus bei Bedarf der Magnet einfach abgeschaltet werden.

Dank der prismatischen Anlagefläche sind dieselben Funktionen auch an Rohren und Profilen möglich und erweitern so das Einsatzgebiet enorm. Die Wasserwaage ist mit präzisen, aus allen Richtungen perfekt ablesbaren Libellen – der verkapselten Flüssigkeit – ausgestattet.

Die konsequente Grafik schafft durch die charakteristische Gliederung ein unverwechselbares Produkt, das durch die Innovation des zuschaltbaren Magneten eine Alleinstellungsposition am Markt erhält. Durch das stabile, eloxierte Aluminiumprofil ist die »Garant 46 7010« robust und liegt gut in der Hand. Sie sticht durch ihre Einfachheit, ihre hohe Funktionalität und ihr Design aus dem konservativen Marktsegment deutlich hervor.

Jury

Sehr sympathisch: in einem kleinen Tool mehrere Funktionen unterzubringen. Wir haben nicht nur eine Kreuz-, Vertikal- und Horizontalwasserwaage sondern auch Anlagemöglichkeiten sowohl für Flächen als auch für Rohre und Profile mit einem Magneten, der an metallischen Flächen eine Anwendung erleichtert, sodass man eine Hand frei hat. Insbesondere überzeugt uns die Funktion des An- und Ausschaltens ohne die sonst bei Permanent-Magneten nachteilige Aktivierung von diversen Kleinteilen in der Umgebung.

Sometimes, assembly work can be so tricky that the tradesman reaches the limits of his co-ordinating powers, and needs three hands. The »Garant 46 7010« gives metalworkers precisely this »third hand«, because an integrated magnet in this innovative spirit level means it no longer has to be held.

It adheres reliably to the workpiece, allowing the tradesman to concentrate fully on the task of marking or assembling. If this magnetic strength is not required in certain situations, an integrated mechanism allows the magnet to be simply switched off.

The V-shaped profile means that the same functions are also available for use on pipes and sections, which considerably widens the spirit level's scope of use. The spirit level is equipped with precise vials that allow an unrestricted view of the bubble from any direction.

The consistently applied graphics with their characteristic structure create an unmistakable product, which is the only spirit level on the market to feature a selectable magnet. The sturdy anodized aluminium profile makes »Garant 46 7010« a hard-wearing product that fits well in the hand. Its simplicity, high degree of functionality and design make it stand out in a market segment characterized by conservatism.

Judges panel

Very appealing: several functions brought together in one tool. Not only a cross, vertical and horizontal spirit level, but also one with different profiles that allow it to be used on flat surfaces as well as pipes and sections. Then there is its magnet, which frees up one hand when working on metal surfaces. We are especially impressed by the on/off function, with none of the activation of diverse small parts in the immediate area, which is the disadvantage of permanent magnets.

miniTwin   Sicherheits-Lichtgitter
Produktion, Montage, Logistik   **Silber**

Safety light curtain
Production, assem

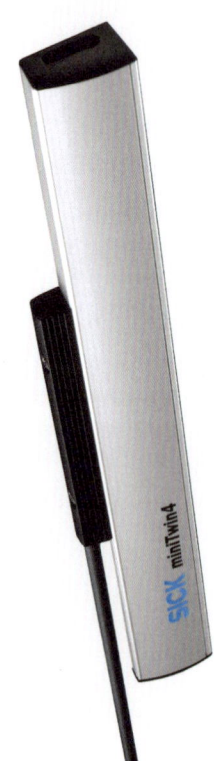

»miniTwin«, der kleinste Lichtvorhang der Welt – er ist gerade mal fingerbreit –, bietet an Handarbeitsplätzen von Maschinen, von Handlings- und Montagesystemen oder an Be- und Entladeöffnungen von vollautomatischen Bestückungsrobotern einen vollständigen, flexiblen und wirtschaftlichen Arbeitsschutz. Er kann in vielen verschiedenen Industriezweigen, wie etwa bei Zulieferern der Automobil- und Luftfahrtindustrie, in der Elektronik- und Pharmaindustrie, in der Lebensmittel- und Getränkeproduktion sowie in der Verpackungsmaschinenindustrie, eingesetzt werden.

Völlig neuartig konstruiert ist die sensorische Ausführung des Geräts: keine getrennten Sender und Empfänger mehr. Bei »miniTwin« sind diese erstmalig in einem einzigen extrem kompakten Gehäuse untergebracht, symmetrisch verteilt auf jeweils eine Gehäusehälfte. Das sichere Lichtgitter entsteht durch eine um 180 Grad verdrehte Montage von zwei baugleichen »miniTwin«-Sticks, sodass die Sender- und Empfängermodule jeweils gegenüberliegen. Diese Miniaturisierung optimiert die Maschinenintegration, erlaubt kostensenkende Standardisierungen und vereinfacht die Handhabung.

Die Montage ergibt sich intuitiv aus dem Produktdesign. Das Gehäuse besitzt eine asphärische und eine gerade Seite. Die letztere wird bündig am Maschinengehäuse befestigt. »miniTwin« gibt es je nach Bedarf in zahlreichen Schutzfeldhöhen von 12 bis 120 Zentimetern. Das Gerät ist biegefest und besitzt eine intelligente Bedien- und Anzeigelogik. So wird die Inbetriebnahme durch eine integrierte LED-Ausrichtanzeige erleichtert. Blaue LEDs melden, wie gut sich Sender und Empfänger erkennen können, was eine schnelle Ausrichtung erlaubt.

Jury
Ein Sicherheits-Lichtvorhang für den Einbau in Maschinen mit einer extrem kleinen und kompakten Bauform. Damit lässt er eine sehr gute Unterbringung in den engen Räumen von Maschinen zu. Die Gestaltung ist zurückgenommen, schlicht und überzeugend, sauber, aufgeräumt und wertig.

»miniTwin« is the world's smallest light curtain, no wider than a finger. At manual workstations, handling and assembly systems, or at the loading and unloading hatches of automatic placement machines, it provides complete, flexible and cost-effective occupational safety. It can be used in many different branches of industry, such as automotive and aerospace suppliers, the electronics and pharmaceuticals industries, foodstuffs and beverage production or in the packaging machinery industry.

One completely new design feature is the way its sensors have been arranged: transmitters and receivers are no longer kept separate. For the first time, »miniTwin« houses both in a single, extremely compact housing, distributed symmetrically so that each takes up half of the housing. This safety light curtain is created by placing two identical »miniTwin« sticks side by side, then turning one of them through 180 degrees. In this way, a transmitter is always opposite a receiver, and vice versa. This miniaturization optimizes integration into machinery, allows cost-cutting standardization to be done, and simplifies handling.

Thanks to the product design, assembly is intuitive. The housing has an aspherical and a straight side. The latter is fixed flush to the machine housing. Depending on requirements, »miniTwin« is available in many protective field heights, from 12 to 120 centimetres. The appliance is bend-resistant, and features an intelligent control and display logic. Putting it into operation is made easier by an integrated alignment indicator. Blue LEDs show how well transmitters and receivers can detect each other, which speeds up alignment.

Judges panel
A safety light curtain for installation in machinery. Its construction is extremely small and compact. This makes it very easy to install in machines, where space is very tight. Its design is unassuming, plain and impressive. Neat, tidy and high-quality.

Quasar[6] Kreuzlinienlaser
Produktion, Montage, Logistik **Silber**

Cross-line laser
Production, asser

Der Kreuzlinienlaser wird zum Nivellieren, Fluchten, Loten und Abtragen rechter Winkel verwendet. Eine waagrechte und vier senkrechte Linien erzeugen an einer Wand und an der Decke je ein Kreuz. Ein zusätzlicher Laserstrahl überträgt das Deckenkreuz auf den Fußboden.

Mit dem »Quasar^6« wird die neue, innovative Formensprache einer Designstudie konsequent umgesetzt, die die Nedo-Produkte wettbewerbsfähiger macht und eine hohe Familienähnlichkeit erzielt. Wesentliches Merkmal seines Designs ist ein einfacher Gehäusekörper, der durch gezielt eingesetzte, überwölbte Flächen und funktionsbezogene Einschnitte und Applikationen spannungsreich ausgestaltet ist. So haben die Laseraustrittsöffnungen facettenförmige Einschnitte, die in der Draufsicht eine Kreuzform bilden und dadurch die Grundfunktion des Gerätes symbolisieren.

Die auffällige Farbgebung ist einerseits ein klares Wiedererkennungs- und Alleinstellungsmerkmal, andererseits macht sie das Gerät am oft unübersichtlichen Einsatzort gut sichtbar. Die Bedien- und Funktionselemente sind durch ihre Farben entsprechend den neuen Nedo-Standards codiert. So ist das anthrazitfarbene Bedienpanel mit weißer Beschriftung und weißen Piktogrammen kontrastreich angelegt. Es liegt geschützt in einem Einschnitt im Gehäusekörper.

Die sichere und kippfreie Drei-Punkt-Aufstellung von »Quasar^6« wird über wohlproportionierte Ausleger erreicht, die mit einstellbaren Standfüßen ausgerüstet sind. Das Gerät projiziert einen Lotpunkt nach unten. Deshalb sind die Stellfüße filigran und schließt der Grundkörper konisch ab. Das garantiert optimale Sicht auf den Lotpunkt.

Jury

Ein technisches Produkt, das durch die Gestaltung Charakter bekommt. Uns gefällt sehr gut die schöne Detaillierung und Farbcodierung der einzelnen Elemente. Intuitive Bedienmöglichkeiten. Ein gelungenes und wertiges Produkt.

This cross laser is used for levelling, aligning, plumbing and creating right angles. One horizontal and four vertical lines create a cross on the wall or the ceiling. An additional laser beam transfers the cross from the ceiling to the floor.

»Quasar^6« consistently puts into practice a new, innovative formal expression. Hatched in a design study, this formal element makes Nedo products more competitive and achieves a high level of family resemblance. The main feature of this design is a simple housing that is made exciting and attractive by the deliberate use of convex surfaces and function-related recesses and applications. The laser apertures, for example, have facetted recesses which, when seen from above, have the form of a cross. In this way, they symbolize the basic function of the device.

The striking colour scheme creates instant recognizability and a unique selling proposition, as well as making the device easy to see in the environment in which it is used. The operating and functional elements are colour-coded in accordance with the new Nedo standard. The anthracite operating panel contrasts with the white lettering and white pictograms, for example. Set in a recess in the housing, the operating panel is well protected.

Three well proportioned, adjustable legs ensure that »Quasar^6« is positioned safely and tilt-free. The device projects a plumb beam onto the ground. This is why the legs have been kept thin, and the housing is conical. In this way, the plumb beam can easily be seen.

Judges panel

A technical product whose design gives it character. We like the nice detail and the way the individual elements have been colour-coded. Intuitive operation. A well made, high-quality product.

Primus²

Rotationslaser
Produktion, Montage, Logistik **Silber**

Rotating laser
Production, assem

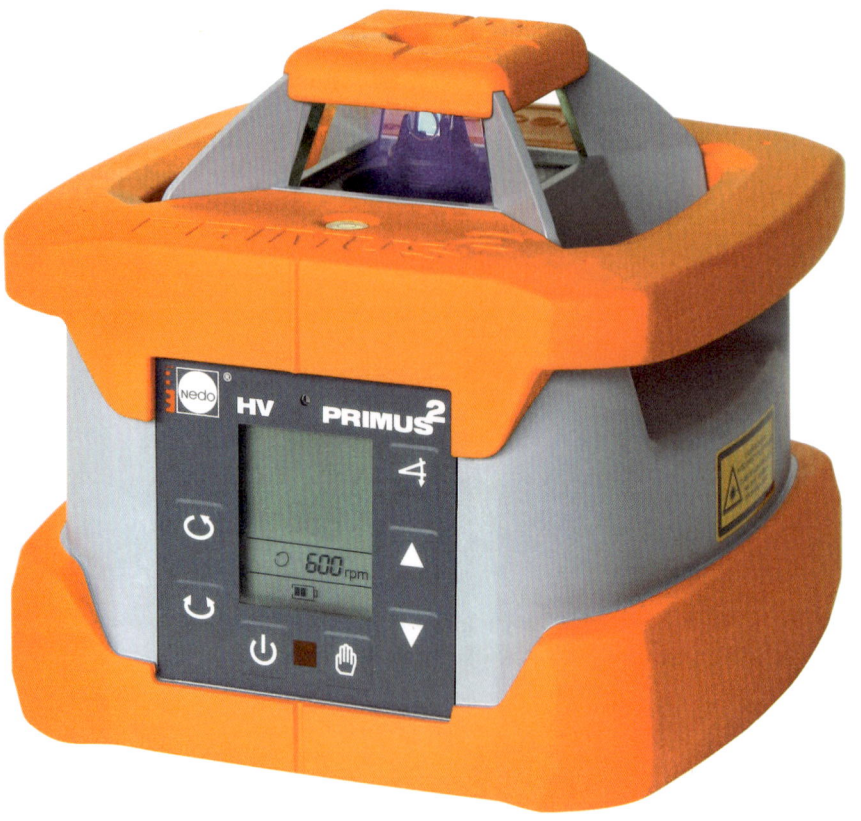

Das kraftvolle und ausdrucksstarke Design des vollautomatischen Rotationslasers führt zu einer äußerst robusten Anmutung. Erreicht wurde dies durch Schutzringe in strahlendem Orange, die mit einer griffigen, gummierten Oberfläche ausgestattet sind und einen Stoßschutz bieten. Diese Gestaltung vermittelt Zuverlässigkeit und Sicherheit im Baustelleneinsatz. Dort wird das Profi-Gerät zum Nivellieren, Fluchten und zur Gefällekontrolle verwendet.

Die Schutzringe werden durch facettenartige Anschnitte strukturiert, die als weiteres Stilelement ebenfalls die Robustheit unterstreichen. Zudem führt dies zu einer technisch orientierten Gesamtanmutung, die den Präzisionsanspruch des Lasers betont. Die Produktgrafik mit Firmenlogo und Produktname ist als Relief ausgeführt. Das ermöglicht auf hochwertige Weise die Markenerkennung und bietet Schutz vor Produktpiraterie. Die neue Farbgebung in hellem Grau und leuchtendem Orange ist zusammen mit dem anthrazitfarbenen Bedienfeld nicht nur ein Alleinstellungs- und Wiedererkennungsmerkmal sondern sorgt auch für gute Sichtbarkeit am oft unübersichtlichen Einsatzort.

Mit dem Layout des Bedienpanels wurde ein für Nedo neuer Designstandard geschaffen, der bei allen nachfolgenden Geräten eingesetzt wird. So sind alle Tastenfelder analog zum Firmenlogo quadratisch angelegt. Die kräftig und eindeutig gestalteten Piktogramme garantieren maximale Ablesbarkeit und somit Bediensicherheit. Mit der neuen Farbgebung wurde eine grundsätzliche Codierung für alle zukünftigen Bedienfelder definiert. So ist der Hintergrund stets anthrazit gehalten, sodass Schrift und Piktogramme in Weiß sich besonders gut hervorheben.

Jury

Uns fasziniert, dass durch die Formgebung zusammen mit den Griffen eine extreme Robustheit vermittelt wird für ein feinelektronisches Gerät wie einen Rotationslaser. Dieser ist wunderschön verpackt und sieht trotzdem aufgrund seines Gehäuses sehr strapazierfähig aus. Er besitzt ein enormes Potential für die vielfältigste Anwendung im Baustellenbereich unter starken Belastungen. Gute Ergonomie durch große, gummierte und ergonomisch ausgebildete Griffe.

The powerful and expressive design of this fully automatic rotating laser creates an impression of extreme sturdiness. This is underlined by the bright orange protective rings, which have a non-slip, rubberized surface, and provide protection against impact. The design gives an impression of reliability and safety on the building site where this professional tool is used for levelling, aligning and grade control.

The protective rings are facetted, and this style element also underscores the tool's sturdiness. This design feature also gives a general high-tech appearance, which emphasizes the laser's claim to precision. The product graphics, with the company logo and the product name, is designed in relief form. This high-quality feature ensures brand recognition and offers protection against copycat products. The new colour scheme, in light grey and bright orange, combined with an anthracite operating panel, is not only a unique selling proposition and a guarantee of recognizability, but also ensures that the tool is easy to see in the environment in which it is used.

In the layout of the operating panel, a design standard has been created for Nedo that is used in all successor products. All the keys are arranged in a square, analogous to the company logo. The powerful, clearly designed pictograms guarantee excellent legibility, and thus operating safety. The new colour scheme applies to all future operating displays and panels. The background is always anthracite, so that the white lettering and pictograms stand out especially well.

Judges panel

What fascinates us is the way the tool's form, together with the grips, creates an impression of extreme sturdiness, and this in a precision electronic tool such as a rotating laser. It is wonderfully packaged, yet looks very hard-wearing thanks to its housing. It has huge potential for a wide range of uses on construction sites, in tough conditions. Good ergonomics, with the large rubberized grips.

Spin Chuck Universal-Werkzeughalter Universal tool hold
Produktion, Montage, Logistik **Silber** Production, assem

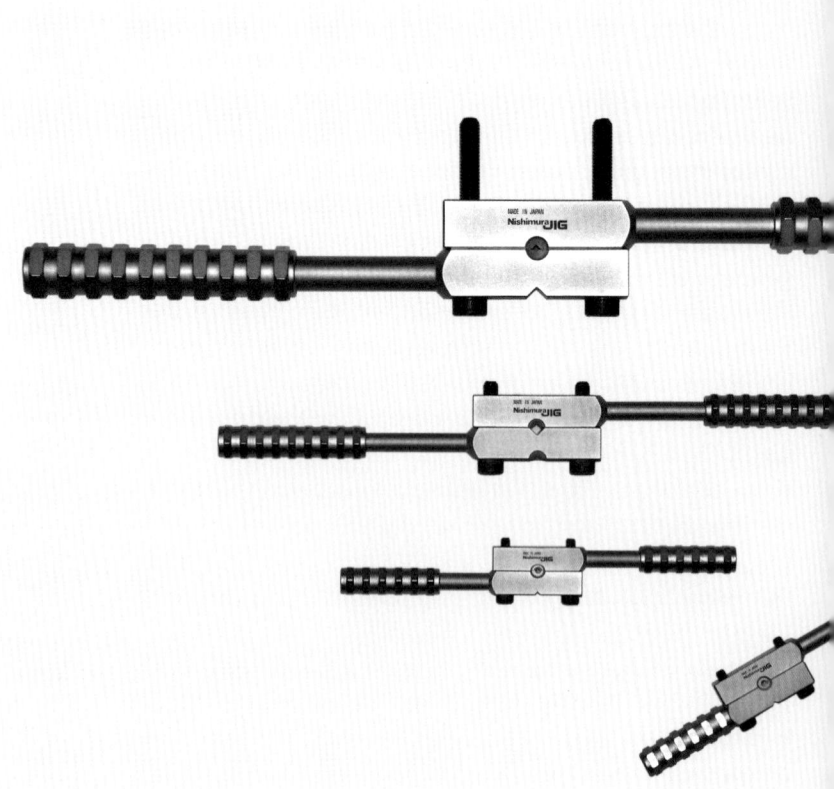

Der »Spin Chuck« ist eine funktionale und ästhetische Neuinterpretation eines traditionellen Handwerkzeuges aus dem Bereich Maschinenbau. Er ersetzt das bisher verwendete Windeisen zur Aufnahme von Gewindebohrern und Handreibahlen. Außerdem können auch alle möglichen Spindeln, Wellen, Achsen, Werkzeuge und Werkstücke sicher und fest aufgenommen werden mittels der Integration verschiedener Formschlusselemente an den Spannbacken.

Die optisch dominanten Griffelemente sind strukturiert und garantieren dadurch einen sicheren Halt selbst bei öligen Händen. Da sie keine scharfen Kanten besitzen, wie sie bei bisher bekannten Kreuzrändelungen vorkommen, bieten sie eine sehr angenehme Haptik. Das Sechskantprofil ermöglicht es, Werkzeugschlüssel zur Montage und zur Demontage zu benutzen. Je nach Montagekonfiguration der Griffelemente kann das Drehmoment vom schmalen zum breit montierten Zustand um das Vierfache erhöht und so dem jeweiligen Einsatzzweck und der Zugänglichkeit angepasst werden.

Das Design ist bewusst reduziert und verwendet ausschließlich Regelgeometrien und Formelemente aus dem Bereich des Maschinenbaus, beispielsweise bei den Handgriffen mit ihrer sechseckigen Grundform, den Einstichen und den typischen Anfasungen, wie sie an Schraubenmuttern zu finden sind. Durch die Wiederholung der Formelemente entsteht jedoch eine neue, interessante Anmutung.

Die präzise Ausführung der Bauteile führt zu einer Hochwertigkeit, die durch die satinierte Chromoberfläche noch gesteigert wird. Dazu trägt auch das Markenemblem bei, das exakt per Lasergravur aufgebracht ist.

Jury
Super Werkzeug-Ästhetik. Die Griffe sind so, dass das Drehmoment verstärkt werden kann. Das finden wir sehr gut. Eine Neuinterpretation oder eine Weiterentwicklung eines alten Präzisionswerkzeuges, und in diesem Sinne ist es sehr sorgfältig umgesetzt. Es hat einen hohen Wiedererkennungswert. Es wurde sozusagen ein eigenes Bild erzeugt, das eine sehr schöne Familien- und Markenbildung in dem Bereich möglich macht.

»Spin Chuck« is a functional and aesthetic reinterpretation of a traditional manual tool from mechanical engineering. It replaces the conventional tap wrench used to position threading taps and hand reamers. And if various elements are integrated in its jaws, it can also safely and securely hold all kinds of spindles, shafts, axles, tools and workpieces.

The visually dominant gripping elements are structured, guaranteeing a secure grip even with greasy hands. As it has none of the sharp edges common in conventional knurled surfaces, it is very pleasant to the touch. The hexagonal profile allows tool keys to be used for assembly and disassembly. Depending on the way the grips are configured, torque can be quadrupled between narrow and wide assembly, and in this way adapted to the respective purpose and level of accessibility.

Its design has been deliberately reduced, using solely regular geometric shapes and form elements from mechanical engineering, such as the handles with their basic hexagonal form, the recesses and the typical chamfers to be found on screw-nuts. The repetition of these formal elements gives rise to a new, interesting appearance.

The precision with which the parts are made gives a high-quality impression, which is made even stronger by the satin-finish chrome surfaces as well as by the brand emblem, which is engraved precisely by laser.

Judges panel
Super machine-tool aesthetic. The grips are made in such a way that torque can be increased using a hexagonal key. We like this a lot. A reinterpretation or further development of an old precision tool. As such, it has been executed very carefully. It has a high level of recognizability. It's as if an independent image has been created that will allow a very attractive family and brand identity to emerge in this area.

MPA-F Ventilinsel
Produktion, Montage, Logistik **Silber**

Valve terminal
Production, assem

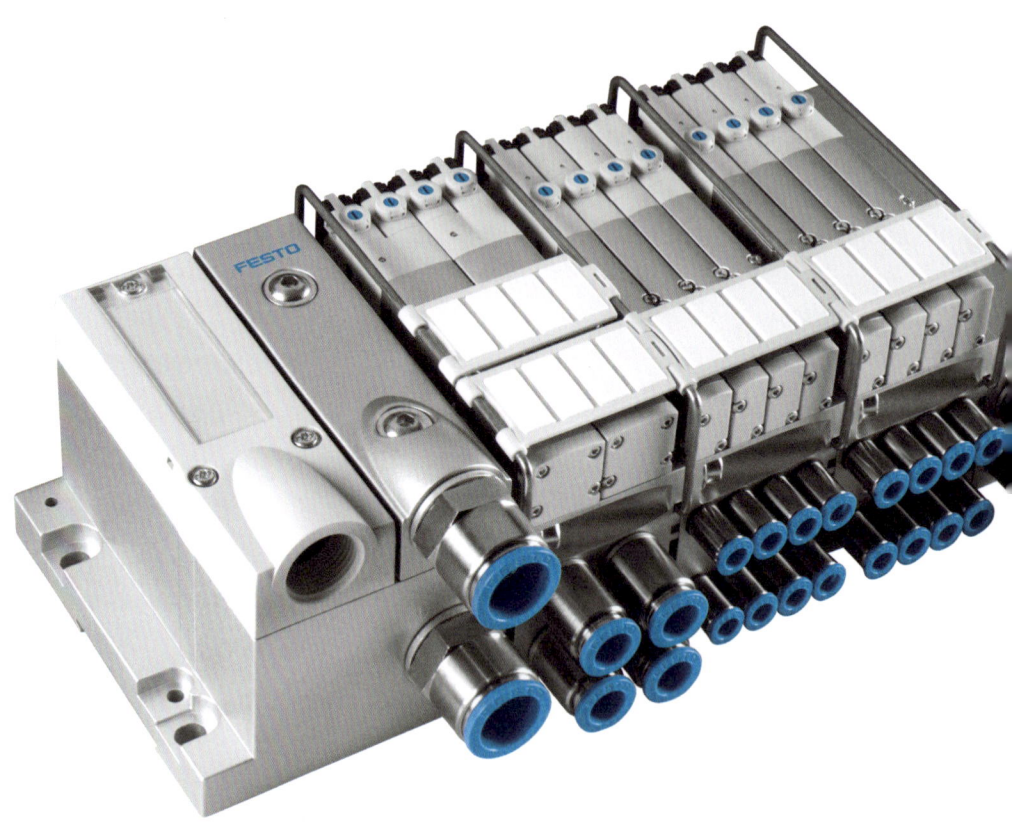

Ventilinseln werden in automatisierten pneumatischen Anlagen benutzt, um Ventile über elektrische Signale anzusteuern und Aktoren zu schalten. Die »MPA-F« ist die Erweiterung einer bestehenden Ventilinselreihe, die im Maschinenbau eingesetzt wird. Sie vereint Ventil-Modularität, Innovation und besonders hohen Durchfluss, wodurch sie deutlich schneller bei der Signalverarbeitung ist. Viele Ventile können gleichzeitig geschaltet und entlüftet werden.

Zusätzlich ist die Ventilinsel mit einem robusten, dauerhaften Kennzeichnungssystem ausgestattet, das sowohl für Papier- als auch für Kunststoffschilder geeignet ist. Diese können ohne Werkzeug montiert werden und befinden sich an den Anschlussplatten und Haltebügeln. Das ist ein großer Vorteil im Servicefall; denn die Schilder sorgen für Klarheit und Eindeutigkeit.

Alle Elemente der »MPA-F« sind aufeinander abgestimmt. Dank ihrer Modularität ist die Ventilinsel leicht umzubauen und zu erweitern. Die Anschlussplatten lassen sich dabei schnell durch drei Schrauben verbinden. Die Ventilinsel integriert sich hervorragend in das Corporate Design von Festo.

Jury

Bei diesem neuen Produkt in dieser Produktkategorie fallen die wiedererkennbare, extreme Hochwertigkeit der Produktausführung und der modulare Charakter auf. Sehr überzeugend und schön gestaltet insbesondere auch mit der blauen, nicht aufdringlichen Farbe. Die Funktionalität der Beschriftungsmöglichkeiten und die Gesamterscheinung machen den langlebigen Charakter des Produktes, dessen Komponenten sicherlich auch gut reparier- und austauschbar sind, deutlich.

Valve terminals are used in automatic pneumatic systems to control valves and switch actuators via electrical signals. The »MPA-F« is a new addition to an existing series of valve terminals used in mechanical engineering. It combines modular valve design, innovation and especially high flow, which means it processes signals significantly faster. Many valves can be simultaneously switched and bled.

In addition, the valve terminal is furnished with a hard-wearing, lasting labelling system, which is suitable for paper and plastic labels. These can be positioned on the connecting plates and retaining brackets, without any need for tools. This is a great benefit during servicing, as the labels provide clear identification.

All the elements of the »MPA-F« are compatible with each other. Thanks to its modular design, the valve terminal can easily be rearranged and extended. Just three screws are needed to attach the connecting plates. The valve terminal harmonizes excellently with Festo corporate design.

Judges panel

Looking at this new product in this product category, you are struck by the extremely high quality of the product design, and the product's modular design. Very convincingly and elegantly designed, also with its unassuming blue colour. The practical labelling solution and the product's overall appearance underscore its long-lasting qualities. Without doubt, its components can easily be repaired and exchanged.

Falk Vision Mobiles Navigationssystem
Kommunikation,
Audio/Video, Optik **Gold**

Mobile navigation
Communication,
audio/video, optic

Die neuen Navigationsgeräte »Vision 700« und »Vision 500« erweitern das hochwertige Produktsortiment von Falk um ein neues Premium-Segment.

Das flache schwarze Gehäuse mit edler Einfassung in Metalloptik wirkt sportlich und klassisch zugleich. Da das Display vollständig in den Rahmen eingelassen ist, entsteht eine plane Oberfläche. Durch die puristischen Formen sowie die kompakte und elegante Erscheinung integriert sich »Falk Vision« sehr gut in verschiedenste Fahrzeug-Interieurs. Das brillante Display wirkt durch das neue anthrazitfarbige Screendesign besonders edel und reagiert dank Sensitive Touch auf leichteste Berührungen. Die TMC-Antenne wurde komplett in das Navigationsgerät integriert und garantiert einen optimalen Empfang von Staumeldungen ganz ohne störendes Kabelgewirr an der Windschutzscheibe.

Die »Falk Vision«-Serie besticht auch durch ihre Technologie auf höchstem Niveau. Neben beeindruckender multimedialer Kompatibilität stellt die Navigation durch Luftbildkarten und 3D-Geländeansicht ein Novum dar, das jede Fahrt zum Erlebnis macht.

Ein weiterer interessanter Menüpunkt sind die Guided Tours, die mit den Baedeker- und Marco Polo-Redaktionen entwickelt wurden. 30 Routen aus Deutschland, Österreich und der Schweiz sind vorinstalliert und bieten interessante Informationen über Land und Leute in Bild und Text. Besonders spektakuläre Sehenswürdigkeiten erläutert ein Sprecher. Dank dem Feature StadtAktiv erreicht man nicht nur sein Ziel mit dem Auto sondern auch mit öffentlichen Verkehrsmitteln. Hier sucht das Navi die beste Verbindung mit S- und U-Bahn, Bus und Zug.

Jury

Das Navigationsgerät ist sehr schön gestaltet, besonders das Metallband, das über drei Flächen läuft, überzeugt uns. Ruhige, sachliche Formgebung, sehr hochwertig, kein Billigprodukt sondern ein echter Wertgegenstand. Ein sehr gutes Produktdetail ist der starke Magnet, der nicht locker sitzt, sondern richtig gut in Position schnappt.

The new »Vision 700« and »Vision 500« navigation devices add a new premium segment to the high-quality Falk range.

The flat black housing, with its metallic-look surround, is both sporty and classic in appearance. As the display is completely flush with the frame, the surface of the device is flat. The purist forms and compact and elegant appearance of »Falk Vision« means that it harmonizes excellently with any vehicle interior. The new anthracite screen design gives the brilliant display an especially high-quality feel. The display's »sensitive touch« function means that it reacts to the lightest touch. The TMC antenna has been completely integrated into the navigation device, and guarantees optimum reception of traffic news, without any irksome tangle of cables at the windscreen.

The »Falk Vision« series also stands out by virtue of its high-end technology. Apart from impressive multimedia compatibility, its navigation function offers aerial maps and 3D terrain views – an innovation that makes every trip an experience.

One further menu item of interest is »Guided Tours«, developed in collaboration with the Baedeker and Marco Polo travel guides. The device comes complete with 30 pre-installed tours in Germany, Austria and Switzerland, offering interesting information about customs and culture in image and text form. A speaker gives a commentary on especially spectacular sights. The »StadtAktiv« feature allows users to reach their destination not only by car, but also by public transport. The navigation device looks for the best rail, bus and train connection.

Judges panel

The navigation device is beautifully designed, and we especially like the metal strip that runs around three sides. Calm, sober form, very high quality. Not a cheap product, but an item of real value. The powerful magnet, which is not loose but snaps really well into position, is an excellent product detail.

Just Mobile Mtable — Monitorständer mit Hideaway für MacBook
Kommunikation,
Audio/Video, Optik **Silber**

Monitor stand wit[h]
Communication,
audio/video, opti[cs]

Der Monitorständer »Just Mobile Mtable« sieht nicht nur schön aus, sondern ist auch überaus nützlich. Er sorgt für einen aufgeräumten Schreibtisch und bietet hohen ergonomischen Komfort beim Arbeiten.

So kann man den iMac oder das MacBook daraufstellen und Tastatur und Maus darunter verschwinden lassen, wenn man sie nicht braucht. Oder aber das MacBook findet seinen Platz unter dem Ständer und das Cinema Display darauf. Der »Just Mobile Mtable« ist kompatibel mit dem 13-Zoll- und dem 15-Zoll-MacBook Pro. Öffnungen links und rechts gestatten den Zugriff zu allen Anschlüssen und zum DVD/CD-Laufwerk.

Eine gute Luftzirkulation gewährleistet die gelochte Rückseite. Der Monitorständer ist mit Gummifüßen ausgestattet und steht somit rutschfest auf dem Tisch. Zwei Gummistreifen verhindern, dass das MacBook beim Reinschieben oder Herausziehen verkratzt. Platz für einen Stift bietet eine kleine Mulde auf der Oberseite.

Nicht nur all diese funktionalen Details unterstreichen seine Hochwertigkeit sondern auch seine Form aus einem Stück Aluminium und sein elegantes reduziertes Design, das optimal zum Mac passt. Ein stilvolles Produkt für Ordnung auf dem Schreibtisch.

Jury

Eine sehr stimmige Lösung, die sich schön in die Produktfamilie der Apple-Notebooks einbindet. Es besitzt auch innen Details, die uns sehr überzeugen, beispielsweise die Gummiapplikation. Dadurch verkratzt das Notebook nicht, wenn man es in den Monitorständer reinschiebt. Oder die Lüftung. Die Anschlüsse liegen innen. Dadurch sieht alles noch sauberer und aufgeräumter aus.

The »Just Mobile Mtable« not only looks good, it is extremely useful as well. It helps keep desks tidy, and provides for excellent ergonomic comfort when working.

An iMac or MacBook can be placed on it, while the keyboard and mouse disappear under it when they are not being used. Alternatively, the MacBook can be placed underneath the stand, and the Cinema Display placed on the top. The »Just Mobile Mtable« is compatible with both 13-inch and 15-inch MacBook Pro models. Openings on the left and right provide access to all ports and to the DVD/CD drive.

The perforated rear panel ensures that air can circulate well. The monitor stand is fitted with rubber feet, which means it will not slide around on the desk. Two rubber strips keep the MacBook from getting scratched when it is slid in or pulled out. A small depression on the top surface provides room for a pen or pencil.

It is not just all these functional details that underline its high quality. There is also its shape, which has been formed from one piece of aluminium, as well as its elegant, reduced design, which goes perfectly with a Mac. A stylish product for a neat and tidy desk.

Judges panel

A very logical solution that harmonizes well with the Apple notebook family. On the inside too, there are details that we found very convincing, such as the rubber strips. They mean that the notebook does not get scratched when it is slid into the monitor stand. Or the ventilation. The connections are on the inside. This gives the whole thing an even neater and tidier look.

Elegance Mobiltelefon für Senioren Mobile phone for
Kommunikation, Communication,
Audio/Video, Optik **Silber** audio/video, optic

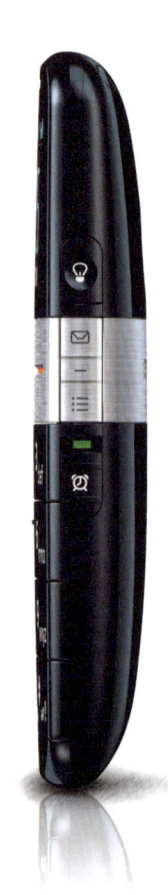

Mit »Elegance« hat der Markt- und Technologieführer für Seniorenhandys ein neues Mobiltelefon herausgebracht, das den Ansprüchen nach attraktivem Design und einfacher Technik besonders gerecht wird. Es bietet Menschen, die einfach nur telefonieren oder über SMS kommunizieren wollen, genau die Funktionen, die sie wirklich brauchen – ohne überflüssige Extras und ohne auf hochwertige, elegante Gestaltung verzichten zu müssen.

Durch seine selbsterklärende Anwendung und leicht verständliche Menüführung ist es so einfach zu bedienen, dass eine Bedienungsanleitung überflüssig wird. So lassen sich etwa Telefonbuch und SMS-Menü direkt und bequem über seitliche Tasten aufrufen.

Das Mobiltelefon für Senioren verfügt über ein breites Farbdisplay mit OLED-Technik, die für »organic light emitting diode« steht und klarere Ansichten durch höhere Helligkeit bei gleichzeitigem starken Kontrast ermöglicht. Die Schrift ist gut lesbar, die Zeichengröße verstellbar.

Das Handy besitzt extragroße Tasten mit ausgezeichnetem Druckpunkt und einen hörgerätetauglichen Lautsprecher. Vibrationsalarm und Klingeltöne können extrastark eingestellt werden. Zusätzlichen Nutzen bieten die eingebaute LED-Taschenlampe, der Wecker und ein einfacher Taschenrechner.

Die puristische Ästhetik und die klare elegante Formgebung ohne Ecken und Kanten charakterisieren das schlanke Design. Das aus hochwertigen Materialien hergestellte Handy wird durch eine Edelstahlverzierung gegliedert. Ein stilvolles Mobiltelefon für einfache Kommunikation.

Jury

Früher waren Handys für Senioren meist eckig, unhandlich und mit so großen Zahlen, dass man sich damit nicht outen wollte. Dieses Mobiltelefon ist kleiner und handlicher – zwar mit großen Zahlen, die aber trotzdem nicht stigmatisierend sind. Es wird den Senioren wirklich gerecht. Die Aufteilung finden wir sehr geglückt. Sehr überzeugend: klare Typografie, leicht ablesbar. Schön die Zusatzfunktion der Taschenlampe. Trotzdem ist das Handy nicht überfrachtet mit technischen Raffinessen. Es ist gut geglückt, haptisch angenehm und weist die richtige Richtung.

»Elegance« is a new mobile phone from the market and technology leader for mobile phones for senior citizens. It meets the demand for attractive design and simple technology especially well. People who simply want to phone or text get precisely the functions they really need, without any superfluous extras, and without having to go without high-quality, elegant design.

Self-explanatory to use and with a navigation menu that is easy to understand, it is so simple to use that there is no need for an instruction booklet. For example, keys on the side of the mobile allow the phonebook and text message menus to be called up directly and conveniently.

This mobile phone for senior citizens has a wide colour display featuring OLED (organic light-emitting diode) technology. The greater brightness and contrast this offers makes the display easier to read. Text is easy to read, and font size can be adjusted.

The mobile phone has extra large keys with an excellent pressure point, as well as a hearing aid-compatible loudspeaker. The vibration alarm and ring tones can be set to extra strong or extra loud. Additional benefits include a built-in LED torch, an alarm function and a simple calculator.

Its slim design is characterized by a purist aesthetic and a clear, elegant form without any sharp corners or edges. Made of high-quality materials, the mobile phone's functional areas are demarcated by a stainless steel trim. A stylish mobile for simple communication.

Judges panel

Most mobile phones for senior citizens used to be angular, unwieldy and furnished with such large numbers that nobody wanted to be seen with one. This mobile is smaller and compacter. The numbers are still large, but without any stigma attached to them. It really delivers what senior citizens need. We really like the way its surface has been divided up. Very impressive. Clear typography, easy to read. The torch is a nice additional function. Even so, the mobile is not overloaded with technological gimmicks. Well done, pleasant to the touch. Points the right way forward.

Diomax® Diodenlaser
Medizin, Rehabilitation,
Geriatrie **Silber**

Diode laser
Medicine, rehabi
geriatric medicin

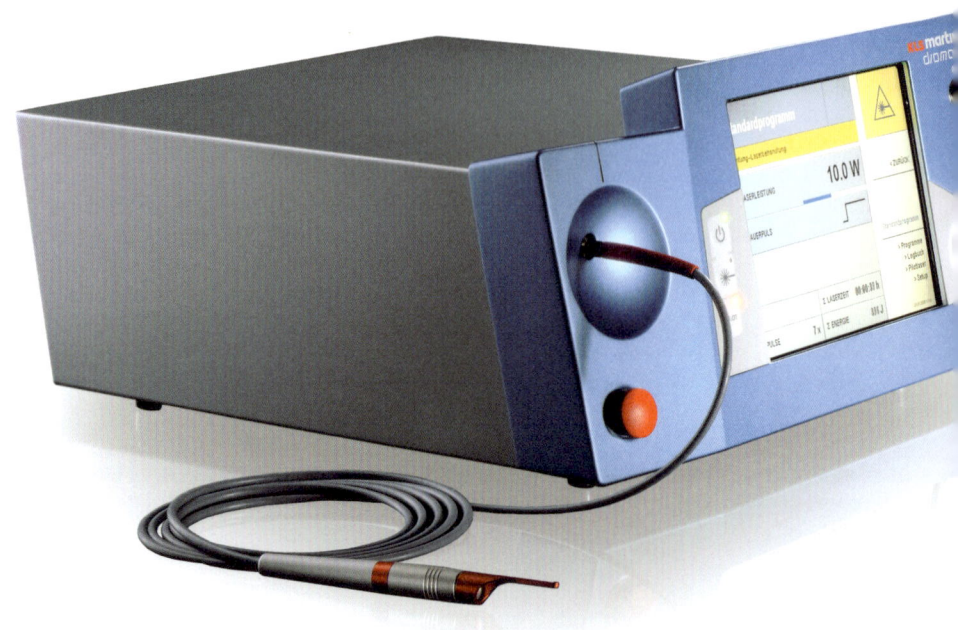

»Diomax®« ist ein echtes Multitalent für die moderne Chirurgie. Der Diodenlaser stellt ein vielseitiges System dar, das von der ambulanten Praxis bis hin zum endoskopischen High-Tech-Operationssaal ein breites Anwendungsspektrum findet. Mit bis zu 20 Watt Laserleistung wird er vorwiegend zur Behandlung von Gefäßerkrankungen mit speziellen Faser- und Kathetersets eingesetzt.

In der Qualität des Laserstrahls setzt er neue Maßstäbe. So weist er eine Strahlqualität auf, die bisher nur mit Festkörperlasern erreichbar war. Aber er besticht auch durch sein durchdachtes Konzept und seine intuitive, komfortable Bedienerführung über Display und Leuchtelemente. So stehen dem Operateur bis zu 50 individuell anpassbare Programme zur Verfügung, aber alle Parameter lassen sich mittels eines einzigen Drehreglers einstellen und werden klar auf dem großen Farbdisplay angezeigt, das optimale Übersicht auch in abgedunkelten Operationssälen garantiert. Alles auf einen Blick – keine verwirrenden Untermenüstrukturen, die die Bedienbarkeit verkomplizieren.

Das kompakte, hochwertige Gerät zeichnet sich durch sein flächiges, polygonales Design, seine funktionale Klarheit und seine übersichtliche, selbsterklärende Bedienoberfläche aus. »Diomax®« erfüllt höchste Ansprüche. Einfach in der Bedienung, erstklassig in der Strahlqualität, kann sich der Operateur voll und ganz auf seine Arbeit konzentrieren.

Jury

Hohe gestalterische Qualität sowohl der Produktgestaltung als auch der grafischen Bedienoberfläche und der Steuerung über einen zentralen Drehregler. Hochwertige Materialien, sehr gelungene Produktgrafik und schöne Farbwahl entsprechend dem CI. Gute Menüführung, sauber gestaltet, hebt sich wohltuend von anderen Geräten in diesem Bereich ab.

»Diomax®« is a true all-rounder for modern surgical procedures. This diode laser is a versatile system with a wide range of applications, from outpatient surgery to endoscopic procedures in state-of-the-art operating theatres. With laser power of up to 20 watts, it is mainly used in combination with special fibre and catheter sets to treat vascular conditions.

The quality of its laser beam sets new standards. Up to now, it has only been possible to generate beams such as this with solid-state lasers. But this is not its only outstanding property. It is also impressive for the clever concept on which it is based, and for the convenient user interface with its display and luminous elements. The surgeon can select from as many as 50 individually adjustable programs, and all parameters, which can be set using a single control knob, are clearly shown on its large colour display, which is easy to read even in darkened operating theatres. Everything is under control at a glance – there are no confusing sub-menus to make operation complicated.

This compact, high-quality appliance features a flat, polygonal design, functional clarity and an easy-to-read, self-explanatory user interface. »Diomax®« satisfies the highest standards. It is simple to use and delivers an excellent beam, allowing the surgeon to concentrate entirely on his patient.

Judges panel

High design quality, in terms of product design, of the graphic interface and of ease of control, which is done via a central control knob. High-quality materials, very well executed product design and good colour scheme that fits in with CI. Good menu navigation, uncluttered in structure. A welcome change from the other appliances in this field.

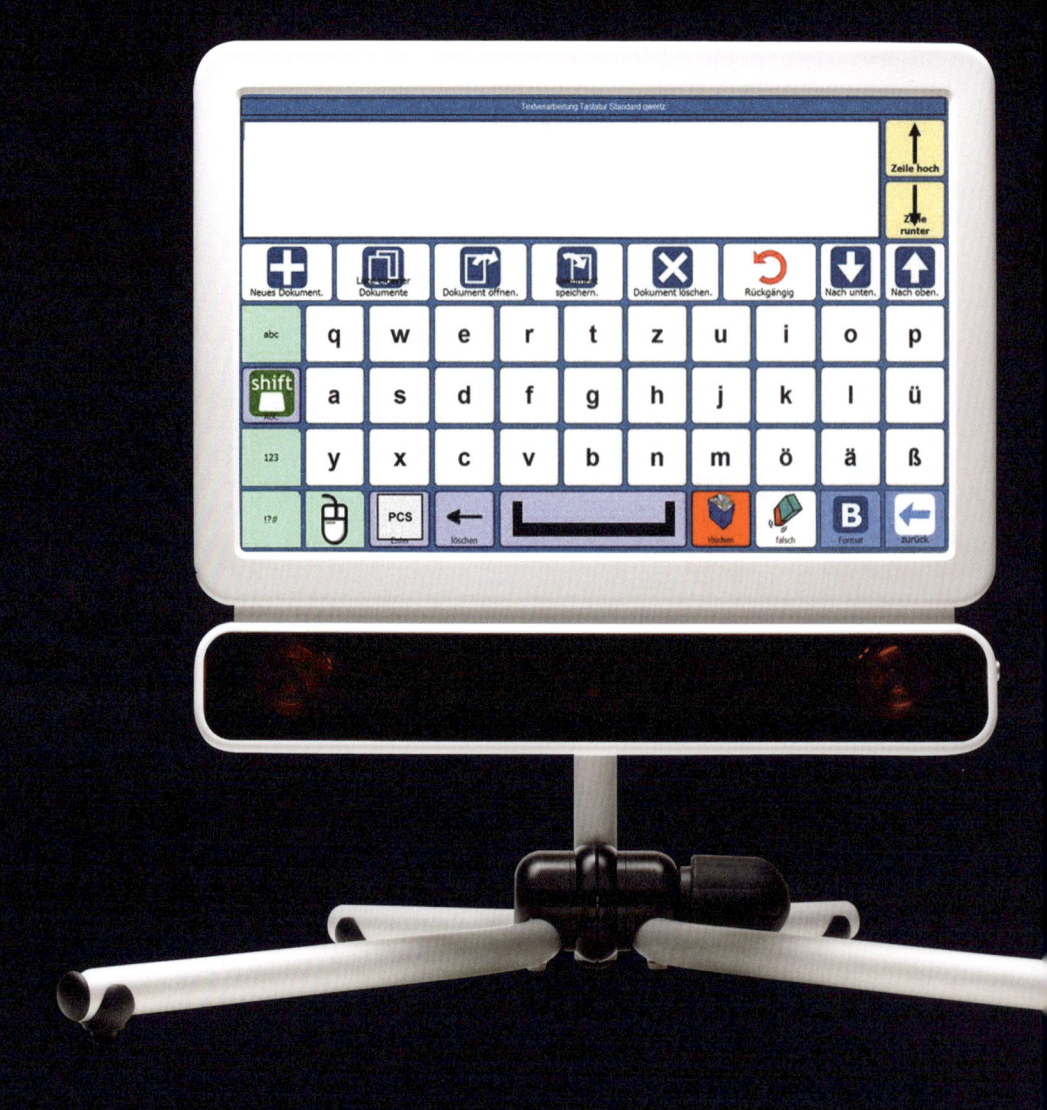

SeeTech® Pro Augensteuerung Eye tracker
Medizin, Rehabilitation, Medicine, rehabil
Geriatrie **Silber** geriatric medicine

»SeeTech® Pro« ist eine computerbasierte Kommunikationshilfe für Menschen, die körperlich so eingeschränkt sind, dass sie nicht mehr selbst kommunizieren können, beispielsweise bei Erkrankungen wie ALS, Multipler Sklerose, Muskelschwäche, Locked-In-Syndrom, ausgeprägter Spastik oder hoher Querschnittslähmung.

Der Monitor ermöglicht die Eingabe und Steuerung per Augenkontakt. Wird ein Bildschirmsymbol mit den Augen fixiert, löst das einen Mausklick aus. Eine integrierte Kamera wertet die Augenbewegungen des Benutzers aus und setzt sie in Aktionen auf dem Bildschirm um. So kann der Benutzer durch einfaches Hinschauen auf ein Symbol oder einen Buchstaben das ganze System selbstständig mit den Augen bedienen. Eingegebene Buchstaben, Wörter und Sätze werden über eine spezielle Software vom Gerät erkannt und in einer akustischen Sprachausgabe über Lautsprecher kommuniziert. »SeeTech® Pro« arbeitet überaus exakt und ist sehr bedienerfreundlich. Ein ständiges Neukalibrieren der Augensteuerung wird dank eines großen Toleranzbereiches überflüssig.

Die Augensteuerung ist ein sehr wirtschaftliches System, da es auf am Markt verfügbare Standardkomponenten zurückgreift. Neu entwickelt wurde das Herzstück des Systems: die Software, die die Augenbewegungen mit Hilfe einer Kamera erfasst, interpretiert und an das Kommunikationsprogramm weitergibt. Das System ermöglicht dank einem Baukastenprinzip individuelle Lösungen für verschiedene Bedürfnisse und kann nach Bedarf erweitert werden.

Der Monitor lässt sich mit Hilfe von Halterungen sowohl am Tisch, am Rollstuhl oder am Bett befestigen.

Jury

Ein sehr wichtiges Thema, das bisher von Gestaltern vernachlässigt worden ist. Deshalb begrüßen wir es sehr, dass dieses Produkt hier eingereicht wurde. Das Augensteuerungssystem funktioniert sehr gut. Es ist ein Bereich, der zwar eine Minderheit betrifft, aber Menschen mit starken körperlichen Einschränkungen eine Möglichkeit schafft, handlungsfähig zu sein. Für Gestalter ist es ein spannendes Feld, in dem sie Selbstständigkeit und Kommunikationsfähigkeit fördern können. Das finden wir ganz wichtig.

»SeeTech® Pro« is a computer-based communication aid for people who are so restricted in their movements that they can no longer communicate without help – in conditions such as ALS, multiple sclerosis, muscular dystrophy, locked-in syndrome, extreme spasticity or quadriplegia.

The monitor registers eye contact to perform input and control functions. If the eyes focus on an icon, a mouse click is triggered. An integrated camera analyzes the user's eye movements and translates them into actions on screen. By simply staring at a symbol or letter, for example, the user can independently control the entire system with his eyes alone. The appliance uses a special software to recognize the letters, words and sentences that are entered, and uses acoustic language output to communicate them via a loudspeaker. »SeeTech® Pro« works extremely precisely, and is very user-friendly. Constant recalibration of the eye tracker is unnecessary, as it has a wide tolerance range.

The eye tracker is a very economical system that makes use of standard, commercially available components. The core of the system, the software, is a new development. This detects eye movements with the help of a camera, interprets them and relays them to the communication program. Thanks to the modular principle on which it is based, the system can provide individual solutions for different needs, and can be enhanced if required.

The brackets provided with the monitor allow it to be fixed to a table, a wheelchair or a bed.

Judges panel

A very important topic that has so far been neglected by designers. This makes us all the more pleased that this product has been submitted. The eye-tracking solution works very well. The target group for a product like this is a minority, but it gives people with extreme physical disabilities a chance to interact with others. For designers this is an exciting field, since it gives them a chance to encourage independence and communicative abilities. We think this is very important.

**Premion Line
Beinbeuger**

Kraftfitnessgerät
Medizin, Rehabilitation,
Geriatrie **Silber**

Strength training
Medicine, rehabili
geriatric medicine

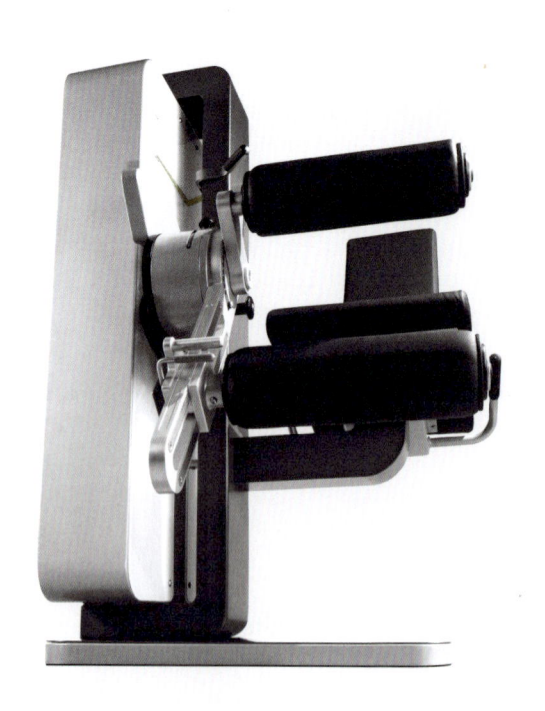

Der Beinbeuger gehört zu insgesamt 17 Trainingsgeräten für den Einsatz in der Rehabilitation und im Fitnessstudio. Die umfassende Produktfamilie ermöglicht nicht nur eine Vielzahl von Trainings- und Therapievarianten, sondern setzt auch neue Maßstäbe. Außergewöhnliche Gestaltung mit markanten Formen, hervorragende Qualität und hohe Funktionalität verbinden sich zu einem homogenen Erscheinungsbild der »Premion Line«.

So lässt sich mit dem patentierten Gewichtsverstellsystem Fast Lock Control direkt aus der Trainingsposition heraus das Gewicht einstellen. Neben der komfortablen Einhandbedienung macht auch der optimale Einstieg über den freischwebenden Sitz die Geräte in hohem Maße barrierefrei und Reha-geeignet.

Der oft martialische Charakter der üblichen Kraft-Fitnessgeräte wird durch den voll verkleideten Gewichtsblock und die sanften Kantenabrundungen gemildert. Das patentierte C-förmige Tragelement – C-Clip Corpus – mit international geschützter Technik und Design dient als funktionale und formale Klammer. Dieses prägnante Gestaltungselement bildet das technische Rückgrat aller Geräte, trägt den Gewichtsblock und löst alle funktionalen Anforderungen.

Weltweit einzigartig sind die frei gestaltbaren Interior Design Displays auf den Geräte-Rückseiten, die es erlauben, jedem Fitness-Studio oder jeder Physiotherapie-Praxis eine ganz individuelle Atmosphäre zu geben und die eigene Marke zu stärken.

Der hohe gestalterische und funktionale Anspruch spiegelt sich in jedem einzelnen Detail und jeder Komponente wider. Beispielsweise wurden erstmalig für die Sitzflächen hochwertige PU-Lederlösungen aus dem Premium-Automobilsektor verarbeitet.

Jury

Hochwertig verarbeitet, sehr modernes Design. Spannend, dass die Gewichte versteckt sind, immer im formal gleichen Block, der so die Benutzerführung über alle Gerätetypen vereinheitlicht. Auf der Rückseite kann er gebrandet werden, was eine fantastische, innovative Möglichkeit zur individuellen Gestaltung ist. Verbesserte Gewichtsverstellmöglichkeit über einen zentralen Hebel, der auch während des Trainings bedient werden kann. Es wirkt nicht so martialisch, wie man das in dem Bereich kennt. Es ist keine Maschine mehr, sondern ein Präzisionsinstrument.

This leg curl apparatus is one of 17 pieces of training equipment for use in rehabilitation and the fitness studio. The wide-ranging product family not only allows many forms of training and therapy, but also sets new standards. An unusual design with striking forms, excellent quality and a high level of functionality combine to produce the homogeneous appearance of »Premion Line«.

The patented Fast Lock Control weight-adjusting system allows the amount of weight to be set directly from the training position. Apart from this convenient one-handed operation, the cantilevered seat provides excellent access to the apparatus, making it barrier-free and perfect for rehabilitation applications.

The completely encased weight block and the softly rounded edges take away some of the frequently martial character seen in conventional strength-training equipment. The technology and design of the patented C-shaped support, or »C-Clip Corpus«, is protected internationally. Formally and functionally, it is common to all the products in this family. This striking design element is the technical backbone of each piece of apparatus: it supports the weight block and fulfils every functional requirement.

One unique feature is the customizable interior design display on the rear side of the apparatus. This allows any gym or physiotherapy practice to create its own individual atmosphere and strengthen its own brand.

The high standards set for design and function are reflected in every single detail and each component. For the first time, for example, the seat surfaces use high-quality PU-leather fabric, which is otherwise used for premium vehicles.

Judges panel

Excellent workmanship, very modern design. It's exciting how the weights have been concealed, always in a block with the same formal appearance, which means all the pieces of apparatus are used in the same way. The rear panel offers room for branding, which is a fantastic, innovative opportunity for individual design. The way weights can be adjusted has been improved. It is now done via a central lever that can also be operated during the workout. It is not as martial as you would expect for products of this kind. It is not so much a machine, more a precision tool.

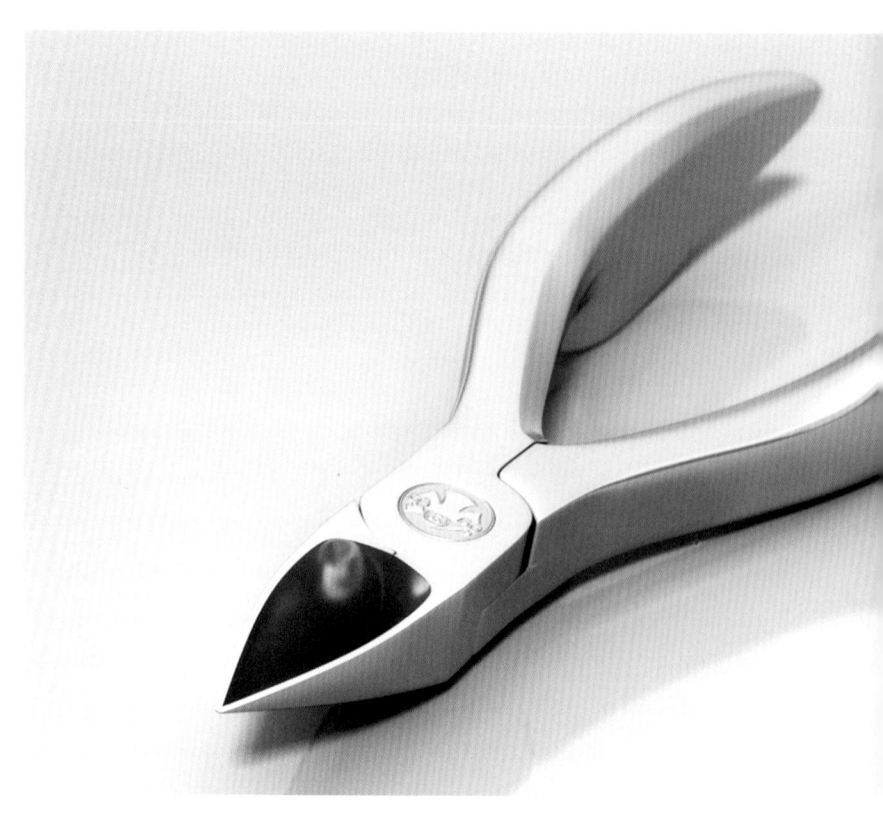

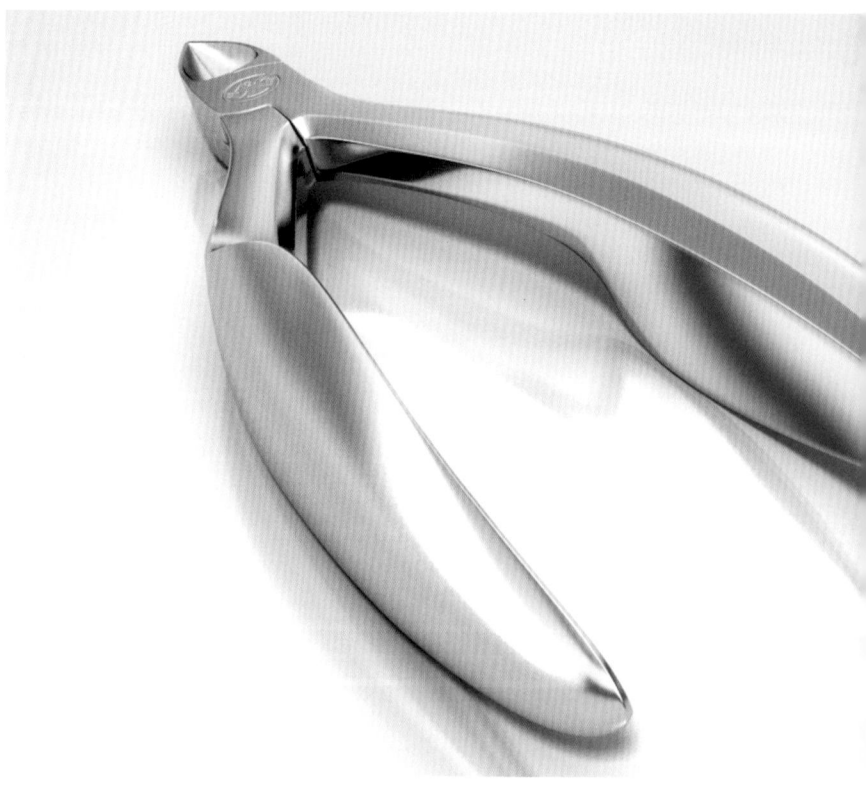

Haptikós Nagelzange Nail nippers
Medizin, Rehabilitation, Medicine, rehabil
Geriatrie **Silber** geriatric medicine

Der Name der Nagelzange ist Programm. »Haptikós« kommt aus dem Griechischen und bedeutet »zum Berühren geeignet«. Ihre außergewöhnliche Form, ihre Größe, ihre Kontur und ihr Gewicht laden zum Betasten und Erfühlen und zur haptischen Wahrnehmung ein. Hautsinne, Muskelanspannung und spielerische Handhabung erschließen das Neuartige von »Haptikós«.

Die Nagelzange für die wachsende Zielgruppe von 50 plus verbindet das angenehme Gefühl des Greifens mit dem günstigen Kraftverhältnis auf der Schneide. Der Drehpunkt wurde näher zur Schneide versetzt, wodurch das Hebelverhältnis optimiert wurde. Dadurch wird der partielle Schnitt des Nagels leicht und angenehm, und die Haltung der Hand ist entspannt.

Durch Gewichtszunahme und Materialerweiterung in den Griffflächen wurde auch die Haptik verbessert. Die Zangengriffe schmiegen sich gut in die Innenflächen der greifenden Hand und sorgen mit ihrer Form für eine optimale Haltung. Durch die breiten Auflagen verteilt sich der Handdruck angenehm auf eine größere Fläche. Das Gewicht gibt eine fühlbare Rückmeldung. Das kurze Gelenk und die kurze Schneide begünstigen das Kraftverhältnis von Handdruck zu Schnittkraft. Das bedeutet gute Führung und ein leichter Schnitt.

Die Nagelzange ist von Linkshändern ebenso zu verwenden wie von Rechtshändern. Sie besteht aus rostfreiem Instrumentenstahl. Ihre reinen, glatten Oberflächen bieten eine angenehme Haptik.

Jury

Die Nagelzange ist nicht nur funktional mit einfacher bequemer Handhabung, sondern auch einfach schön. Sie liegt gut in der Hand und wirkt wie eine kleine Skulptur mit harmonischen Übergängen. Uns überzeugen auch die handschmeichlerischen Qualitäten. Schöne matte Oberfläche, sehr angenehme Haptik.

The nail nippers' name is a manifesto: the Greek word »haptikós« means »fit to be touched«. Their unusual form, size, contours and weight are an invitation to touch and feel, to experience the product tactually. The user senses what is new about »Haptikós« through the skin, the tension of the muscles and the pleasure of handling.

Developed for the growing target group of consumers aged 50 plus, the nail nippers combine a pleasant grip with good transfer of cutting force to the blade. The fulcrum has been moved closer to the blade, thus optimizing leverage. Cutting nails thus becomes easy and pleasant, and the hand is relieved of any tension.

Adding weight to and expanding the size of the grips also improves the feel of the nippers. The grips fit snugly into the palm of the hand, and their form ensures an optimum grip. The broad surface of the grips means that pressure is applied to a broader area of the hand. The nippers' weight means the user can feel when he is using them correctly. The short joint and short blade facilitate the translation of hand pressure into cutting pressure. This means the nippers can be guided well, and cut easily.

The nippers can be used by both left-handers and right-handers. They are made of stainless surgical steel. Their pure, smooth surface makes them pleasant to the touch.

Judges panel

The nippers are not only functional – easy and comfortable to use – but also simply beautiful. They fit nicely in the hand, and have the appearance of a small sculpture with harmonious transitions. We also liked the fact that the nippers' are a joy to touch. Elegant matt surface, very pleasant to the touch.

Snodo® Fingerorthese
Medizin, Rehabilitation,
Geriatrie **Silber**

Finger splint
Medicine, rehabilit
geriatric medicine

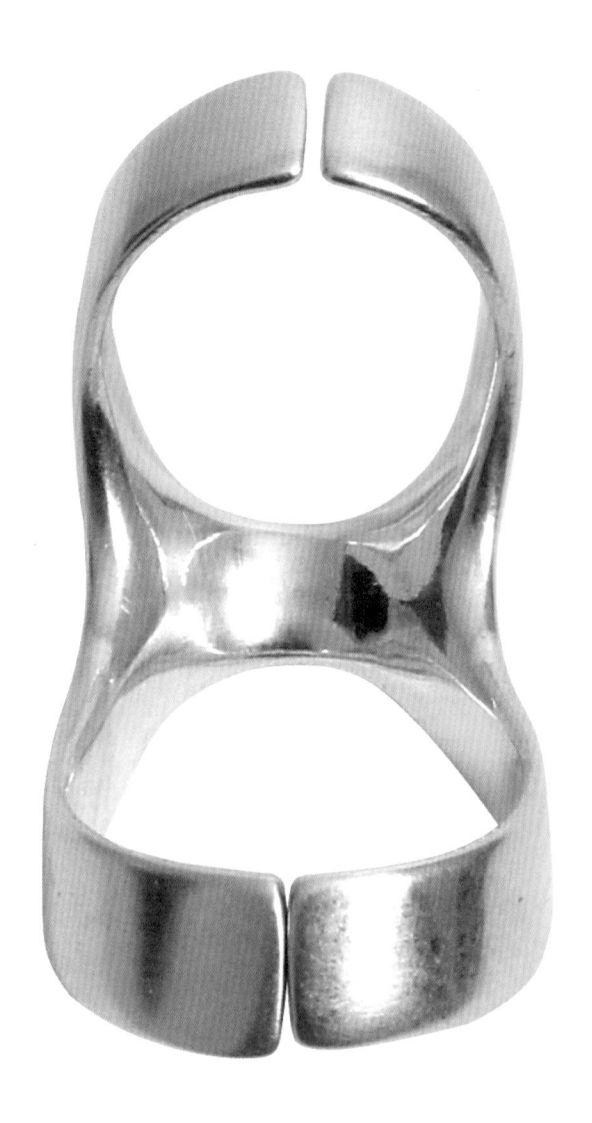

»Snodo®« ist eine Fingerorthese für Menschen mit rheumatischen Erkrankungen, bei denen das Finger-Mittelgelenk schmerzhaft und dauerhaft überstreckt und das Endgelenk in einer Beugestellung fixiert ist – die sogenannte Schwanenhals-Deformität.

Innovativ ist, dass die aus Sterlingsilber gefertigte Schiene eine geöffnete Form hat und damit nach Bedarf enger und weiter gestellt werden kann. Beide Bügel sitzen in optimalem Abstand zum Mittelgelenk und sind breit gearbeitet. Das bringt dem Träger Bequemlichkeit beim Bewegen und Greifen der Finger und verhindert die Überstreckung des kranken Mittelgelenkes. Die antibakterielle Wirkung des Silbers macht »Snodo®« hautsympathisch.

Mit der Orthese kann man alle Arbeiten des täglichen Lebens verrichten. Dabei sieht die Orthese nicht wie ein orthopädisches Produkt, sondern wie ein Schmuckstück aus. So wirkt sie nicht stigmatisierend ganz im Gegensatz zu den unästhetischen und kurzlebigen handelsüblichen Orthesen.

»Snodo®« verbindet nicht nur Funktionalität mit hochwertiger Verarbeitung und klarer attraktiver Formensprache, sondern erfüllt auch hohe Ansprüche an Nachhaltigkeit. So ist sie stabil, dauerhaft haltbar und damit langlebig. Zudem lässt sie sich zu 100 Prozent recyceln.

Jury

Ein Hilfsmittel für Rheuma-Kranke, das aber nicht so aussieht, sondern wie ein attraktiver Fingerschmuck aus Silber gestaltet ist. Die Orthese vereint formale Qualitäten mit der ergonomischen Verbesserung für die Benutzer. Sie ist leicht zu reinigen, langlebig und von hoher Wertigkeit.

»Snodo®« is a finger splint for people with rheumatoid arthritis, in which the middle joint of the finger is painfully and permanently hyper-extended and the joint closest to the fingertip is permanently bent toward the palm – also known as swan-neck deformity.

The innovative feature of this splint, which is made of sterling silver, is that it is open in form, and can thus be made wider or narrower as required. The two clamps have a large surface area, and are set at an optimum distance from the middle joint. Moving the finger and gripping is thus comfortable for the wearer, and hyper-extension of the middle joint is prevented. The antibacterial effect of the silver makes »Snodo®« kind to the skin.

The splint allows everyday tasks to be carried out without hindrance. Moreover, it does not look like an orthopaedic product at all, but like a piece of jewellery. Unlike the ugly, short-lived splints available on the market, it does not have any stigmatizing effect.

»Snodo®« not only combines functionality with high-quality workmanship and clear, attractive formal expression, it also satisfies high standards of sustainability. It is robust and long-lasting, and thus has a long service life. It can also be completely recycled.

Judges panel

For people suffering from rheumatoid arthritis, an aid that doesn't look like one, but like an attractive piece of silver jewellery for the finger. The splint combines formal qualities and an ergonomic benefit for the user. It is easy to clean, long-lasting and high-quality.

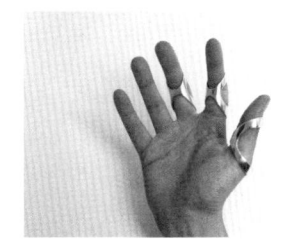

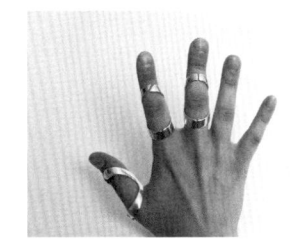

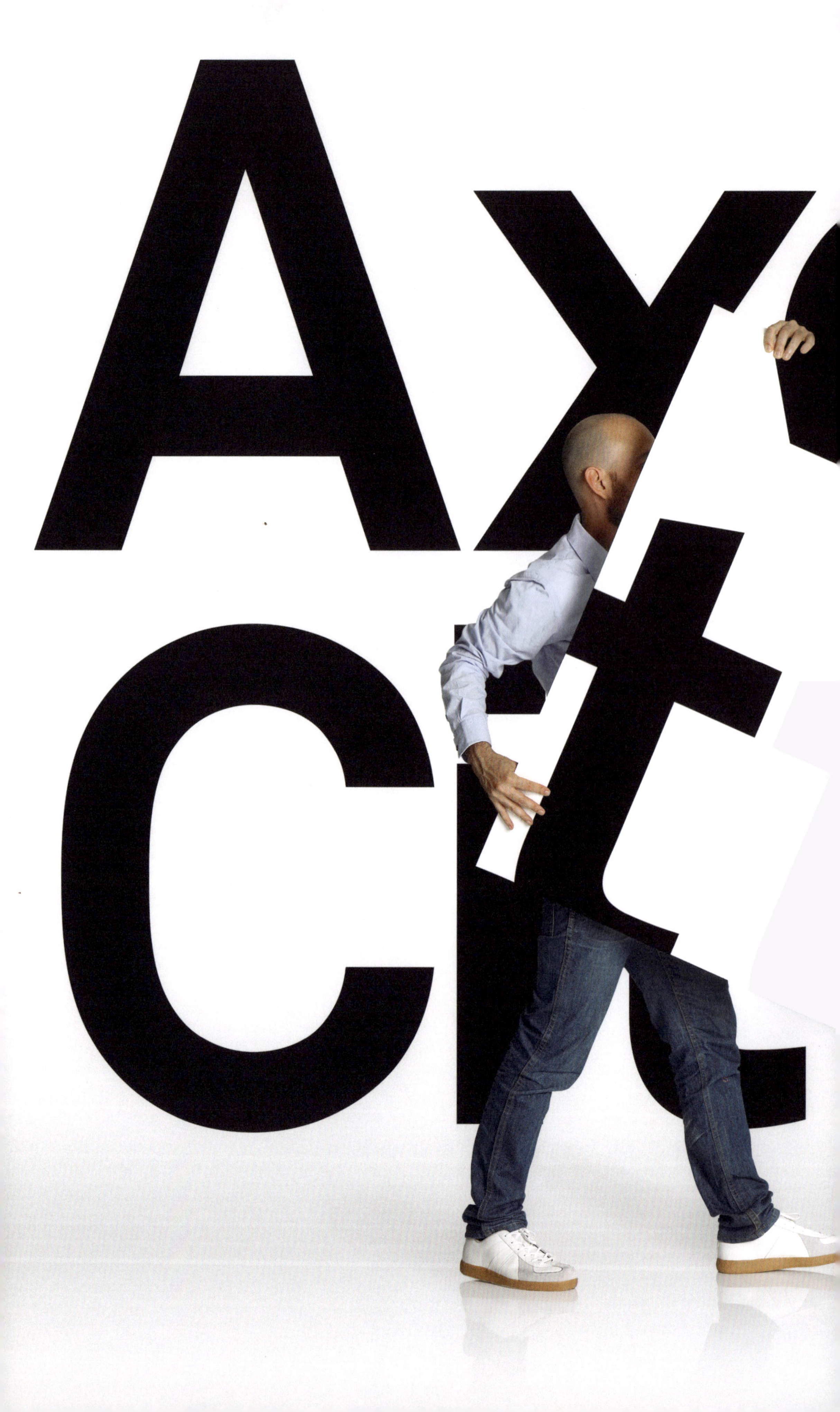

Ax
C

erio

Axor Citerio WTM
180 mm

Waschtischmischer
Bad, Sanitär, Wellness **Gold**

Wash stand mixer
Bathrooms, sanita
wellness **Gold**

Der Einhebel-Waschtischmischer erweitert die Badkollektion »Axor Citterio«, die für höchste Design- und Fertigungsqualität steht. Sie ist charakterisiert durch das Spannungsverhältnis von hochwertigen Flächen und klaren Linien, von runden und eckigen Formen, die sich bis ins kleinste Detail durchziehen.

So besticht auch die neue Armatur durch ihre Formensprache, die sanfte, harmonische Radien – Sinnbild für das kostbare Lebenselement Wasser – und präzise, geradlinige Kantenführung, Zeitlosigkeit und Modernität perfekt verbindet. Edle Materialien und brillante Oberflächen unterstreichen die Hochwertigkeit.

Der 180 Millimeter hohe Waschtischmischer steht für höchsten Bedienkomfort. So lässt er sich bequem über einen Joystick steuern. Höhe und Länge des Auslaufs stehen im wohlproportionierten Verhältnis zueinander und machen die Nutzung besonders komfortabel. Mit dem bündig integrierten Strahlformer lässt sich der Strahlwinkel einfach einstellen. Der weit auskragende Auslauf ermöglicht, die Armatur noch vielfältiger bei unterschiedlichen Waschtischgeometrien einzusetzen. Damit eröffnet sie zusätzliche Kombinations- und Gestaltungsmöglichkeiten für den Waschtischbereich.

Dank der Hansgrohe EcoSmart-Technologie wird der Wasserdurchfluss auf rund fünf Liter pro Minute begrenzt – und dies ohne jeden Komfortverlust.

Jury

Eine Armatur für den privaten Bereich, die formal sehr schön gelöst ist. Die Möglichkeit der handlosen, fingerlosen Bedienung mit dem Handgelenk oder dem Arm erlaubt, auch mit schmutzigen Händen den Waschtischmischer zu bedienen ohne ihn anfassen zu müssen. Sehr überzeugende Produktpräsentation. Besonders ansprechend finden wir die Lösung der Kreisfunktion für die Warmwassermischung, die mit einer gut erkennbaren Nullstellung versehen ist und auch in einer mechanisch sehr schönen Ausführung erfolgt.

This single-lever wash stand mixer tap is an addition to the »Axor Citterio« bathroom collection, which stands for the highest design and manufacturing quality. It is characterized by the tension between high-quality surfaces and clear lines, between round and angular shapes, a tension which is continued down to the last detail.

This new fitting stands out by virtue of its formal expression, which perfectly combines timelessness and modernity in its soft, harmonious radii – symbolic of the precious vital element water – and precise, straight edges. Precious materials and brilliant surfaces underline its high quality.

180 millimetres high, the wash stand mixer tap stands for outstanding ease of operation. It can be controlled comfortably by means of a joystick. The height and length of the spout are well proportioned, and make the tap especially convenient to use. The spray former, which is integrated flush with the tap, allows simple adjustment of the angle of the water jet. The spout's long overhang means that the fitting can be used with even more different wash-stand geometries. In this way, it opens up additional possibilities for combination and new design possibilities in the wash stand area.

Hansgrohe's EcoSmart technology means that water flow is reduced to roughly five litres per minute, yet without any loss of comfort.

Judges panel

A fitting for the private sphere, formally very well done. Since a hand or finger is not needed to operate it – a wrist or arm will also do – the mixer tap can be used without having to put dirty hands on it. Very convincing product presentation. We thought the solution with the circular function for mixing hot water was especially appealing. It is easy to tell when the tap is off, and the mechanical design is very well done.

Celis E Elektronische Waschtisch-Armatur
Bad, Sanitär, Wellness **Silber**

Electronic wash st
Bathrooms, sanita
wellness **Silver**

Die elektronische Waschtisch-Armatur »Celis E« ist für den Einsatz in öffentlichen und gewerblichen Sanitärräumen entworfen, wie beispielsweise in Gastronomie und Hotels, Sportstätten und Flughäfen, Rasl- und Campingplätzen, Verwaltungsgebäuden und Arztpraxen. Sie lässt sich aber ebensogut im privaten Bereich, etwa im Gäste-WC, verwenden.

Die komfortable Waschtisch-Armatur funktioniert berührungslos mit Infrarot-Sensor für hygienische Bedienung. Ihre robuste Ganzmetallausführung macht sie vandalensicher.

»Celis E« besticht durch ihr zeitloses, elegantes Design. Mit ihrer kleinen Bauhöhe und ihrem schlanken Körper präsentiert sie sich in harmonischen, ausbalancierten Proportionen.

Die nahtlosen Übergänge des Armaturenkörpers, der aus einem Stück gefertigt ist, zeugen nicht nur von hochwertiger Perfektion, sondern sorgen auch für optimale Hygiene, da sie die vollständige Reinigung ermöglichen.

Die Waschtisch-Armatur wird in zwei Ausführungen angeboten, zum einen für kaltes, beziehungsweise vorgemischtes Wasser, zum anderen mit Temperaturregler für Mischwasser. Bei Bedarf kann eine automatische 24-Stundenspülung zugeschaltet werden, um auch bei unregelmäßig genutzten Sanitärräumen Hygiene in der Anschlussleitung zu gewährleisten.

Jury

Eine Armatur für den öffentlichen Bereich. Sie ist aus einem Stück gefertigt und damit fugenlos und sehr gut und rückstandsfrei zu reinigen. Vom Preis-Leistungs-Verhältnis gut positioniert. Eine formal sehr schöne und wertige Lösung.

»Celis E«, an electronic wash stand fitting, has been designed for use in public and commercial washrooms, such as in restaurants and hotels, gymnasiums and airports, service stations and camp sites, administrative buildings and surgeries. However, it can be used equally well in the private sphere, such as the guest toilet.

This convenient wash stand fitting works without any contact, being activated by an infrared sensor, which makes it hygienic to use. Its sturdy all-metal design makes it vandalism-proof.

»Celis E« is exceptionally timeless and elegant in design. Low in overall height, and with a slim body, its proportions are harmonious and balanced.

The seamless transitions of the body of the fitting, which is made from one piece, bear witness not only to a marked sense of perfection, but also ensure optimum hygiene, since they allow it to be cleaned completely.

The wash stand fitting is available in two designs – one for cold or pre-mixed water, and the other with a mixing battery. On request, it can be furnished with a flushing function that automatically runs the tap every 24 hours, which ensures that the water in the pipes remains clean even if the washroom is not in regular use.

Judges panel

A fitting for the public sphere. It is made of one piece, and so has no joints, which means it can be cleaned very well, without any residues. Well positioned in terms of value for money. A formally very elegant and high-quality solution.

T44

3NO

T44T43N0 FlexInduktion-Kochfeld mit TwistPad FlexInduction hob
Küche, Haushalt **Gold** Kitchen, househol

Das FlexInduktion-Kochfeld bietet alle bekannten Vorzüge der Induktion, jedoch darüberhinaus noch mehr Freiheit und Komfort beim Kochen. So passt sich das Kochfeld den Töpfen flexibel an. Die linke Seite des Kochfeldes besteht aus einer großen Kochzone, die getrennt über eine Sensortaste geschaltet werden kann und dadurch maximale Flexibilität bei der Positionierung und der Größe der Töpfe – von der Espressokanne bis zum Bräter – ermöglicht. Auf der rechten Seite befinden sich zwei Einzel-Induktions-Kochzonen.

Das Kochfeld verfügt zusätzlich über die intelligente TwistPad-Bedienung. Das bedeutet grenzenlosen Bedienkomfort mit dem magnetischen, abnehmbaren TwistPad: aufsetzen – antippen – drehen. Supereinfach.

Dabei wird der Bedienknebel neben die Digitalanzeige auf die Keramikoberfläche gelegt, wo er durch Permanentmagnete unter der Oberfläche in Position gehalten wird. Sensoren im Kochfeld registrieren die Richtungsänderung beim Bewegen des Reglers und nehmen die gewählte Einstellung vor. Wird der Knebel verschoben oder entfernt, schaltet die Kochstelle automatisch ab.

Das Bedienfeld ist übersichtlich und selbsterklärend gestaltet. Das hochwertig designte Kochfeld wird von einem eleganten Edelstahlrahmen umgeben.

Jury

Eine hochinnovative Interaktionsgestaltung – intuitiv und gleichzeitig spielerisch. Es macht Spaß, mit dem Objekt umzugehen, bietet aber auch funktionale Vorteile, beispielsweise was Verschmutzung angeht. Es ist eine absolut geschlossene Oberfläche, die leicht zu reinigen ist. Variable Kochfelder erlauben unterschiedliche Funktionalitäten beim Kochen. Diese Kindersicherung, denken wir, ist attraktiv, weil sie nicht als Lösung für den Notfall eingesetzt wird, sondern eine Hightech-Lösung ist.

The »FlexInduction« hob offers all the benefits of induction, but with even more freedom and comfort when cooking. For example, the hob adjusts flexibly to the size and position of the pots and pans. The left half of the hob is one large cooking zone that can be switched on separately by means of a sensor button, allowing maximum flexibility when it comes to the position and size of the pots and pans –whether an espresso maker or a roasting tin. The right half of the hob comprises two individual induction cooking zones.

The hob also comes with the TwistPad, a intelligent new control. The magnetic, removable TwistPad offers boundless cooking convenience: simply position, touch lightly, and turn. Nothing could be easier.

The control knob is placed on the ceramic surface next to the digital display, where it is kept in place by permanent magnets under the surface. Sensors in the hob register the change in direction when the control knob is moved, and adjust to the desired setting. If the knob is displaced or removed, the hob switches off automatically.

The layout of the controls is clear and self-explanatory. An elegant stainless steel rim runs around the stylish hob.

Judges panel

Highly innovative, interactive design. It is both intuitive and playful. Using it is fun, but the hob also offers functional benefits – when it comes to cleaning, for example. Its surface is absolutely flush, which makes it easy to clean. Variable cooking zones provide different cooking functions. What makes the child lock attractive for us is that it is a high-tech solution, not just a solution for emergencies.

B46E74N0 Backofen Oven
Küche, Haushalt **Silber** Kitchen, household

Der Einbau-Backofen besticht durch sein neues, faszinierendes Design. Ein Grundcharakteristikum ist sein nach oben offener Rahmen als Matrix, an dem sich alles ausrichtet. Eine interessante Spannung erzeugt das Zusammenspiel von feiner Facettierung der Kanten als markantem und der Ellipse als hintergründigem Designelement. Herausragend sind die geprägte Bedienblende, auf der die Einknopf-Bedienung zentral platziert ist, und der darüberliegende Glaseinleger mit Klartext-Elektronik.

Aber der Backofen aus Edelstahl zeichnet sich nicht nur durch seine hochwertige klare Gestaltung aus sondern besitzt auch eine Vielzahl an technischen Vorzügen. So gestatten der ergonomisch mitdrehende Türgriff Slide® und die voll versenkbare Backofentür Hide® ein bequemes Öffnen des Backofens. Man kommt an alles ran und kann viel besser arbeiten.

Das DUO-Backofensystem mit zwölf Betriebsarten ermöglicht eine perfekte Zubereitung der Speisen. Es bietet zwei voneinander unabhängige Beheizungsarten: neben der konventionellen Ober- und Unterhitze das CircoTherm®-Heißluftsystem. Bei dieser einzigartigen Rundumhitze wird Heißluft mit hoher Gechwindigkeit gezielt um die Speisen gelenkt. Das Menükochen ist auf bis zu drei Ebenen gleichzeitig möglich. Ohne Geschmacksübertragung, kein Saftverlust, schnelles Schließen der Poren beim Brat- und Backgut.

Jury

Überzeugend gelöst, wie man den Backofen steuert, sehr gute Handhabung, selbsterklärende, intuitive Bedienerführung. Wir finden es auch schön, dass der Griff mit der Tür mitgeht und immer horizontal bleibt und sich die Tür vollständig versenkt. Das ist sehr praktisch. Man hat dadurch einen guten Zugriff auf die Speisen. Hohe Funktionalität.

The impressive thing about this built-in oven is its new and fascinating design. Its hallmark is its frame, designed as a matrix which is left un-enclosed the top, and which acts as the point of reference for all the other features. The interplay between the sophisticated bevelling of the edges as a striking design element, and the ellipse as a subtle design element, creates an interesting tension. Other outstanding design features are the embossed control panel, with the single-knob control placed at its centre, and the glass insert above it with its clear text electronic display.

But this stainless steel oven does not only stand out because of its high-quality, sleek design. It also offers many technical benefits. The oven can be opened comfortably, for example, thanks to the Slide® handle, which turns as the door opens, and the Hide® oven door, which retracts completely. Everything is more accessible, making cooking easier.

The DUO oven system with 12 programmes means that food can be prepared perfectly. It heats food in two completely different ways: apart from the conventional top and bottom heat feature, there is also the CircoTherm® fan-oven system. This unique fan system rapidly circulates hot air around the food. This allows an entire menu to be cooked on three levels at once. The different tastes do not mingle, and meat loses none of its juices, as the pores are quickly sealed.

Judges panel

The way the oven is controlled has been very well solved, excellent handling, self-explanatory and intuitive user interface. We also like the way the handle moves with the door, always remaining horizontal, and the way the door is completely drawn back into a recess. This is very practical. It gives you good access to the food in the oven. Very functional.

C49C62N0   Dampfgarbackofen   Steam oven
           Küche, Haushalt   **Silber**   Kitchen, househol

Der hochwertige Dampfgarbackofen überzeugt durch seine zeitlose Emotionalität und seine elegante und schlichte Formgebung. Auffallend ist das wiederkehrende Designelement der Facette, das an den Edelstahlkanten und Tasten sowie bei Griff und Drehwähler auftaucht – wie bei allen Neff Einbaugeräten – und damit perfekt mit ihnen kombinierbar ist.

Er besticht aber nicht nur durch sein klares Design, sondern auch durch zahlreiche technische Highlights, die hohen Komfort bieten.

So dreht sich der Türgriff Slide® automatisch beim Öffnen der Tür mit, sodass man ihn bequem mit der Hand führen kann. Hohen Komfort bietet auch die Tür Hide®, die vollständig versenkbar ist und damit dem Nutzer reichlich Platz zum bequemen Hantieren schafft. Oder die revolutionäre CircoSteam® Technik. Diese vereint Heißluft und Dampfgaren, was perfekte Ergebnisse erzielt: die Speisen bleiben innen saftig und werden außen kross. Insgesamt bietet der Dampfgarbackofen neun verschiedene Betriebsarten.

Herausragend ist die Bedienblende mit facettiertem, aufgesetztem Glaseinleger mit Klartext-Elektronik und Einknopf-Bedienung. Wird er gerade nicht gebraucht, lässt sich der Bedienknebel vollständig versenken.

Jury

Wir finden ihn gut, weil zum einen die Handhabung mit der versenkbaren Tür sehr schön ist. Das ist faszinierend und etwas Besonderes. Sehr funktional, man verbrennt sich nicht die Finger und kommt gut an die Speisen. Zum anderen ist ein Dampfgarer mit dem kleineren Backofen auch etwas für kleine Haushalte und für schonendere Zubereitung. Im Alter achtet man ja besonders auf gesunde Ernährung, so kann man ihn auch als Universal-Produkt sehen. Die digitale Benutzerführung, das Interface, ist sehr intuitiv, gutes Feedback, einfach und selbsterklärend.

This high-quality steam oven stands out by virtue of its timeless emotionality, and elegant and unassuming design. One striking feature is the bevelling, as a recurring design element that can be found on the stainless steel surround, on the knobs, on the handle and on the rotary selector. This element is common to all Neff built-in appliances, which means the oven can be combined perfectly with them.

But its clear design is not the only reason it stands out. It also features many technical highlights that add up to a high level of convenience.

The Slide® door handle, for example, turns automatically as the door opens, so that the cook's hand is not twisted uncomfortably. The Hide® door also makes life easier, because it is completely retractable, and so provides the user plenty of room to work unimpeded. Or then there is the revolutionary CircoSteam® technology, which combines circulating hot air and steam to deliver perfect results. Food remains moist on the inside and crisps up nicely on the outside. With this steam oven, cooks can choose from nine operating modes.

One outstanding feature is the control panel, with its bevelled, superimposed glass insert with plain-text electronics and single-knob control. And when it is not in use, the control knob can be completely depressed to form a flush surface.

Judges panel

On the one hand, we like it because the retractable door makes it convenient to use. This is fascinating, as well as something special. Very functional, you don't burn your fingers and can get at the food easily. On the other hand, a steam oven with a smaller oven is something for smaller households, as well as for gentler food preparation. In old age, healthy eating is especially important. In this way, you could see it as a universal product. The digital navigation menu, the interface, is very intuitive, good feedback, simple and self-explanatory.

Varithek® 2.0 Kochmodul
Küche, Haushalt **Silber**

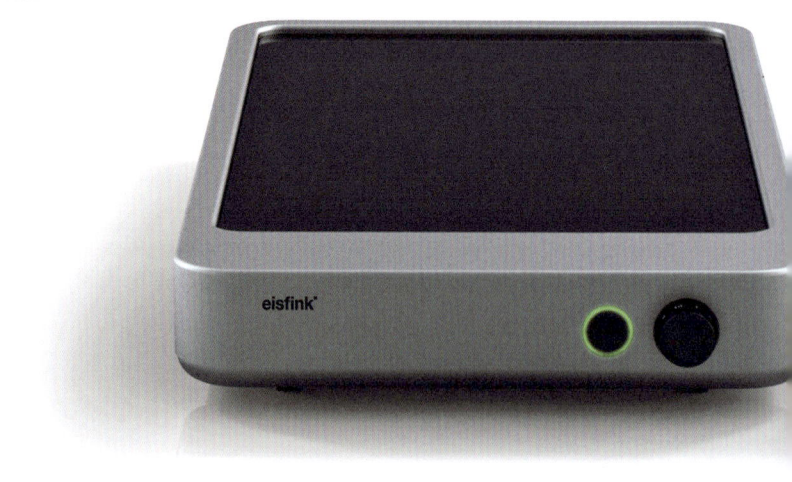

Cooking module
Kitchen, household

Kochen, Grillen, Braten, Frittieren, Woken oder Kühlen – mit einem einzigen Gerät? All diese Garprozesse ermöglicht »Varithek®«. Dieser Klassiker des Frontcookings erscheint nun mit »Varithek® 2.0« in neuem Gewand.

Das hochwertige Kochmodul mit einem Gehäuse aus Edelstahl besticht durch seine puristische, klare Gestaltung. Es hat aber nicht nur ein frisches Design erhalten, sondern auch seine Technik wurde optimiert, die jetzt noch mehr Flexibilität, Funktionalität und Unabhängigkeit garantiert. Die innovative automatische Steuerung erlaubt erstmals auch halbautomatisches Kochen. Mit Hilfe von vordefinierten Programmen kann der Koch unterschiedlichste Speisen automatisch fertig garen. Das gestattet ihm, alleine mehrere Geräte auf einmal zu bedienen, ohne zu riskieren, dass ihm etwas anbrennt.

Dank des neuen Designs – »Varithek® 2.0« besitzt einen integrierten Fixierrahmen für das Gastronorm 1/1-Maß – kann das Gerät nun auch ohne Systemträger als Auftischgerät verwendet werden. Neu ist auch, dass der Thermoplate, der erste Kochtopf im Gastronormformat, die gesamte Fläche – eckig, statt rund – nutzt und unmittelbar auf der Energiequelle steht. Dadurch wird die Energie um 75 Prozent reduziert.

Jury
Eine Neuinterpretation eines traditionellen Themas im Bereich Catering. Überzeugend die hervorragende neue Gestaltung und die Tatsache, dass ein einziges Gerät verschiedenste Garmöglichkeiten wie Dämpfen, Frittieren, Braten, Kochen erlaubt. Sehr positiv, dass durch eine effizientere Art der mobilen Eventbekochung eine Energieersparnis erreicht wird.

Boil, grill, roast, deep-fry, stir-fry or cool – with just one appliance? All these cooking processes are possible with »Varithek®«. The front-cooking classic has now been given a fresh new design as »Varithek® 2.0«.

The high-quality cooking module with its stainless-steel housing stands out by virtue of its clear, purist design. However, it is not just its design that is new. Its inner workings have also been optimized, and now provide even more flexibility, functionality and independence. The innovative automatic control also permits semi-automatic cooking for the first time. With the help of pre-defined programmes, the cook can automatically cook the widest variety of foods to perfection. This allows him to operate several appliances at once on his own, without any risk of food burning.

Thanks to its new design – »Varithek® 2.0« has an integrated fixing frame for Gastronorm 1/1 size containers – the appliance can now also be used as a table-top appliance, without any supporting frame. One further new feature is that the thermoplate – the first Gastronorm-size pot – uses up the entire heating surface, since it is rectangular rather than round. This results in an energy saving of up to 75 percent.

Judges panel
A re-interpretation of a traditional theme from the catering field. An attractive product family with various elements. The excellent new design is impressive, as is the modularity of the system, which allows food to be prepared in all kinds of ways – steamed, deep-fried, fried, boiled. It is also very positive that this more efficient form of mobile event-cooking also allows energy to be saved.

CoolDeLuxe
K8345 X0

Einbau-Kühl-Gefrierkombination
Küche, Haushalt **Silber**

Built-in fridge-fre
Kitchen, househol

Die Kühl-Gefrierkombination besticht durch ihre Fülle an ergonomisch hervorragend gestalteten Details und Besonderheiten, die große Flexibilität und hohen Komfort bieten.

So ist zum Beispiel das Butter- und Käsefach mit einer Slide & Hide®-Funktion – mit einer versenkbaren Klappe – ausgestattet. Das Gerät besitzt flexible Ablageelemente wahlweise für Eier oder Flaschen. Zwei Abstellflächen können durch ihre EasyLift-Funktion einfach und leicht in der Höhe verstellt werden. Man kann bequem unterschiedlich hohe Getränkeflaschen in der Tür aufbewahren, da der niedrige Türabsteller darüber sich stufenlos verschieben lässt. Dank des Teleskop-Vollauszuges, mit dem zwei Lagerschalen ausgestattet sind, kommt man einfach an die Speisen heran.

Die Kühl-Gefrierkombination bietet auch zahlreiche technische Vorteile. So taut sie vollautomatisch im Kühlraum ab. Der Clou dabei: Das Gefrierteil mit separater Tür muss dank »NoFrost«-Technologie nie mehr abgetaut werden. In den VitaFresh®-Frischhaltezonen bei nahe Null Grad wird automatisch die Feuchtigkeit reguliert. Das erhält deutlich länger die Frische und den Nährwert der Lebensmittel. Die trockene Zone besitzt eine mittlere Luftfeuchtigkeit um circa 50 Prozent für Fleisch und Milchprodukte und die feuchte Zone eine hohe Luftfeuchte um circa 95 Prozent für Salat, Gemüse und Obst.

Durch die Türschließhilfe mit Dämpfung und Softeinzug lässt sich die Tür komfortabel schließen.

Jury

Uns überzeugen verschiedene Innovationen, zum Beispiel die EasyLift-Funktion, bei der man Fächer stufenlos verstellen kann. Das Licht ist gut gelöst in Richtung Produkt, es strahlt nicht die Personen an, sondern die Speisen. Dann finden wir die Typografie und die Farbigkeit deutlich souveräner und einheitlicher, einfacher und klarer gelöst als bei Konkurrenzprodukten.

This fridge-freezer features a wealth of ergonomically excellently designed details and special features that offer a high level of both flexibility and convenience.

The butter and cheese compartment, for example, is fitted with a Slide & Hide® function, which means that the lid is fully retractable. The appliance is equipped with flexible shelves that can be used for eggs or for bottles. Two further shelves feature an EasyLift function, which means that their height can be adjusted simply, without effort. Bottles of different heights can easily be kept in the door, as the height of the low door shelf above them is infinitely variable. Two telescopic, fully extending shelves make it easy to get at food stored in the fridge.

The fridge-freezer also has many technical benefits. The fridge compartment defrosts fully automatically. More cleverly, the freezer compartment, with its separate door, never has to be defrosted, thanks to NoFrost technology. In the VitaFresh® compartments, where food is stored at close to zero, moisture is regulated automatically. This means food stays fresh, and nutritional value is preserved, much longer. Average humidity in the dry zone is roughly 50 percent, which makes it ideal for meat and dairy products. In the moist zone for salad, fruit and vegetables, by contrast, humidity is roughly 95 percent.

The door can be closed softly and without effort, thanks to a damping door-closing mechanism.

Judges panel

We are impressed by a number of innovations, such as the EasyLift function, which allows shelves to be infinitely varied. The lighting issue has been resolved well. It lights up the products in the fridge rather than the person opening it. And we think that the typography and colour scheme have been handled with much more confidence, and are more coherent, simpler and clear than in rival products.

SMS69M28 EU   Standgeschirrspüler
Küche, Haushalt   **Silber**

Free-standing dis
Kitchen, househo

Der neue Standgeschirrspüler ist der Weltmeister unter seinesgleichen. Er ist der sparsamste Spüler weltweit; denn er verbraucht im Normalprogramm gerade mal sieben Liter Wasser. Möglich macht das eine von Bosch erfundene wegweisende Technologie: ActiveWater, ein neues Spülsystem, das jeden Tropfen Wasser maximal nutzt.

Schnellere Erwärmung, optimierte Filtertechnik, gezielte Wasserverteilung und bessere Pumpenleistung ermöglichen weniger Wasser- und Energieverbrauch bei mehr Leistung. Zusammen mit Wärmetauscher sowie Aqua- und Beladungssensor schafft der ActiveWater Geschirrspüler so beste Energiewerte. Zudem sorgen Dosierassistent und Reinigerautomatik für ein optimales Ergebnis. Während des Spülvorgangs fällt dabei das Reiniger-Tab in eine spezielle Auffangschale, wo es kontrolliert vollständig aufgelöst wird. So kann es bestmöglich seine Wirkung entfalten.

Der ActiveWater Geschirrspüler in Silver-Inox besitzt eine Antifingerprint Oberfläche. Die klare Gliederung der Blende erleichtert die Wahl der sechs Programme und der fünf Sonderfunktionen.

Das Korbsystem bietet zahlreiche Varianten und hohen Komfort, da es vielfach einstellbar ist. Ergänzt wird es durch eine Vario-Schublade als dritte Beladungsebene für Besteck und kleinere Geschirrteile, die mehr Stellfläche im Unterkorb schafft.

Jury

Der Standgeschirrspüler beeindruckt uns vor allem durch seine ökologischen Aspekte, durch die Technologie, die den Wasserverbrauch senkt. Er weist den richtigen Weg. Auch sonst besitzt er sehr gut gelöste Details in der Variabilität im Innenraum, die Bedienung ist eindeutig.

This new stand-alone dishwasher leads the class in its field. It is the world's most economical dishwasher, consuming just seven litres of water in standard operation. This is possible thanks to a pioneering technology invented by Bosch: Active Water, a new dishwashing system that gets the most out of every drop of water.

Faster heating, optimized filter technology, targeted distribution of water and improved pump performance means lower consumption of water and power but better performance. In combination with a heat exchanger, a water sensor and a load sensor, the Active Water dishwasher achieves excellent energy ratings. The dishwasher's outstanding results are also helped by a DosageAssist and »detergent aware« system. During the washing process, the dishwasher tab falls into a special container, where it is gradually and completely dissolved. This allows it to be used to the best possible effect.

The surface of the stainless silver version of the dishwasher does not show any fingerprints. The clearly organized control panel makes it easy to select the six programmes and five special functions.

The variable basket system is extremely convenient, since it can be adjusted in many different ways. This is complemented by the VarioDrawer, a third loading level for cutlery and small pieces of crockery, which also creates more space in the bottom basket.

Judges panel

What especially impresses us about this freestanding dishwasher is its ecological aspects, and the technology that reduces water consumption. It points the right way forward. But in other respects too, the way more variability has been provided in the interior is very good, and the controls can clearly be understood.

A la carte | Modulküche | | Modular kitchen
| Küche, Haushalt **Silber** | | Kitchen, household

Das unkonventionelle Küchensystem bietet vielseitige Möglichkeiten. Es eignet sich sowohl für den Office- oder Event- als auch den privaten Bereich und besteht aus einzelnen allseitig gut gestalteten Funktionsmodulen, die wie Möbelstücke wirken. Diese können individuell zusammengestellt werden – als Block oder Zeile – und auf die jeweilige Raum- und Anschluss-Situation reagieren: wandgebunden, freistehend oder raumteilend. Ein großer Vorteil auch bei Umzügen – es lässt sich zudem zu einem handlichen Transportvolumen zusammenpacken.

Die einzelnen Module werden untereinander per Magnet verbunden. In den entstehenden Zwischenraum lässt sich ein Bechereinsatz mit einem Schneidbrett aus Buche oder einem Abtropfgitter einstecken, der als zusätzliche Ablage, als Schneidunterlage, Abfallsammler oder für Küchenkräuter genutzt werden kann.

Die einzelnen Nutzbereiche lassen sich individuell bespielen. So kann man das Mittelfach sowohl für ein Gerät der Kompaktklasse, wie Backofen, Dampfgarer, Geschirrspüler und Mikrowelle, als auch für Stauraum mit Drehtür oder Schubkästen verwenden. Die zweiteilige Rückwand erlaubt eine problemlose Installation ohne handwerkliche Eingriffe. Das Fach der Unterschale wird mit einer Klappe verschlossen, die Oberschale enthält entweder die Spüle oder einen Schubkasten mit Selbsteinzug.

Die robusten Außenschalen bestehen aus Buchenholzformteilen, die mit weißem stoß- und abriebfestem Schichtstoff belegt sind. Durch verstellbare Edelstahlfüße lassen sich die Module in der Höhe anpassen. Wahlweise können sie auch mit Rollen ausgestattet werden.

Jury

Wir finden es super. Es ist eine andere Art, eine Küche zu sehen, als Solitär. Man kann sie da anordnen, wo man will, und vielleicht sogar mitnehmen, wenn man auf Messen geht. Sie lässt sich auch ganz klein zusammenbauen. Wenn man die Elemente verbindet, finden wir gut, dass man noch Add-ons hat, mit denen man die Ritzen schließen kann. Die Flexibilität ist interessant, der visuelle Eindruck auch. Mal etwas ganz anderes in der Küche.

This unconventional kitchen system is full of possibilities. It is suitable for the office, for an event or for the private sphere. The individual, well designed functional modules it is made up of are like individual pieces of furniture. They can be combined as desired, as a block or as a range, and react to the space and connections available in the individual room – attached to a wall, free-standing or as a partition. A great advantage, also when moving house, is that the modules can be knocked down to a manageable size.

The various modules are held together by magnets. A cup-holder, a beech cutting board or a drying rack can be inserted in the resulting space between the modules. The drying rack can also be used as an additional shelf, as a base to cut on, as a waste collector, or for kitchen herbs.

The individual compartments can also be used as desired. The middle compartment, for example, can house a compact kitchen appliance such as an oven, a steam oven, a dishwasher or a microwave. But it can also be fitted with a hinged door or drawer and used as storage space. The two-part rear panel allows elements to be installed without the need for professional help. A flap seals off the bottom compartment, and the upper compartment then provides space for a sink or a self-retracting drawer.

The sturdy outer panels are made of moulded beech coated with white shock-resistant and anti-wear laminate. Adjustable stainless steel legs allow the height of the modules to be varied. Casters are also available as an option.

Judges panel

A super idea. A different way of seeing a kitchen, as a stand-alone furniture element. It can be put up where it is wanted, perhaps even taken along on visits to trade fairs. It can be folded down to a very small pack size. And when the elements are linked up, we like the way that there are add-ons that allow the gaps to be closed. Its flexibility is interesting, and so is the visual impression it makes. Something completely new in the kitchen for a change.

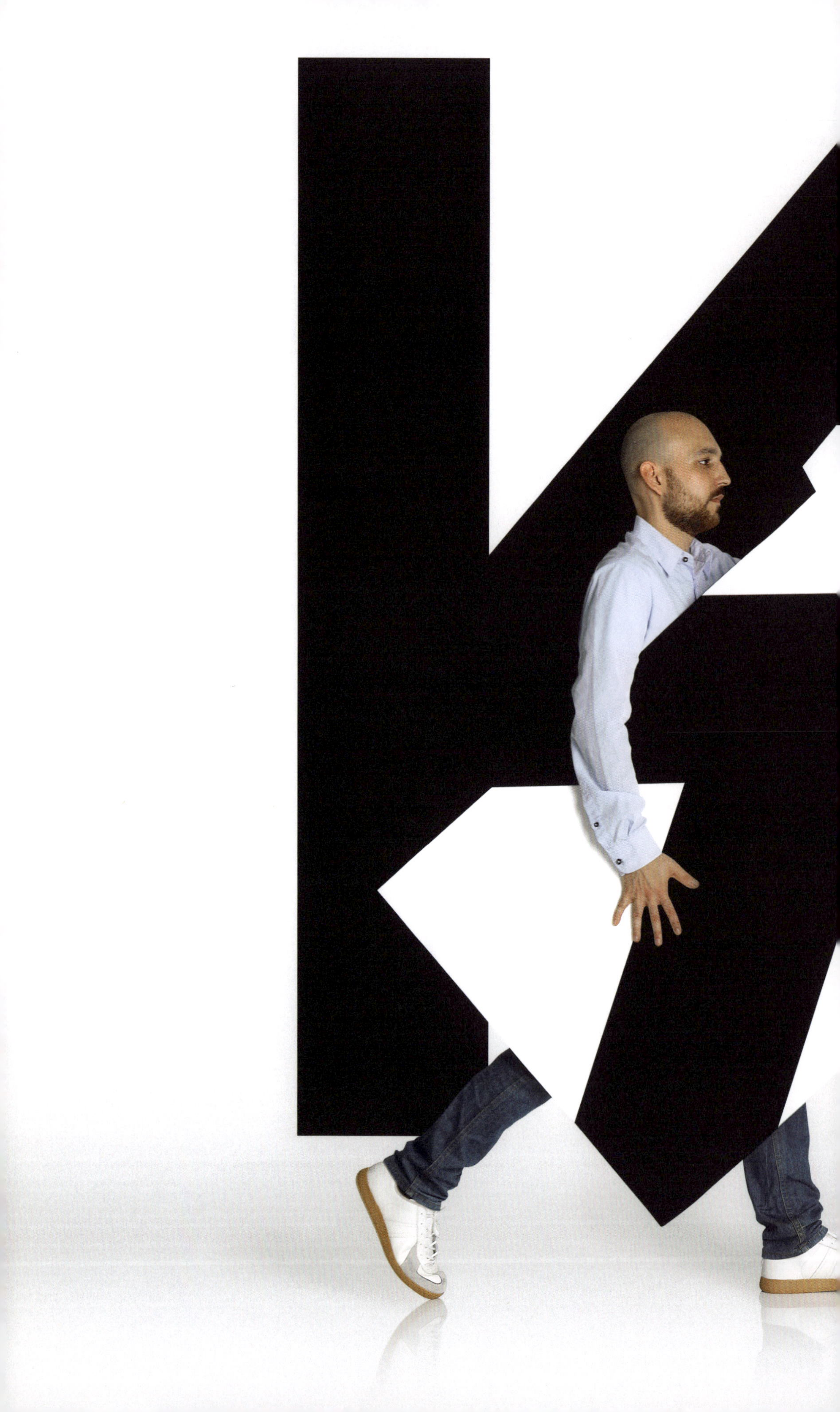

2

K2   Kleines Kochmesser   Small chef's knife
       Tisch- und Küchenkultur   **Gold**   Tableware and kit

»K2« ist ein kleines Vielzweckmesser in erstklassiger Qualität und mit einem hohen Anspruch für das Kochen. Mit seiner gerade mal elf Zentimeter langen aber breiten Klinge mit dem sanften Bogen bietet es hervorragende Schnitteigenschaften; denn die Schneide verläuft vergleichbar wie bei einem großen Kochmesser. So lässt sich das Messer ganz ähnlich beim Schneiden führen. Es besitzt aber den großen Vorteil, dass es gleichzeitig sehr handlich ist durch die deutlich geringere Größe.

Das kleine Kochmesser mit einer Gesamtlänge von 23 Zentimetern eignet sich für alle Arbeiten auf dem Brett. Ob Gemüse oder Kräuter, Fleisch oder Gewürze – das kleine Messer schneidet glatt und präzise durch.

Es ist mit vier verschiedenen Griffvarianten zu haben: in Pflaumen- oder Olivenholz, in schwarzem POM- oder weißem Acryl-Kunststoff. Seine Klinge ist im traditionellen Handwerk dünngeschliffen und auf höchste Schärfe von Hand blaugepließtet. Sie ist wahlweise aus rostfreiem Chrom-Molybdän-Vanadium-Stahl oder aus nicht rostfreiem Karbonstahl. Die Variante mit der rostfreien Klinge wiegt gerade mal 60, die andere 68 Gramm.

Jury

Ein sehr schönes Messer auch durch die Kombination von Holz und Metall, sehr ästhetisch. Es liegt gut in der Hand. Uns gefällt das Archaische, genietet, ein wunderschönes Werkzeug, ungeheuer scharf. Die hohe Klinge ist wichtig fürs Schneiden, damit man an den Fingern gut entlangfahren kann, ohne sich zu verletzen. Formal erinnert es an die ersten wunderschönen Messer mit vernieteten Handschalen, wobei man bei der Klingenform eher an japanische Messer denkt. Hier wurde das Beste aus zwei Welten kombiniert.

»K2« is a small, all-purpose knife, made to the highest quality standards for discerning cooks. Although only 11 centimetres long, its blade is also broad. As it is gently curved, it has excellent cutting qualities, since the line of the cutting edge is comparable with that of a large cook's knife. This means the knife can be used in a very similar way to a large knife. At the same time, it has the great advantage of being very handy because of its significantly smaller size.

With an overall length of 23 centimetres, this small knife is suitable for all kinds of cutting work. Whether vegetables or herbs, meat or spices, the small chef's knife cuts cleanly and precisely.

It is available with a choice of four handles: in plum or olive wood, in black polyoxymethylene or white acrylic plastic. Its blade is ground thin using traditional craft methods, and honed by hand for extreme sharpness. It is available either in stainless chromium-molybdenum-vanadium steel or in non-stainless carbon steel. The stainless variant of the knife weighs just 60 grams, while the non-stainless version weighs 68 grams.

Judges panel

A very beautiful knife, also because of the combination of wood and metal, very aesthetic. It fits snugly in the hand. We like its archaic qualities, with the rivets. It is a wonderful tool, incredibly sharp. The broad blade is important when cutting. Your can run your fingers along the blade without injuring yourself. Formally, it is reminiscent of the first beautiful knives with their riveted handles, although the blade is more evocative of Japanese knives. The best of both worlds has been combined here.

Pâtisserie Backzubehör-Kollektion Bake-ware collect
Tisch- und Küchenkultur **Silber** Tableware and kitc

Die neue Backzubehör-Kollektion »Pâtisserie«, die 40 Backhelfer und drei Schüsseln umfasst, präsentiert sich durch ihre ganz eigene Handschrift und ihre individuelle Formensprache als eigenständige Produktfamilie.

Eine gestalterische Klammer bildet die sich konisch erweiternde Form, die an jedem Griff wiederzufinden ist. Leichte, gezielte Variationen dieser Form sind individuell auf die Funktion der einzelnen Werkzeuge abgestimmt, womit ergonomischen Aspekten Rechnung getragen wurde. Die Griffe liegen gut in der Hand. Ihre sich öffnende Form verhindert, dass der Nutzer in Richtung Werkzeug abrutscht.

Auch die Schüsseln lassen sich visuell eindeutig der Formensprache der Kollektion zuordnen. Ihr umlaufender breiter Rand nimmt in seinem Schwung die stilisierte und dynamische Wirkung der konischen Griffe auf. Durch seine konsequente Ausformung erlaubt er ein bequemes Umgreifen während des Rührens. Die Schnaupe formt sich wie selbstverständlich aus dem Rand der Schüssel heraus und betont die kontrastierende Zweifarbigkeit zwischen innen und außen. Da die Deckel rotationssymmetrisch sind, lassen sie sich in jeder Richtung einsetzen und schließen durch leichtes Andrücken dicht mit der Schüssel ab. Die flächenfüllende Gummierung des Schüsselbodens sorgt für einen sicheren Stand.

Durch die formale Reduktion, die klare und elegante Gestaltung, die durchdachte Deklination und die hochwertige Verarbeitung der Produkte spricht die gesamte Serie eine gemeinsame, ganz eigene faszinierende Sprache.

Jury

Die ganze Kollektion finden wir sehr harmonisch, alles passt wunderbar zusammen. Sehr funktional, vor allen Dingen sind die Schüsseln super. Durch die Aussparung im Deckel kann man das Rührgerät reinhalten, ohne dass etwas herausspritzt. Sehr schöne Ästhetik, haben wir bisher so noch nicht gesehen. Hochwertige Materialität, angenehme Haptik. Auch eine gelungene Integration des Rutschschutzes in den Boden. Die hochglänzenden weißen Flächen mit Holz bieten eine sehr natürliche und sympathische warme Anmutung für die Küche.

With its own distinctive character and its individual formal expression, »Pâtisserie«, the new bake-ware collection that comprises 40 baking aids and three bowls, is a self-contained product family.

The design element common to all elements is the conically extended form that characterizes every handle. Slight variations of this form have been individually customized to the function of the individual utensils, taking account of ergonomic criteria. The handles fit well in the hand. Their conical form prevents the user's hand sliding toward the utensil.

In their formal expression, the bowls are also clearly part of the collection. The curve of the broad band running around their edge takes up the stylized and dynamic effect of the conical handles. This uninterrupted form makes them easy to grip when stirring. The spout is a logical extension of the bowl edge, and accentuates the contrast between the colour on the inside and outside. As the lids are rotationally symmetric, they can be used in any position. Slight pressure is all that is needed to form an airtight seal with the bowl. The rubber material fixed to the entire base surface of the bowl helps it to stand firm.

Because of the products' formal reduction, clear and elegant design, clever declination and excellent workmanship, the entire series speaks a common language – one which is distinctive and fascinating.

Judges panel

In our view, the entire collection is very harmonious, everything goes excellently with everything else. Very functional, the bowls in particular are super. The opening in the lid means a mixer can be inserted, and nothing will splatter out. Aesthetically very pleasing, like nothing we have ever seen before. High-quality materials, pleasant to the touch. The anti-slip base has been very well integrated. The combination of highly polished white surfaces and wood creates a very natural and appealing warmth for the kitchen.

Tupper®-Turbo-Chef Kräuter-Zerkleinerer mit Zugmechanismus
Tisch- und Küchenkultur **Silber**

Herb chopper with
Tableware and kit

»Tupper®-Turbo-Chef« zerkleinert für die Pestosoße nicht nur das Basilikum turboschnell, sondern auch die Pinienkerne und den Knoblauch. Parmesan und Olivenöl dazu, noch mal durchmischen und fertig ist eine der beliebtesten Pastasoßen.

Das herausragende faszinierende Produkt ist vielseitig, schnell und einfach in der Bedienung. Man muss nur den kinderleichten Zugmechanismus bedienen und schon zerkleinert der rasante Küchenhelfer Kräuter, wie Petersilie, Majoran oder Koriander ebenso wie Nüsse, Zwiebeln, Oliven, kleine Mengen von Äpfeln, Schinken und vieles mehr. Damit ist er auch ideal zum Zubereiten von Dips und Aufstrichen. Das Zerkleinern mit dem »Tupper®-Turbo-Chef« entspricht 288 Messerschnitten in weniger als 15 Sekunden.

Das handliche Gerät besteht aus drei Teilen: einem transparenten Behälter – so sieht man, wie fein die Lebensmittel bereits zerkleinert sind –, einem Messerhalter mit drei rostfreien, scharfen Schneideblättern und einem Deckel mit Zugmechanismus für müheloses Zerkleinern. Die ergonomische Form des Deckels, der dank einem Bajonettverschluss sicher den Behälter verschließt, erlaubt einen exzellenten Griff und die Nutzung sowohl für Rechts- als auch Linkshänder sowie für kleine Hände ebenso wie für große. Das rutschfeste Material sorgt dafür, dass das Gerät stabil auf der Arbeitsfläche steht und beim Gebrauch nicht weggleitet.

Der Kräuter-Zerkleinerer ist ungeheuer effektiv, dabei leicht und kompakt und braucht wenig Platz zur Aufbewahrung.

Jury

Einfache und spielerische Funktionsweise, ein mechanisches Gerät zum Zerkleinern von Küchenkräutern und damit auch für gesundes Kochen. Ein wunderbarer Ersatz zu den elektrisch betriebenen Geräten. Einfach zu reinigen, sicher und eine schöne Verbindung von Funktion und spielerischem Bedienen. Das Gerät besitzt einen ungewöhnlichen Mechanismus ähnlich dem einer Salatschleuder. Es ist einzigartig, sowas haben wir noch nie gesehen.

If you are making pesto, the »Tupper®-Turbo-Chef« will chop up not only the basil at lightning speed, but also the pine nuts and the garlic. All that then has to be done to make this popular pasta sauce is to add the parmesan and olive oil.

This excellent and fascinating product is versatile, fast and simple to use. All that has to be done is to pull on the draw string, and this fast little kitchen aid will chop herbs such as parsley, marjoram or coriander, as well as nuts, onions, olives, small quantities of apple, ham and much more. This also makes it ideal when preparing dips and spreads. Chopping with the »Tupper®-Turbo-Chef« is equivalent to 288 knife-chops in less than 15 seconds.

This handy little appliance comprises three parts: A transparent container – which allows the user to see how chopping is progressing – a knife holder for the three sharp blades made of stainless steel, and a lid with a draw mechanism for easy chopping. The ergonomic shape of the lid, which locks onto the container by means of a bayonet catch, makes it very easy to grip, as well as making it suitable for right-handers or left-handers, for small hands as well as large hands. The anti-slip material ensures that the appliance stays firmly on the worktop, and does not move around when being used.

The herb chopper is extremely effective, but at the same time light and compact, taking up very little storage space.

Judges panel

Simple, playful functionality, a mechanical appliance to chop herbs, and thus also an appliance for healthy eating. A wonderful substitute for appliances that tend to be electrically driven. Simple to clean, a safe and attractive combination of function and playful operation. The appliance has an unusual mechanism, a little bit like a salad spinner. Quite extraordinary, we've never seen anything quite like it.

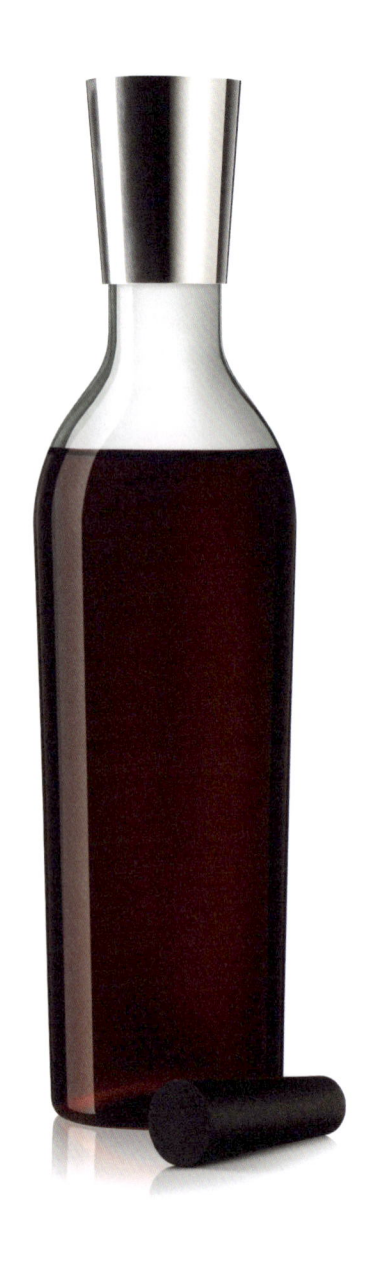

Bag-in-Box-Karaffe Weinkaraffe
Tisch- und Küchenkultur **Silber**

Wine carafe
Tableware and kitc

Das Ziel der Designer war es, Wein aus der Bag-in-Box zur akzeptierten Alternative zu Flaschenweinen zu machen. Dafür gestalteten sie ein innovatives Produkt mit einer einfachen, ästhetischen Designlösung für das Servieren von Wein aus dem Karton. Herausgekommen ist eine attraktive Karaffe, die den Wein nicht nur stilvoll präsentiert, sondern es auch ermöglicht, im Auge zu behalten, wieviel konsumiert wird.

Sie hat eine elegante Formensprache und ist nicht nur ideal für das Servieren am Tisch, sondern auch für die Aufbewahrung des Weines im Kühlschrank. Sie ist aus Glas und in der praktischen Größe von 0,75 Liter erhältlich, dem Standardmaß von handelsüblichen Weinflaschen. So passt sie in die Kühlschranktür zum Kühlen von Weiß- und Roséwein und zu deren Aufbewahrung.

Oben besitzt sie eine große Öffnung, durch die man leicht Wein aus der Box in die Karaffe umfüllen kann. Der Einsatz aus Edelstahl sowie die Form bewirken, dass der Wein beim Abfüllen auch dekantiert wird. Die Karaffe ist nicht nur tropffrei, sondern mit ihr lässt sich der Wein auch perfekt dosieren. Mit einem schwarzen Stopfen aus Silikongummi lässt sie sich verschließen, sodass der abgefüllte Wein gut bis zum nächsten Tag aufbewahrt werden kann. Sie ist leicht zu reinigen und spülmaschinenfest.

Jury

Für diesen Bereich, Umfüllen von Weinkartons, haben wir noch keine so schöne Lösung gesehen. Man hat eine wohlgeformte, wertige Glaskaraffe auf dem Tisch, die man auch verschließen und luftdicht im Kühlschrank aufbewahren kann. Sie ist elegant, sie hat für die Genusssache Wein trinken die richtige Ästhetik, die Weinkartons natürlich nicht besitzen. Man wertet den Wein damit noch mal auf.

The designers wanted to make wine from a Bag-in-Box an acceptable alternative to wine from a bottle. To achieve this, they designed an innovative product with a simple, aesthetic solution for serving wine from a carton. The result is an attractive carafe that not only presents the wine stylishly, but also allows the user to keep an eye on how much wine has been consumed.

It has an elegant formal expression, and is ideal not only for serving wine at the table, but also for keeping wine in the fridge. Made of glass, it comes with a capacity of 75 centilitres, which is the standard size of commercial wine bottles. This means it fits into the fridge door, so that white or rosé wines can be cooled.

The mouth of the carafe is wide, so that wine can easily be poured into it from the Bag-in-Box. The stainless steel insert's form means that the wine is decanted when it is filled into the carafe. The carafe is not only drip-free, but also allows just the right amount of wine to be drunk. A black silicone rubber stopper allows it to be sealed, so that the decanted wine can be kept until the next day. It is easy to clean and dishwasher-safe.

Judges panel

We have never seen such an elegant solution for serving wine from a box. Here you have a beautifully shaped, high-quality glass carafe on the table – one that can also be stoppered and kept air-tight in the fridge. It is elegant, with the appropriate aesthetic appearance for the pleasurable activity of wine-drinking – something that a Bag-in-Box clearly does not have. This carafe gives the wine an extra quality boost.

Balance

Schale
Tisch- und Küchenkultur **Silber**

Bowl
Tableware and kitc

Muscheln und ihre stromlinienartige Gestalt dienten als Vorbild für die extravagante Schale. Dank der unverwechselbaren Formgebung überzeugt »Balance« als eigenständige Tischskulptur und bietet einen hohen ästhetischen Genuss. Die längliche Schale ist klar gestaltet und sanft geschwungen. Je nach Betrachtungswinkel scheint sie fast zu schweben.

Ihr Charakteristikum ist der leicht verschobene Schwerpunkt, der außerhalb der Mitte liegt. Dadurch entsteht eine dynamische Asymmetrie. Ein präzise gezogener Rand führt die beiden Außenflächen der Doppelschale schwungvoll zusammen. Die unterschiedlich stark geformten Ober- und Unterseiten geben der länglichen Form ein elegantes Volumen.

Die klare Linienführung und die hochwertige Gestaltung wird durch augenfällige Effekte unterstrichen: Im hochglanzpolierten Edelstahl spiegelt sich die Umgebung in den Oberflächen wider, und die Reflexionen betonen die spannungsvollen Krümmungen der Schale.

Jury

Wir finden die Schale sehr elegant. Sie besitzt eine schöne dynamische Form, wir können sie uns als Inszenierung auf dem Tisch gut vorstellen, wenn man etwas darauflegt, hat sie spannende Reflexionen. Diese Zweiteiligkeit, dass die Schale einerseits kompakt und andererseits trotzdem leicht ist, ist sehr gelungen, weil sie aus zwei Teilen gefertigt und innen hohl ist.

The streamlined shape of a shell was the model for this extravagant bowl. Thanks to its unmistakable shape, »Balance« can stand on its own as a sculpted object for the table. Its appearance gives aesthetic pleasure. The oblong bowl is clearly shaped, with gentle curves. Depending on the angle of view, it appears almost to float.

Its defining characteristic is its slightly shifted centre of gravity, which is off-centre. This gives rise to a dynamic asymmetry. A precisely described edge vibrantly brings the two outer surfaces of this double bowl together. The difference in thickness between the upper and lower edges gives the oblong form an elegant volume.

The clear lines and high-quality design are underscored by striking effects. The bowl's surroundings are reflected in its highly polished surfaces, and these reflections emphasize the bowl's exciting curves.

Judges panel

We think the bowl is very elegant. It has a wonderful dynamic shape, we can well imagine it as a dramatic centrepiece on the table. When something is placed on it, the reflections are fascinating. The bowl's duality – compact on the one hand and light on the other – is extremely well done. It comes from the fact that the bowl is made of two pieces, and is hollow on the inside.

Paper & Poetry Aufbewahrungsschalen
Tisch- und Küchenkultur **Silber**

Storage bowls
Tableware and kit

Wer braucht sie nicht – kleine Behältnisse für all die Dinge, die einen Platz auf dem (Schreib)tisch benötigen. Für Büroklammern, Radiergummi und Co. Oder zum Sammeln von Kleinigkeiten. Dafür sind die »Paper & Poetry« Schalen bestens geeignet.

Aber sie bieten noch wesentlich mehr: Sie können eine Denkpause zwischen den Arbeiten und ein Lächeln zwischen Akten und Ablagen zaubern; denn sie erzählen von Gedanken und Taten, Ordnung und Chaos. Etwa »Gedanken sind der Anfang von Taten« und »Lebenskunst ist die Kunst des Weglassens« oder der Satz von Albert Einstein »Ordnung braucht nur der Dumme, ein Genie beherrscht das Chaos.«

Mit diesen und anderen Motiven sind die Schalen »Paper & Poetry«, die aus Porzellan gefertigt sind, verziert. Sie sind in zwei Größen erhältlich. Die kleinen Schalen haben einen Durchmesser von sechs mit einer Höhe von zweieinhalb Zentimetern, die großen einen Durchmesser von zehn mit einer Höhe von drei Zentimetern. Sowohl die großen als auch die kleinen Schalen gibt es mit jeweils sechs verschiedenen Motiven.

Die Schalen gehören zu der Kollektion »Paper & Poetry«, die Produkte zum Ordnen, Sortieren, Ablegen und Verschönern herausbringt. Diese Gegenstände verbinden Alltag und Poesie in Büro und Arbeitszimmer. Sie sollen nicht nur für Ordnung auf dem Schreibtisch sorgen, sondern auch den Alltag bereichern.

Jury

Sehr nette Idee sowohl in der Kombination von Schale und Motiv als auch in der Machart. Es ist ein Siebdruck mit keramischen Glasuren. Typografisch ist es sehr schön umgesetzt, das wird auch nach einiger Zeit noch nicht langweilig. Die Schalen kann man sowohl im Büro als auch privat gut verwenden. Durch ihre schlichte elegante Form sind sie vielseitig einsetzbar. Sie haben auch eine Art Sammelcharakter.

There is hardly anyone who does not need somewhere to put all the things that have to go on a table or desk. For paperclips, erasers, and the like. Or for collecting small trifles. The »Paper & Poetry« bowls are excellently suited for this.

But they can do much more. They can conjure up a pause for thought in the middle of work, a smile between documents and filing; for they tell a story about thoughts and deeds, order and chaos. There are quotes such as »Thoughts are the origin of all deeds«, »The art of living is the art of letting go« or Albert Einstein's »Order is for idiots, genius can handle chaos.«

Made of porcelain, the »Paper & Poetry« bowls are decorated with these and other quotes. They are available in two sizes. The small bowls are six centimetres in diameter and two-and-a-half centimetres high. The large ones are ten centimetres across and three centimetres high. Both the large and the small bowls are available in six different designs.

The bowls are part of the »Paper & Poetry« collection, whose products serve the purpose of ordering, sorting, stowing away and embellishing. These products combine poetry and the everyday in the office and the study. They are intended not only to keep desks tidy, but also to enrich everyday life.

Judges panel

Very nice idea – both the way the bowls and the quotes have been combined and the way they have been made. This is a screen print with a ceramic glaze. Typographically very well done, so that they won't become boring even after a while. The bowls can be used equally well in the office and at home. Their unassuming elegant form means they can be used in a variety of ways. There is also something of the collector's item in them.

K

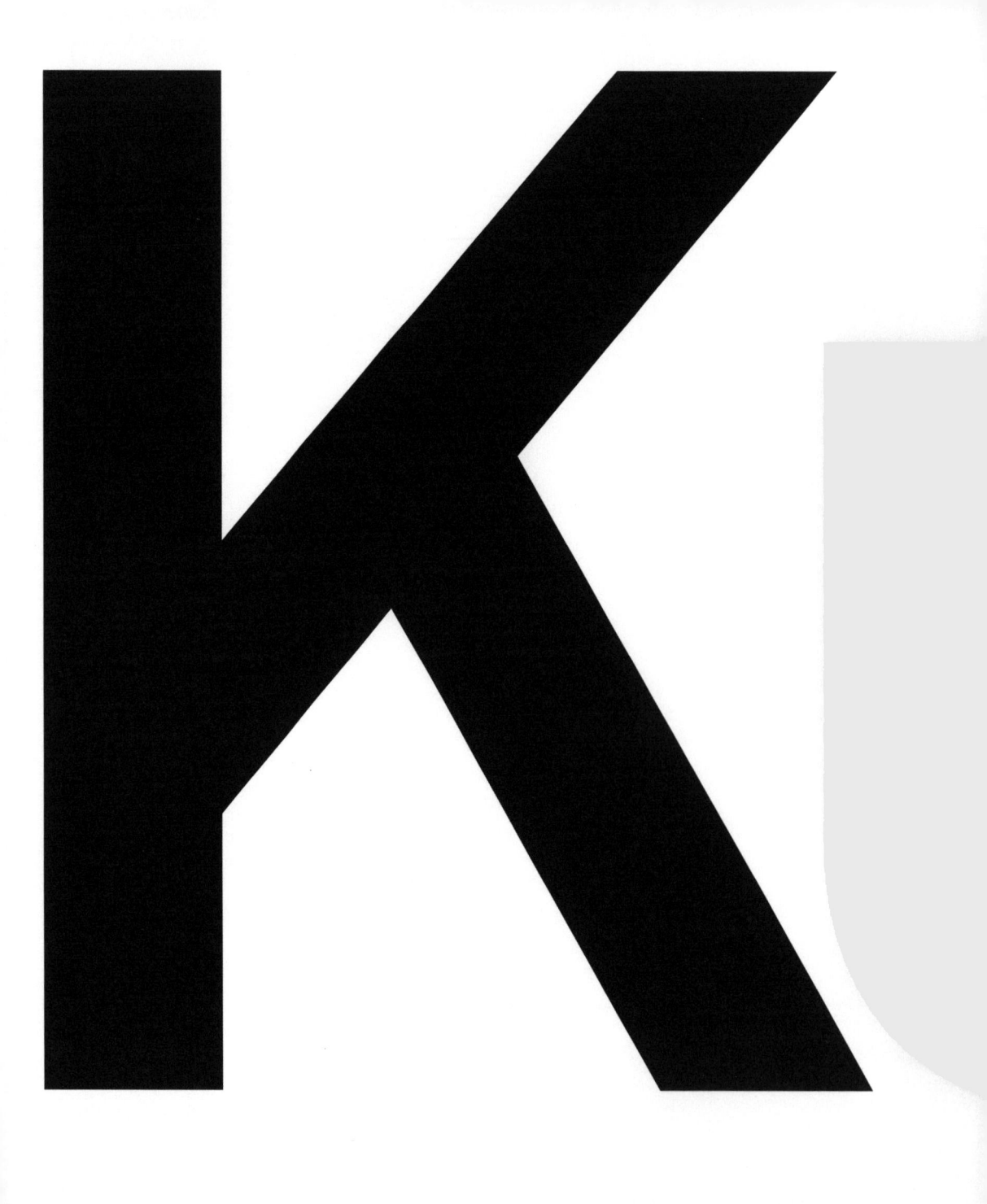

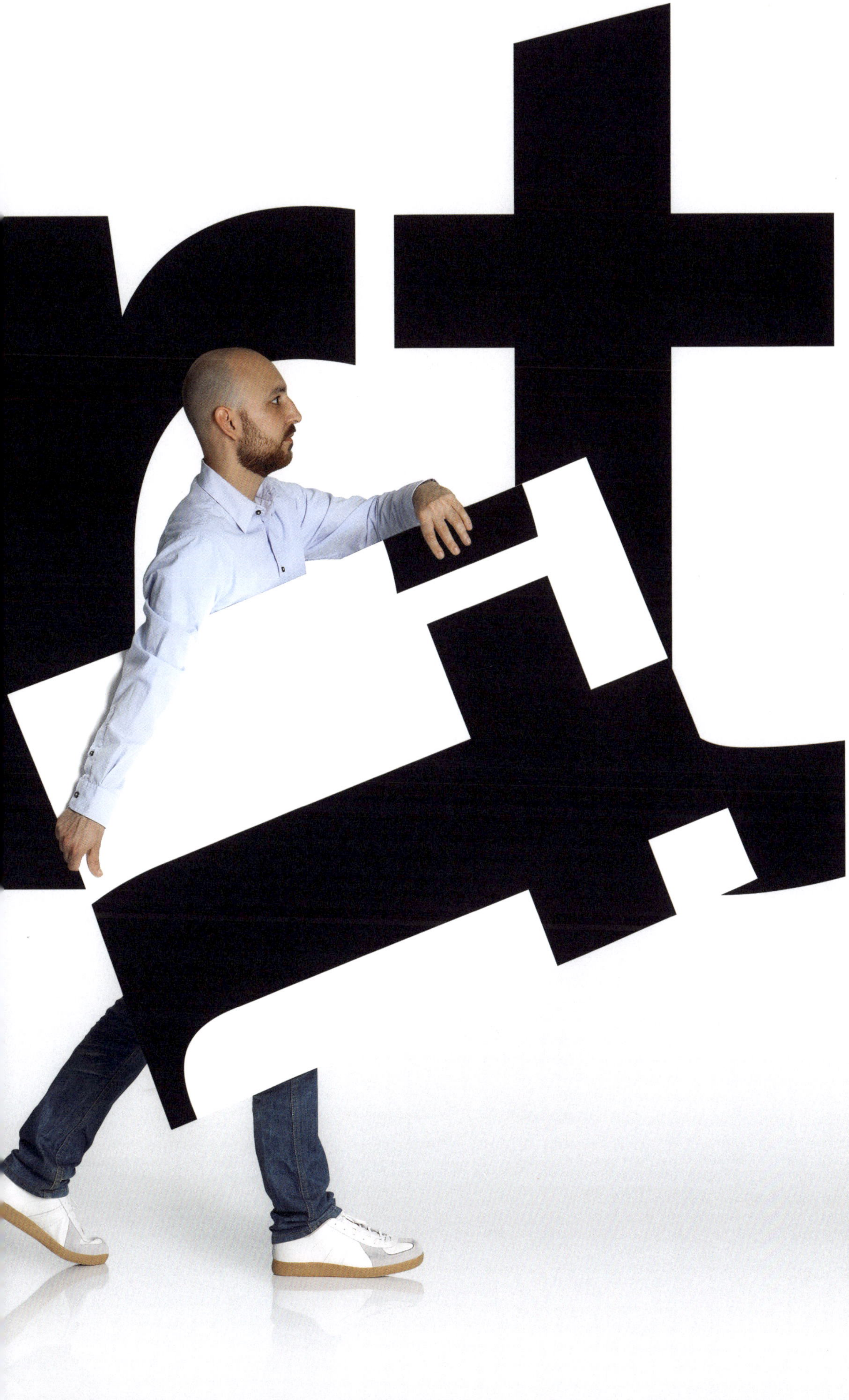

Kurt   Sofabett   Sofa bed
Wohnen **Gold**   Living **Gold**

Was ist »Kurt«: Sofa oder Bett? Sofabett oder Bettsofa? »Kurt« ist alles in einem, geht weit über den Urbegriff des Schlafsofas hinaus und erfüllt damit die besonderen Anforderungen von heute: bequem und flexibel, zum Sitzen und zum Schlafen, einfach zu verwandeln und an verschiedenen Standorten einzusetzen.

Dieses Two-in-One-Sofa bietet in jeder seiner Funktionen reichlich Komfort und viele Facetten. Offen dient der tiefliegende Hochlehner als bequemes Sofa und als markanter Blickfänger durch seine architektonische Linienführung und seine ungewöhnlichen Proportionen. Seine angeschrägte Sitzfläche erlaubt eine bequeme, zurückgelehnte Position. Die Armlehnen bieten dabei eine breite Ablagefläche.

Das Sofa lässt sich ganz einfach und schnell schließen, indem die Rückenlehne mit einem Griff nach vorne geklappt wird. So entsteht ein gleichmäßiger Korpus in Form eines Quaders. Dieser dient als Couch oder Daybed für den Mittagsschlaf zu Hause, als Sitzbank oder Büroliege für eine kreative Siesta zwischendurch. Mit seiner angenehmen Schlafhöhe kann es aber ebensogut als vollwertiges Gästebett eingesetzt werden.

Seine hohe Flexibilität macht sich auch bei einem Umzug bezahlt. Dank seinem klappbaren Rücken lässt sich »Kurt« ganz flach im Umzugswagen verstauen. Das Gestell besteht aus massiver Buche, der Rahmen aus Stahlrohr und die Füße aus schwarz lackierter Buche.

Jury

Viel einfacher und schöner geht es eigentlich nicht. In allen Einsatzfunktionen macht es eine in sich stimmige Figur im Raum, seine Form ist auch als Bett intakt. Das unterscheidet es von anderen Bettsofas, bei denen Elemente herausgezogen werden und Seitenteile stehen bleiben. Besonders angenehm, dass der Matratzenkern weich ist, weil der Rahmen außen ist. Man liegt nicht nur, sondern sitzt auch gut. Es gibt kaum Schlafsofas, bei denen das so ist. Clever: Die keilförmige Anschrägung sorgt für eine bessere Ergonomie und eine formale Eigenständigkeit. Ein gutes Produkt beispielsweise für Menschen mit wenig Platz wie etwa in New York nicht nur für Gäste, sondern für sich selbst.

Is »Kurt« a sofa or a bed? A sofa bed or a bed sofa? »Kurt« is all these at once, going far beyond the original idea of the sleeping sofa to meet the special demands of our modern age: It is comfortable and flexible, for sitting and sleeping. It is easy to convert and suitable for different settings.

In each one of its functions, this two in-one sofa offers plenty of comfort and many features. When it is open, the low-slung, high-back seat is a comfortable sofa. Its architectural lines and unusual proportions make it a real eye-catcher. Its slightly sloping seating surface makes for a comfortable, laid-back position. The arm rests offer a broad, shelf-like surface.

The sofa is simply and quickly closed in one single movement, by tipping the back rest forward. This results in a regular cuboid shape. It can then be used as a couch or as a day bed for an afternoon nap at home, as a bench or as an office lounger for a quick creative siesta. The pleasant height of its sleeping surface means it can equally well be used as a perfectly adequate spare bed.

Its extreme flexibility also pays off when moving home. Thanks to its fold-down back, Kurt can be stowed away very flat in a removal van. Its structure is made of solid beech, its outer frame of tubular steel, and its legs of black stained beech.

Judges panel

Things hardly get much simpler or more attractive than this. In all its uses, it creates a coherent presence, and its form remains intact even when it is a bed. This sets it apart from other sofa beds, where elements have to be pulled out, and side elements stay where they are. One especially pleasant feature is that the mattress core is soft, because the frame runs around the edge. It is not only pleasant to lie on, but also to sit on. There are scarcely any sofa beds this could be said of. One clever feature is the wedge-like slope of the seating surface, which makes for better ergonomics and formal autonomy. A good product for people like New Yorkers, who have little room not only for guests, but also for themselves.

Bucky Beistelltisch Side table
Wohnen **Silber** Living **Silver**

»Bucky« ist ein durchdachter Beistelltisch, der formstabil, robust und vielseitig einsetzbar ist: als Beisteller fürs Sofa, als Telefontisch, Schirmständer und Schlüsselablage in der Garderobe, als nützlicher Tisch für Utensilien im Badezimmer, als Nachttisch im Gästezimmer – den Nutzungsmöglichkeiten sind keine Grenzen gesetzt.

Dank seiner praktischen Kaffeetischhöhe von 62,5 Zentimetern passt er sich geschickt an Couchtisch oder Sofa an. In seinem Bauch lassen sich Zeitschriften, Zeitungen, die Fernbedienung oder auch andere Dinge bequem und stilvoll aufbewahren.

»Bucky« ist ein nicht zu übersehender Hingucker dank seiner ungewöhnlichen Gestalt und Proportion. Im Raum bildet er in der grasgrünen oder warmen roten Variante einen Farbtupfer, in der cremeweißen Version nimmt er sich dezent zurück. Er besteht aus gebogenem pulverbeschichtetem Stahlblech, seine im Fuß eingelassenen Filzgleiter schützen den Boden.

Jury

Formal einfach und multifunktional: Man kann ihn nicht nur als Beistelltisch, sondern auch als Zeitschriftenständer sowie als Schirmständer verwenden. Wir finden ihn sehr eigenständig, und uns gefällt, wie seine Form aus den Blechverformungen entwickelt ist. Die Proportion ist ungewöhnlich, sie macht ihn interessanter und er wirkt jung – ein Eyecatcher. Schön auch, dass unten Filz eingelassen ist, um den Boden zu schonen. Dadurch scheint er etwas zu schweben.

»Bucky« is a well designed side table. Its shape makes it strong and sturdy, and very versatile. It can be used as a side table next to the sofa, as a telephone table, as an umbrella stand, as somewhere to deposit keys, as a useful table for bathroom things, as a bedside table in the guest room – there is no limit to its uses.

Thanks to its practical height – 62.5 centimetres – it harmonizes well with a coffee table or sofa. The hollow base on which it stands offers plenty of room for tidily and stylishly storing away magazines, newspapers, remote controls and other items.

But it is not only its unusual form and proportions that make »Bucky« a magnet for attention. Its grass-green or warm red variants provide a splash of colour in any room, while its cream-white variant is modestly unassuming. It is made of curved, powder-coated sheet steel. The felt glides embedded in is base protect the floor.

Judges panel

Formally simple and multifunctional: It can be used not only as a side table, but also as a magazine rack or umbrella stand. We like its self-contained design, and the way its form has been developed by bending metal. Its proportions are unusual. They make it more interesting, as well as giving it a young appearance – an eye-catcher. We also like the way felt has been embedded in its base to protect the floor. As a result, it seems almost to float.

Vladi

Beistelltisch
Wohnen **Silber**

Side table
Living **Silver**

Der ungewöhnliche Beistelltisch spielt mit der Balance von Leichtigkeit und Spannung. So scheint die Tischplatte auf dem Netz aus filigranen Schnüren zu schweben. Stabilität liefert der dünne, dezente Stab im Innern. Kraft und Gegenkraft wirken zusammen. Dadurch erhält »Vladi« seinen ganz eigenen herausragenden Charakter.

Der Beistelltisch ist in zwei Größen und in verschiedenen Ausführungen erhältlich. So ist die Tischplatte aus Massivholz – amerikanischer Nussbaum oder Wenge – oder aus einer Variante in schwarzem Softlack.

Das Gestell besteht aus einem Stahlstab und einer Bodenplatte, – beide sind schwarz beschichtet – sowie einem schwarzen Synthetik-Schnurgeflecht, das feine Linien auf der Tischplatte zeichnet. Wahlweise ist der Tisch mit Kunststoffgleitern für Stein- und Teppichböden ausgestattet oder mit Filzgleitern, die Holzböden schonen.

Jury
Aus der Architektur bekanntes Bauprinzip, spannungsvoll, interessant umgesetzt in einem Beistelltisch mit sehr überzeugender Anmutung.

This unusual side table plays with the balance between lightness and tension. The table top appears to float on a mesh of delicate strands. It gets its stability from the slim central column. Strength and grace interact. This interplay gives »Vladi« a quite unique quality.

The side table is available in two sizes and various designs. The table top is available as solid wood – American walnut or wengé – or in a variant that has been coated with soft black lacquer.

The base comprises a steel column and a base plate – both with a black coating – and a black mesh of nylon threads which traces fine lines on the table top. The table is available either with plastic glides for stone floors and carpets, or with felt glides for wooden flooring.

Judges panel
A construction principle that is well known in architecture, excitingly and interestingly applied to a side table. The overall impression is very convincing.

Cuoio

Stuhl
Wohnen **Silber**

Chair
Living **Silver**

Der Stuhl »Cuoio« zeichnet sich durch seinen Minimalismus aus, der Form und Materialien – Leder und Stahl – bestimmt. So besteht das Gestell aus hochglanz pulverbeschichtetem schwarzen Stahl. Die Sitzfläche und der Rücken sind aus Leder gefertigt, das vollständig in schwarz oder in verschiedenen Brauntönen, aber immer mit schwarzer Rückseite, zu haben ist.

Seine typische Form erhält er durch Ausschnitte in Sitz und Rücken. Der flexible Rücken sorgt für Komfort und die Taillierung für bequemes Sitzen.

Ein auf das Wesentliche reduzierter und zeitloser Stuhl, der zudem auch nachhaltig ist; denn Bezug und Gestell lassen sich leicht trennen und recyceln. »Cuoio« ist in einer Variante ohne und einer mit Armlehnen aus hochglanz pulverbeschichtetem schwarzen Stahl erhältlich, die mit schwarzem Leder ummantelt sind.

Jury

Eine Neuinterpretation eines alten Themas. Ein leichter und eleganter Metallstuhl kombiniert mit Leder. Die Einschnitte auf der Sesseloberfläche sorgen für Spannung. Eine schöne und einfache Form, filigran und trotzdem durch das dickere Leder substantiell – eine interessante Kombination, sehr minimalistisch.

What is striking about »Cuoio« is its minimalism, which determines its form and the materials used – leather and steel. The chair frame is made of highly polished, powder-coated black steel. The seat and back surfaces are made of leather, and are available either in black only, or in various brown tones in combination with a black back.

It takes its typical form from slits in the seat and back surfaces. The flexible back and the shape of the seat provide for comfortable seating.

This is a timeless chair that has been reduced to the essentials. Yet it is also sustainable, for the coverings and frame can easily be separated and recycled. »Cuoio« is available with or without armrests, which are made of highly polished powder-coated black steel sheathed with black leather.

Judges panel

A re-interpretation of a well known theme. A light, elegant metal chair, combined with leather. The slits on the chair surface create added fascination. A beautiful, simple form, delicate yet at the same time sturdy thanks to the thickness of the leather – an interesting combination, very minimalistic.

WK 695 aero   Wohnsessel / Loungesessel   Easy chair / Lounge
                 Wohnen   **Silber**   Living   **Silver**

Der Loungesessel mit skulpturalen Qualitäten wirkt schwerelos, ist aber dennoch von starker visueller Präsenz. Er bietet von allen Seiten interessante Perspektiven und behauptet sich frei im Raum. Dank seiner kompakten Abmessungen und seiner organischen Formgebung – er gleicht einem gefalteten Blatt, das sich dem Körper anpasst – setzt er eindrucksvolle Akzente.

»aero« ist sowohl ein Solitär als auch ein ideales vielseitiges Ergänzungsmöbel. So beherrscht er den Dialog mit einem Sofa und ist durch seine schmale, aber kantige Außenkontur und die straffe Polsterung zu vielen Polstermöbeln kompatibel. Dank seiner eleganten puristischen Gestaltung lässt er sich auch sehr gut mit vielen Wohnstilen kombinieren.

Er bietet hohen Komfort, der durch die unsichtbare Verstärkung der Polsterauflage zur Sitzmitte hin noch erhöht wird. Ein zentrales, eingebettetes Kissen bietet nicht nur ein Plus an Bequemlichkeit, sondern setzt auch einen formalen Akzent und eröffnet die Möglichkeit zur mehrfarbigen Gestaltung.

»aero« ist in verschiedenen Varianten zu haben – mit drehbarer Lagerung entweder auf einem leichten Metallkreuzgestell oder auf einem lackierten runden Tellerfuß – und in verschiedenen Stoff- und Lederbezügen.

Jury
Elegant, leicht, komfortabel, das Leder ist sehr schön verarbeitet. Ein Understatement-Thron. Wir finden ihn repräsentativ auf eine sehr zurückhaltende Art und Weise, sehr sophisticated. Er erinnert an die Klassische Moderne, an die Fünfziger Jahre und ist trotzdem topaktuell. Er ist ausgesprochen bequem, dafür, dass er so schlank wirkt.

With its sculptural qualities, this lounge chair has a weightless appearance, yet its visual presence is still strong. It is interesting to look at from any angle, and speaks for itself in any setting. Thanks to its compact dimensions and organic form – like a folded leaf that fits snugly around the body – it creates an impressive accent.

»aero« is both a stand-alone piece of furniture and an ideal supplementary item. It harmonizes perfectly with a sofa, and is compatible with most upholstered furniture thanks to its narrow, angular outer contours and streamlined upholstery. Its elegant, purist shape also means that it goes very well with many furnishing styles.

It is extremely comfortable, not least due to the invisible stiffening of the upholstery towards the middle of the seat. An embedded cushion in the middle of the seat not only creates extra comfort, but also sets a formal accent, and opens up possibilities for different colour combinations.

»aero« is available in different variants – as a swivel chair either on a five-prong light metal base or on a painted round base – and with various fabric and leather coverings.

Judges panel
Elegant, light, comfortable, the leather has been very beautifully crafted. An understatement throne. With its very unassuming manner, it is both prestigious and very sophisticated. It is reminiscent of classic modernism and the 1950s, but is nonetheless very up to date. For a chair that is so slim in appearance, it is outstandingly comfortable.

Polsterbank
Wohnen **Silber**

Cushion bench
Living **Silver**

Die schlichte Polsterbank »b3« ist nicht nur Sitzgelegenheit, sondern bietet auch eine versteckte Aufbewahrungsmöglichkeit für verschiedenste Utensilien. Sie lässt sich vielseitig einsetzen beispielsweise im Wohnraum, im Schlafzimmer oder im Eingangsbereich.

Eine Variante von »b3« ist die L-Bank, die ebenfalls in viele verschiedene Situationen passt. Sie steht einzeln im Entrée oder in Kombination mit der Polsterbank am Esstisch. Beide zusammen geschoben bilden eine Liege als Tagbett für die Siesta oder als Übernachtungsbett für unvorhergesehene Gäste. Außerdem lassen sich mit ihr Räume definieren, in denen man sich gerne trifft beispielsweise im öffentlichen Raum als Lobby-, Lounge-, Konferenz- oder Meetingsituation. Obendrein schafft sie viel Stauraum.

Die Polsterbänke sind in verschiedenen Ausführungen erhältlich. So können die Farben des Linoleums, mit dem der Sockel belegt ist – pearl, olive, mauve oder nero –, beliebig mit zwei verschiedenen Stoffarten kombiniert werden: zum einen mit Bouclé Nya Nordiska in beige, olive, melange oder ebony, zum anderen mit Woodnotes Sand aus gezwirntem Papier und Baumwolle in white-natural oder black.

Jury

Besonders überzeugt uns die Möglichkeit, dass man mit den Bänken verschiedene Konfigurationen bei Partys oder in anderen Situationen bilden kann. Der Stauraum ist ein wunderbares, funktionales Plus. Wir finden es schön, dass er gut versteckt ist und man ihn nicht als solchen erkennt. Man denkt, dass man nur ein Polstermöbel hat und erhält dennoch den Zusatznutzen. Der Stoff ist sehr strapazierfähig.

The unpretentious »b3« cushion bench is not just somewhere to sit. It also offers a discreet possibility for storing away a wide variety of utensils. It can be used for many purposes – in the living room, bedroom, or entrance hall.

One variant of »b3« is the L-shaped bench, which can also be used in many different situations. It can stand alone in an entrance hall, and be combined with the cushion bench at the dining table. In combination, the two variants form a surface for an afternoon nap, or can be used as a bed for unexpected guests. They can also be used to define spaces in which people can meet. Set up in public spaces, they can create a lobby, lounge, conference space or meeting space. In addition, these benches create a lot of storage space.

The cushion benches are available in different designs. The pearl, olive, mauve or nero linoleum covering the pedestal can be combined with two different types of fabric – either with Bouclé Nya Nordiska, which is available in beige, olive, melange or ebony, or with Woodnotes Sand, which is made of paper yarn and cotton, and is available in white-natural or black.

Judges panel

We are especially convinced by the way these benches allow different configurations to be formed – at parties or in other situations. The storage space is a wonderful, functional extra. We like the way this space is well hidden, and is not immediately recognizable. It looks as though all you have is a piece of upholstered furniture, yet there is an additional benefit as well. The material is very hard-wearing.

sixteen

Hocker / Beistelltisch
Wohnen **Silber**

Stool and side table
Living **Silver**

»sixteen« ist ein Universalgenie. Als Hocker mit der grauen Sitzauflage aus Filz bietet er auch unangekündigten Besuchern schnell einen Sitzplatz. Belegt man ihn stattdessen mit der Glasplatte mit polierten Kanten, wird er zum Beistelltisch, der sogar groß genug für ein spontanes Dinner for two ist.

Der Hocker fungiert außerdem dank eines Adapters als Lampenfuß für die Tischleuchte Tolomeo. So sorgt er für mehr Platz auf dem Schreibtisch. Er kann ferner zur Blumenvase werden. Mit bis zu neun einsteckbaren Vasen aus Duranglas lassen sich nach Belieben blühende Arrangements bilden. »sixteen« sorgt auch für romatische Stimmung, wenn er mit bis zu neun einsteckbaren Kerzenhaltern aus Edelstahl bestückt wird. Zudem dient er als Aufbewahrungsmöbel beispielsweise für Zeitungen, Telefonbücher oder CDs.

Die massiven lackierten Eichenstäbe schaffen eine architektonische Struktur, die an Manhattan erinnert: gewaltige Bauwerke und tiefe Straßenschluchten. Die Stäbe sind in einem strengen Raster angeordnet. Alle Proportionen entsprechen dem Verhältnis phi (1,618) – und somit dem goldenen Schnitt. »sixteen« besitzt eine Kantenlänge der Stäbe von 42 Millimetern, eine Stablänge von 42 Zentimetern und eine Grundfläche von 26 x 26 Zentimetern.

Jury

Uns gefällt die einfache klare Form kombiniert mit dem Werkstoff Holz: ein Quadrat als Grundform, verbunden mit vielen kleinen Quadraten. Wir finden die verschiedenen Möglichkeiten der Nutzung sehr schön: Hocker, Tisch, mit Kerzen, mit Blumen oder für Zeitschriften – eine wunderbare spielerische Umsetzung eines bekannten Themas.

»sixteen« is an all-round genius. As a stool, with its grey felt cushion, it quickly provides unannounced guests with somewhere to sit. If, instead of the cushion, the glass top with its polished edges is placed on top, it becomes a side table, which is even big enough for a spontaneous dinner for two.

The stool can also be used as a lamp base, thanks to an adapter for the Tolomeo table lamp. In this way, it creates more space on the desk. It can also be turned into a vase for flowers. Up to nine Duran glass vases can be inserted into it, creating plenty of scope for flower arrangements. »sixteen« can also provide for a romantic mood. All that has to be done is insert up to nine stainless steel candleholders. It can also serve as a storage module – for newspapers, for example, or for telephone directories or CDs.

The solid, varnished oak columns create an architectural structure that is reminiscent of Manhattan: towering buildings and deep, canyon-like streets. The columns are arranged according to a strict pattern. All their proportions approximate the constant phi (1.618) – and thus the golden section. The sides of the table are 42 millimetres long, while the columns themselves are 42 centimetres long. The base of »sixteen« measures 26 by 26 centimetres.

Judges panel

We like the simple, clear form in combination with wood. A square as the basic shape, in combination with many small squares. We are very impressed by the many different ways it can be used: as a stool or a table, with candles or flowers, or for magazines – a wonderfully playful interpretation of a well known theme.

Piano   Regalsystem   Shelving system
             Wohnen **Silber**   Living **Silver**

»Piano« bedeutet im Italienischen neben Klavier oder sacht und leise auch Etage und Fläche. Nomen est omen. So wird Etage auf Etage gebaut. Die Horizontale prägt und akzentuiert das Regalsystem. Die Borde scheinen wie Tragflächen zu schweben, tragen große und kleine Schiebetüren in zahlreichen Farben und schaffen neben Stauraum auch Schauraum. Sie bestechen durch ihre ausladende Großzügigkeit so breit wie das Möbel ist – bis zu 362 Zentimeter am Stück.

Klar und schlicht ist die Form, vielfältig und zahlreich sind die Anwendungs- und individuellen Gestaltungsmöglichkeiten: raumgreifende Regalskulptur oder elegantes Sideboard, individuelles Mediencenter oder luftige Ausstellungsebene, schlankes Hängeboard oder raffinierte Wohnwand.

Stabilität und Statik erhält das Regal durch filigrane Wangen, die dezent im Hintergrund bleiben. Die Wangen und Rückwände können im Breitenraster von 30 Zentimeter beliebig positioniert werden.

»Piano« bietet zwei Rastertiefen – 32 Zentimeter für Bücher und 48 Zentimeter für Stauraum und HiFi-Lösungen. Neben Klappen und Schubkästen lässt sich das Regalsystem auch mit Schiebetüren ausrüsten. Letztere können mit LED-Lichtschienen ausgestattet werden, die die transluzenten Farbflächen erstrahlen lassen. Es ist in verschiedenen Lackausführungen und Holzarten erhältlich.

Jury

Ein ausgesprochen gut und detailliert ausgearbeitetes Regalsystem sowohl was die Montage als auch die Gebrauchsfähigkeit betrifft. Uns gefällt besonders, dass es zahlreiche Variationen bietet und sich mit ihm unterschiedlichste Strukturen und Konfigurationen erzeugen lassen. Insgesamt eine sehr schöne und ästhetisch überzeugende Lösung.

Apart from being the name of a musical instrument, »piano« is also the Italian word for gentle and quiet, as well as storey or floor and surface. Nomen est omen. Here, one floor is built on top of another. Horizontal lines characterize this shelving system, and give it its special feel. The shelves appear to float like wings, provide a base for large and small sliding doors of various colours, and create display space as well as storage space. The system's expansive, generous dimensions are striking – one single element can be up to 362 centimetres wide.

While its form is clear and unpretentious, the possibilities for use and individual configuration are many and varied: from a shelving system that fills the room to an elegant sideboard, a customized media centre or a light display shelf, a slim wall-mounted sideboard or a sophisticated wall-to-wall shelf unit.

The shelving system gets its stability and robustness from delicate vertical cheeks that remain unassumingly in the background. The cheeks and back panels can be positioned as desired at 30-centimetre intervals.

»Piano« is available in two depths – 32 centimetres for books and 48 centimetres for storage space and hi-fi. Apart from sliding doors, which can be fitted with LED lighting rails that make them shine like translucent planes of colour, the shelving system can also be equipped with hinged doors and drawers. It is available in various colours and wood types.

Judges panel

An outstandingly well designed shelving system that shows plenty of attention to detail. This goes for the way it is put together and for the possibilities for use. We particularly like the many variants it offers, and how it allows a great variety of structures and configurations to be created. All in all, a very elegant and aesthetically convincing solution.

jp 003　　Medienmöbel　　　　　　　　　　　　　　　Media furniture
　　　　　Wohnen **Silber**　　　　　　　　　　　　Living **Silver**

Dieses neuartige flexible Medienmöbel, das sich individuell den eigenen Bedürfnissen und Wünschen anpassen lässt, bietet Platz für Receiver, DVD Player, Flachbildschirm, Minianlage und Medienträger.

Es besteht aus einem Kabelkanal, der als Rückgrat des Möbels fungiert, und unterschiedlich großen Kuben mit und ohne Schubkästen. Zunächst befestigt man den Kabelkanal an der Wand nahe einer Steckdose. Die Kuben werden anschließend in der gewünschten Höhe in die Nuten an der Frontseite des Rückgrats eingeschoben und mit einfachen Laschen in seinem Innern fixiert. Durch die seitlichen Kabelauslässe schließt man die einzelnen eingestellten Geräte an die innenliegende Stromversorgung an und verbindet sie miteinander.

Nach dem Schließen der Frontseite kann der Flachbildschirm eingehängt und die Kuben beliebig in die gewünschte Position geschoben werden. In einem der Schubkästen lässt sich eine Mehrfachsteckdose als Ladestation für Mobiltelefon, Digitalkamera oder MP3-Player nutzen.

Das Medienmöbel ist in verschiedenen Ausführungen zu haben. Die kleinere Variante eignet sich ideal für den Eingangsbereich. Wird es nahe dem Telefonanschluss angebracht, kann es Telefon und Anrufbeantworter beherbergen. Die Schubkästen bieten Platz für Modem oder Router.

Jury
Neuer Archetyp eines Medienmöbels mit vielen klugen Detaillösungen insbesondere bei der Frage des Kabelmanagements, innovativ und überzeugend gelöst. Die Verschränkung ist clever.

This novel, flexible piece of media furniture, which can be adapted to individual needs and wishes, offers room for a receiver, a DVD player, a flat-screen TV, a mini-hi-fi, and media carriers such as discs.

It comprises a cable duct, which acts as the element's spine, and cubes of various sizes, which come with and without drawers. The cable duct is first attached to the wall near a power socket. The cubes are then slotted into the grooves on the front of the spine at the desired height. They are fixed by means of simple lugs on the inside of the spine. The cable outlets arranged along the side of the spine serve to connect the individual appliances to the power supply on the inside of the spine, as well as to each other.

Once the front has been closed, the flat-screen TV can be mounted, and the cubes pushed into the desired position. One of the drawers is equipped with a multiple socket, so that mobile phone, digital cameras or MP3 players can be recharged.

This piece of furniture is available in various designs. The smaller variant is ideal for entrance halls. If it is located near a telephone socket, it can house a telephone and answering machine. The drawers offer room for a modem or router.

Judges panel
A new archetype of a media furniture element, with many clever details, especially when it comes to the issue of cable management, which has been solved innovatively and convincingly. The way the elements interleave is clever.

Zeugwart Schuhgarderobe Shoe cupboard
Wohnen **Silber** Living **Silver**

Dieses außergewöhnliche und leichte Möbel bietet zwei Funktionen in einem: Schuhregal und Garderobe. Auf kleiner Standfläche ermöglicht es die Unterbringung von bis zu 26 Paar Schuhen. Ein zusätzliches Garderobenteil lässt sich bei Bedarf einfach in die in einem festen Raster sitzenden Stäbe werkzeuglos einsetzen, und schon kann man Mäntel und Jacken aufhängen sowie Hüte und Mützen ablegen.

So leistet »Zeugwart« seinen Dienst an verschiedenen Plätzen mit unterschiedlichem Nutzen: in der Kammer als Schuhregal, das maximal (aus)genutzt werden kann oder im Flur als Kombimöbel für Garderobe und Schuhe.

Der Hüter und Wächter über Schuhe und Mäntel lehnt einfach an der Wand und lässt sich zusätzlich mit einer Wandsicherung befestigen. Er besteht aus weiß beschichtetem Multiplex mit Stäben aus Eschenholz.

Jury

Die Leiteridee, wenn sie wie hier gut ausgeführt ist – dieses einfach an der Wand Lehnen –, fasziniert uns. Die Schuhgarderobe ist ideal für beengte Wohnverhältnisse wie Studentenwohnungen und kleine Apartments. So passen die Schuhe einer dreiköpfigen Familie hinein. Wir finden sie leicht und elegant wie eine schöne Skulptur. Sie ist vielseitig einsetzbar und nicht nur auf Schuhe, Jacken und Mäntel beschränkt. Wir würden sie auch als Spontanablage beispielsweise für Handtücher oder Schals verwenden. Superhohe Flexibilität.

This unusual and light piece of furniture offers two functions in one: it is both a shoe rack and a wardrobe. Although it takes up little space, it has room for as many as 26 pairs of shoes. If desired, an additional wardrobe element can be attached without the need for any tools to the columns, which are arranged according to a fixed pattern. Coats and jackets can then be hung up, and there is also room for hats and caps.

Wherever and however it is used, »Zeugwart« is a useful piece of furniture: stowed away in a small utility room, it can serve as a shoe rack that can be used to the full. In the entrance hall, it can serve as a combined wardrobe and shoe cupboard.

This guardian of shoes and coats is simply leaned against the wall, and can also be held in place with a wall bracket. It is made of white laminated plywood, while the columns are made of ash.

Judges panel

We were fascinated by the ladder idea, which has been excellently executed here, as well as by the idea of lounging against a wall. The shoe cupboard is ideal wherever living space is at a premium – in student quarters, for example, or in small flats. There is enough room for the shoes of a family of three. It is light and elegant, like a beautiful sculpture. It is very versatile, and not simply restricted to shoes, jackets and coats. We would use it as somewhere to »dump« things, such as towels or scarves. Really very flexible.

QuickClick Silencer Geräuschabsorbierendes Gleitsystem
Wohnen **Silber**

Sound-absorbing
Living **Silver**

»QuickClick Silencer« ist ein revolutionärer Möbelgleiter. Er sorgt nicht nur dafür, dass Stühle nicht ruckeln, bockeln und hoppeln, sondern auch nicht mehr quietschen.

So löst er – erstmals überzeugend – ein ewig auftretendes Problem: Filigrane Rundrohrstühle erzeugen beim Bewegen laute, stark störende Geräusche, vibrieren und lassen sich nur mühsam verschieben. Durch einen neu entwickelten, elastischen Schwingungsdämpfer, der über den Gleiteinsatz gestülpt und in das Rohr eingesteckt wird, werden die unerwünschten Vibrationen erstmals nahezu komplett absorbiert. So reduziert der erste vibrationsabsorbierende Gleiter den Geräuschpegel um bis zu 80 Prozent.

Stühle, die mit dem »QuickClick Silencer« ausgerüstet sind, gleiten bodenschonend, sanft und geräuschlos auf jeder Art von Bodenbelag, da aus dem QuickClick-System jederzeit ohne spezielles Werkzeug unterschiedliche austauschbare Gleiteinsätze mit verschiedenen Materialeigenschaften mit einem einfachen »Click« eingesetzt werden können.

Jury

Das ist ein intelligentes Fußgleitersystem, bestehend aus verschiedenen Endmaterialien, wie Filz oder Kunststoff, das durch eine neuartige Technik Geräusche absorbiert. Wir zeichnen hier vor allem diese Leistung von Wagner aus, da wir denken, dass es weltweit das einzige Unternehmen ist, das sich mit so einer kleinen Problematik auseinandersetzt und dadurch sehr flexibel Lösungen für die verschiedensten Bodenarten und Oberflächen entwickelt – und das zu einem niedrigen Preis.

»QuickClick Silencer« is a revolutionary furniture glide. It not only ensures that chairs are no longer banged or scraped along the floor, but also stops them from squeaking when they are moved.

This is the first convincing solution to an age-old problem: delicate round-tubing chairs make a loud, disturbing noise when they are moved. They also vibrate and can only be pushed across the floor with difficulty. For the first time, unwanted vibrations are almost completely absorbed by a newly developed, elastic vibration damper, which is slipped over the glider and plugged into the tubular frame. This vibration absorber reduced noise level by as much as 80 percent.

Chairs fitted with the »QuickClick Silencer« slide gently and noiselessly across the floor, and are gentle to the floor at the same time. The various types of gliders, whose materials vary according to the type of flooring, are interchangeable and can be simply clicked into place without any need for special tools.

Judges panel

This is an intelligent glider system, the bases of which are made of various materials such as felt or plastic. An innovative design means that they absorb noise. Our award especially honours the work done by Wagner. As far as we know, it is the only company in the world that has devoted itself to such an issue and has come up with extremely flexible solutions for the widest variety of floorings and surfaces – and this at a low price.

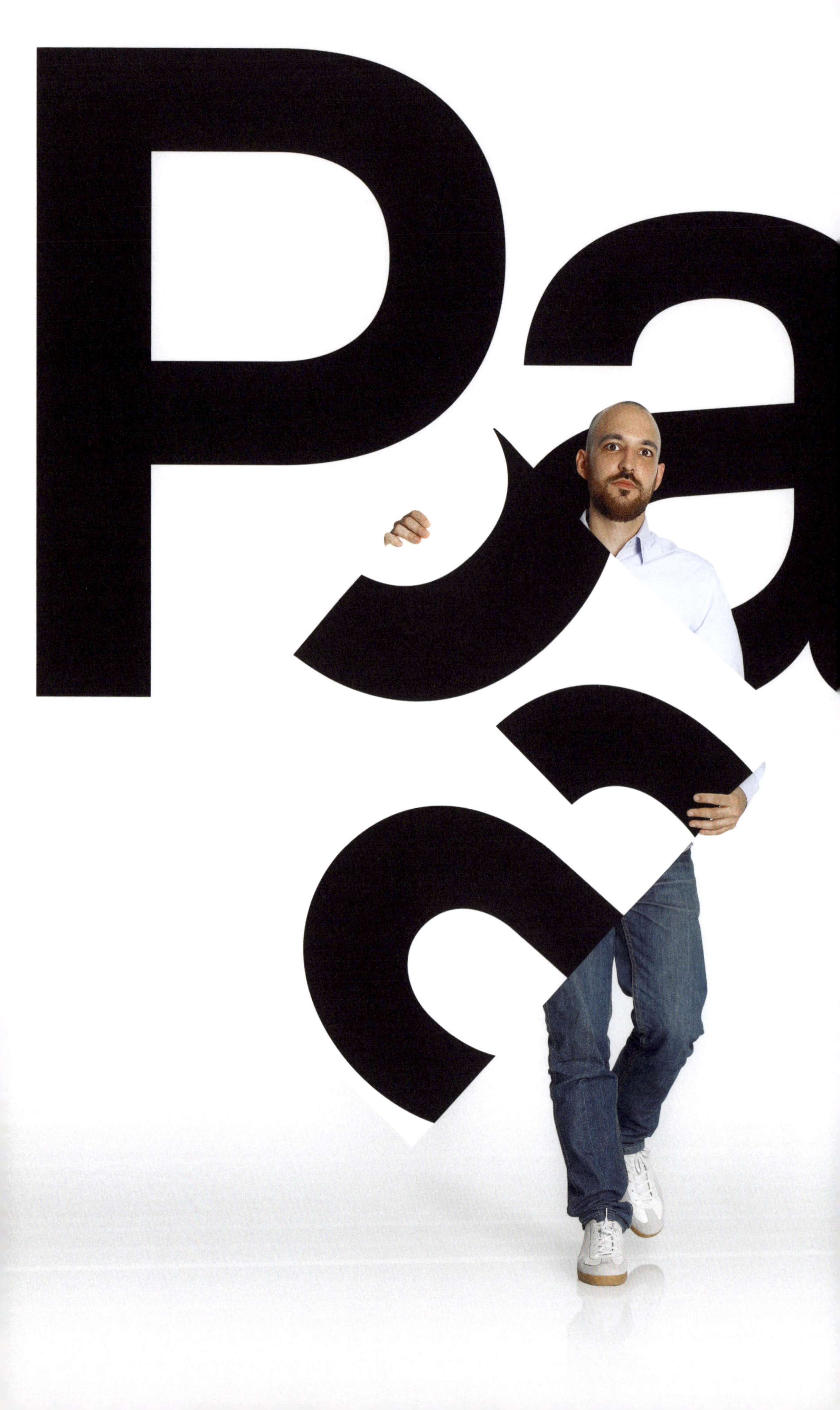
Pa

CS

Parcs Raumbildendes Möbelensemble Zone-creating furn
Objekt **Gold** Contract furniture

»Es bedarf Aufgeklärtheit, Realitätssinn und Progressivität, um zu erkennen, dass auch jemand, der auf einem Sofa sitzt, Mehrwert für das Unternehmen schafft«, meint Tom Lloyd vom Designstudio PearsonLloyd, das »Parcs« entworfen hat. Dieses raumbildende Möbelprogramm schafft ein inspirierendes Arbeitsumfeld für spontanen Austausch, persönliche Begegnungen, Teamarbeit und Meetings.

Die Designer analysierten zunächst, wie Menschen im Büro arbeiten und interagieren, wenn sie sich außerhalb des formellen Umfeldes wie Sitzungssälen, Konferenzräumen und ihren Schreibtischen bewegen. So entstand »Parcs«, eine andere Art der Möblierung für die zentralen Kommunikations- und Arbeitszonen – das Büro als eine frei gestaltbare Stadtlandschaft. Es besteht aus einer Vielzahl beliebig kombinierbarer Einzelmöbel für viele unterschiedliche Situationen ohne eine fest diktierte Nutzungsart.

Dabei gibt es vier Typologien. »Causeways« besteht aus Sitzbänken, Fence-Modulen, Schränken und Wänden und lädt zum Sitzen, Stehen und Anlehnen ein. Bei den Sesseln und Sofas der »Wing Series« schirmen Seitenkopfstützen visuell und akustisch ab. So ermöglichen sie konzentrierte Gespräche, fokussiertes Arbeiten oder Erholung. Für Brainstormings oder kurze Meetings im Sitzen oder Stehen bietet die markant geformte »Toguna« einen kreisrunden, akustisch geschützten, halb offenen Raum. Die »Idea Wall« ist ein freistehendes, winkelförmiges Wandelement mit integrierter Kommunikations- und Medientechnik. Kombiniert man sie mit einem Stehtisch oder Causeway-Elementen, wird sie zu einem idealen Ort für medienunterstützte Präsentationen und Diskussionen.

»Parcs« schafft neue Trends, motiviert zu Bewegung, fördert Initiative und Innovation.

Jury
Ein raumbildendes Möbelensemble, das auf das Bedürfnis, in Großraumbüros separate Zonen zu schaffen, eine überzeugende Antwort gibt. Es schafft atmosphärisch einen abgeschirmten Raum, auch akustisch, für verschiedenste Gesprächssituationen. Man hat das Gefühl, man ist ganz für sich. Man kann ungestört Besprechungen abhalten oder mit dem Handy telefonieren, kann sich aber trotzdem durch die Offenheit insbesondere in Armlehnenhöhe, was funktional sehr schön gelöst ist, gut bewegen. Es hat etwas von Cocooning. Weckt Emotionen, sehr überzeugend, großartig.

»It needs progressiveness to recognize that someone who sits on a sofa can still be creating value for the company«, says Tom Lloyd from the design studio PearsonLloyd, which created »Parcs«. This zone-creating range of furniture shapes an inspiring working environment for spontaneous exchange, personal encounters, team work and meetings.

The designers first analyzed how people in the office work and interact when they are outside the formal environment of meeting rooms, conference halls, and their desks. The result was »Parcs«, a different kind of furniture for the central communicative zone in the office, which now becomes an area that can be structured as desired. It comprises a wide variety of individual furniture elements that can be combined as desired, for any kind of situation. There is no pre-determined use for the elements.

There are four »typologies«. »Causeways« comprises benches, fence modules, cupboards and walls, and invites the user to sit, stand or lean. The wings on the headrests of the armchairs and sofas in the »Wing Series« provide visual and acoustic privacy. In this way, they allow focused discussions and work, or relaxation. With its striking shape, »Toguna« creates a round, acoustically protected, semi-open space for brainstorming sessions or brief meetings, in which participants can sit or stand. The »Idea Wall« is a free-standing, angled wall element with integrated communication and media technology. If it is combined with a high desk or Causeway elements, it is an ideal place for media-based presentations and discussions.

»Parcs« creates new trends, motivates people to move, and encourages initiative and innovation.

Judges panel
A zone-creating furniture series that provides a convincing answer to the need to create separate zones in open-plan offices. It creates the atmosphere of a separate room – also acoustically – for the most diverse meeting situations. It gives you a feeling of privacy. You can talk or use your mobile without interruption. At the same time, however, the elements' openness, especially at arm-rest height, gives you freedom to move. Functionally very well done. The whole thing has a cocooning touch. It arouses emotions, very impressive, great.

K1 Kirchenstuhl
Objekt **Silber**

Church seat
Contract furniture

Der Kirchenstuhl »K1«, der für Saalbestuhlungen und Kirchenbauten entworfen worden ist, wird von Loony-Design hergestellt. Loony ist ein gemeinsames Projekt der Staatlichen Akademie der bildenden Künste Stuttgart und des Diakonischen Werks Baden, um psychisch kranke und behinderte Menschen mit sinnvollen Arbeitsmöglichkeiten zu versorgen. Loony-Produkte zeichnen sich durch ihre hohe Design- und Verarbeitungsqualität aus. Sie sind von Hand gearbeitet, und bei den Materialien wird auf Umweltverträglichkeit und Nachhaltigkeit geachtet.

So wird auch »K1« manufakturell aus hochwertigem Stahl und heimischen Hölzern in einer anerkannten Werkstatt für behinderte Menschen gefertigt. Der Kirchenstuhl besticht durch seine schlichte Eleganz und bodenständige Solidität. Seine formale Klarheit verleiht ihm auch in großen Räumen und ungewöhnlichen architektonischen Situationen Souveränität. In der Reihung nimmt sich der Stuhl zurück und schafft so ein ruhiges Gesamtbild.

Sitz und Rückenlehne bestehen aus konkav ausgefrästen massiven Eichenplatten. Das bewirkt nicht nur eine skulpturale Leichtigkeit, sondern bietet auch ergonomische Vorteile. So macht die konkave Form den Stuhl bequemer. Durch die Unterkonstruktion der Stahlzarge wird außerdem der Sitzkomfort noch verstärkt. Die Lehne gibt leicht nach und passt sich unterstützend dem Rücken an. Die zusätzlichen Reihenverbinder aus Stahl dienen gleichzeitig als Gesangbuchablage. Für eine hervorragende Statik und für eine nahezu unbegrenzte Haltbarkeit sorgt die schwere Konstruktion des Gestells.

Jury

Eine neue Sitzqualität für kirchliche Bereiche. Durch die Flexibilität der Rückenlehne ist er auch für längeres Sitzen komfortabel. Er integriert sich sehr gut in Kirchenräumen durch die kubische Formensprache und sachliche, strenge Gestaltung, die auf subtile Art an ein Kreuz erinnert. Positiv finden wir, dass er von Loony in Werkstätten für behinderte Menschen produziert wird. Schön sind die kleinen Details, wie die Gebetbuchablage, die gleichzeitig Reihenverbinder ist, oder wie das Rahmengestell aus Stahl in die Kanten läuft.

The »K1« church seat, which was designed for assembly halls and churches, is manufactured by Loony Design. Loony is a joint project of the Stuttgart Academy of Fine Arts and the Diakonisches Werk, a welfare organization run by the church in Baden. Its aim is to give physically and mentally handicapped people meaningful work. Loony products stand out by virtue of the high quality of their design and workmanship. They are hand-crafted, and the materials are chosen with a view to environmental impact and sustainability.

»K1« is manufactured out of high-quality steel and locally sourced timber in a recognized workshop for the handicapped. The church seat gives an impression of unpretentious elegance and down-to-earth sobriety. Its formal clarity gives it an air of composure, even in large rooms and unusual architectural surroundings. When placed in a row with other seats, it fades into the background, creating an overall impression of tranquillity.

The seat surface and back rest are made of solid oak, cut to a concave shape. This not only creates an impression of sculptural lightness, but also has ergonomic benefits. The concave shape makes the seat more comfortable, for example. This comfort is further enhanced by the steel-frame substructure. The back rest gives slightly, providing support for the back. The steel row connectors, available as an extra, also provide space to deposit a hymn book. The heavy construction of the frame makes the seat extremely stable and practically indestructible.

Judges panel

A new seating quality for church settings. The flexible backrest makes it comfortable to sit in even for longer periods. Its cubistic formal expression and sober, strict design, which is subtly reminiscent of a cross, means that it harmonizes excellently with a church setting. A further positive aspect for us is that Loony produces it in workshops for the handicapped. There are also some nice small details, such as the row connector that also provides room for a hymn book, or the way the steel frame continues into the chair legs.

easySit® Bürodrehstuhl Office swivel chair
Objekt **Silber** Contract furniture

Nomen est omen. Der »easySit®« ermöglicht dem Benutzer so viel individuelle Bewegungsfreiheit wie wohl kaum ein anderer Bürostuhl – und das ohne aufwändige Einstellungen. Aufgrund seiner Konstruktion muss einfach nur mit einem Handgriff Sitzhöhe und -tiefe gewählt werden.

»easySit®« passt sich selbstständig den Bewegungswünschen des Körpers an und sorgt mit sanfter Unterstützung des gesamten Muskelsystems dafür, dass man intuitiv die beste Körperhaltung für die jeweilige Tätigkeit und Sitzposition wählt. Die innovative Gleitmechanik unterstützt dabei die Körperbewegung – die gleitende Bewegung von Sitz und Rückenlehne folgt dem Körper regelrecht. Beim Zurücklehnen gleitet die Sitzfläche automatisch in die entgegengesetzte Richtung und der Winkel zwischen Bildschirm und Auge bleibt so fast unverändert.

Es werden alle Wirbelsäulenbereiche wirkungsvoll entlastet. Durch seine Bewegungsanreize kräftigt der Bürostuhl die feinen Strukturen in der Rückenmuskulatur und regt zusätzlich den Stoffwechsel an. Fazit: Wie man auch sitzt, man sitzt komfortabel und ergonomisch.

Klares Design, klassische Linienführung, sorgfältige Verarbeitung und hochwertige Materialien unterstreichen seinen hohen Anspruch an Individualität und Stil. Für »easySit®« gibt es eine Vielzahl an Kombinationsmöglichkeiten. So ist er in Stoff oder in Leder, in verschiedenen Farben, beispielsweise schwarz, weiß oder knall-orange oder mit farbigen Ledernähten und wirkungsvollen Kontrasten der Polsterung zu haben.

Jury

Ein innovativer Bürodrehstuhl, der sich durch eine neue Sitzmechanik auszeichnet. Die Rückenlehne ist mit der Sitzfläche verbunden. Wenn die Rückenlehne nach hinten geht, verschiebt sich die Sitzfläche nach vorne. Die zurückhaltende Gestaltung ist sehr angenehm, der Stuhl ist repräsentativ ohne protzig zu wirken.

Nomen est omen. »easySit®« offers its user a level of individual freedom of movement that is rarely seen in office chairs, and this without the need for complicated adjustments. Its design means that all the user has to do is select seat height and depth. One hand movement is sufficient to do this.

»easySit®« adjusts automatically to the body's movements, and the gentle support it provides for the entire muscular system ensures that the user intuitively chooses the best posture for each activity and seating position. Its innovative sliding mechanism supports body movements, with the seat and the back rest literally tracking every move the body makes. When the user leans back, the seat automatically slides in the opposite direction, so that the angle between computer screen and eye remains practically unchanged.

All areas of the back are effectively supported. In encouraging the user to move, the office chair strengthens the fine structures of the muscles of the back, and gives an additional stimulus to metabolism. In short, no matter how you sit, you sit comfortably and ergonomically.

Clear design, classic lines, careful workmanship and high-quality materials emphasize its high standards of individuality and style. »easySit®« is available in many combinations. It is available with a fabric or leather covering, in diverse colours such as black, white or bright orange, or with coloured seams and strikingly contrasting upholstery.

Judges panel

An innovative office swivel chair that stands out by virtue of its novel seat mechanism. The back rest is connected to the seat. If the back rest moves backwards, the seat slides forwards. The restrained design is very pleasant, the chair is prestigious without being ostentatious.

Cobi Konferenzdrehstuhl
Objekt **Silber**

Conference swivel
Contract furniture

Teamarbeit nimmt einen immer größeren Teil der Arbeitszeit ein. Meist gibt es aber gerade in Projekt- und Konferenzräumen keinen ergonomischen Sitzkomfort. Folgen von unbehaglichem Sitzen sind Müdigkeit und nachlassende Konzentration. Teamarbeit im Sitzen erfordert deshalb nicht nur völlig andere Sitzhaltungen, sondern auch andersartige Stühle, die ein Maximum an Bewegungsfreiheit bieten.

»cobi« ist ein Konferenzdrehstuhl, der diese Anforderungen erfüllt. Er sorgt für hohen Komfort. So kommt er mit nur einem einzigen manuellen Bedienhebel zur Sitzhöhenverstellung aus – ganz wichtig; denn, ist das nicht der Fall, bleiben bei Teamstühlen die Einstellmöglichkeiten meist ungenutzt.

Alles andere erledigt ein innovativer und intuitiver gewichtsaktivierter Mechanismus und alle Einzelkomponenten, die sich dem Körper flexibel anpassen. Der Gegendruck der elastischen Rückenlehne wird automatisch auf das Körpergewicht des Nutzers angepasst. Lehnt man sich auf die Rückenlehne, so gibt die Oberkante aus Elastomer angenehm nach und bietet eine bequeme Auflage für den Arm. »cobi« besticht auch mit seiner nach drei Seiten biegsamen Sitzschale. Er unterstützt viele verschiedene Sitzhaltungen – vor- oder zurückgelehnt, aufrecht, nach links oder rechts gedreht – und fördert so dynamisches Sitzen.

Für die Rückenlehne mit atmungsaktivem Connect 3D Netzbezug stehen acht Farben zur Auswahl, der Atlantic-Bezug der Sitzfläche ist wahlweise in der gleichen oder einer Kontrastfarbe erhältlich. Fußgestell, Sitz- und Rückenlehnenschale gibt es in schwarz oder weiß.

Jury

Einfacher, eleganter Konferenzdrehstuhl. Ausgezeichnet, wie Rücken- und Armlehnen direkt nach unten zur Mechanik geführt werden und in ihnen der innovative Mechanismus integriert wurde. Schön und formal ansprechend gelöst durch die Flexibilität der Materialien im Rücken und die Aufgrätung in verschiedene Bahnen. Dadurch erhält man eine sehr gute Lüftung im Rückenbereich. Die Flexibilität der Oberkante lässt zusätzliche Sitzpositionen zu, also auch mit dem Arm auf der Rückenlehne. Eine innovative, verbesserte Sitzergonomie.

More and more working hours are taken up with team work. Usually, however, project and conference rooms are ergonomically uncomfortable places. If people cannot sit comfortably, fatigue sets in and concentration falters. Sedentary teamwork thus requires not only completely different postures, but also different chairs that offer maximum freedom of movement.

»cobi« is a conference swivel chair that meets these needs. It ensures that people can sit comfortably. It requires just one manually operated lever to adjust seating height. This is very important, since if this is not the case, people will generally not try to adjust chairs to the right height.

All the other adjustments are taken care of by an innovative mechanism that reacts intuitively to weight, while every individual component adjusts flexibly to provide the support needed. The level of counter-pressure exerted by the elastic backrest adjusts automatically to the weight of the user. If the user leans on the back of the chair, the elastomer top edge yields pleasantly and offers a comfortable armrest. A further striking feature of »cobi« is its flexing seat pan, which yields to pressure on three sides. It supports many different seating postures, leaning forward or back, upright, turned to the left or right – and encourages users to move around in their seats.

The backrest made of breathable Connect 3D Knit fabric is available in eight colours, and the Atlantic seat fabric can be selected in the same colour or in a contrasting shade. The base, seat pan and back frame are available in black or white.

Judges panel

Simple, elegant conference swivel chair. Excellent, the way the back and arm rests are guided directly to the mechanism below, and the way the innovative mechanism has been integrated in them. The flexibility of the materials in the back area and the fishbone structure with its various bands is elegant and formally appealing. This keeps the back very well ventilated. The flexible top edge of the back rest allows other postures to be adopted – with the arm resting on the back rest, for example. Innovative, enhanced seating ergonomics.

Setu™ Mehrzweck-Sitzmöbel Multipurpose cha
Objekt **Silber** Contract furniture

»Setu™« ist eine zeitgemäße Stuhlreihe, die sowohl in moderne Arbeitsumgebungen als auch in Wohnräume passt, und neue Maßstäbe in Bezug auf Einfachheit, Vielseitigkeit und Komfort setzt.

Zu der Stuhlreihe, die noch erweitert werden soll, gehören heute Stühle mit vier- und fünfstrahligem Fußkreuz, mit und ohne Rollen und Armstützen, sowie ein Lounge-Sessel mit dazu passender Fußbank. »Setu™« kann vielseitig eingesetzt werden beispielsweise für Teamarbeitsplätze, Konferenzräume oder Cafés.

Die Kinematic Spine™, eine Kombination aus zwei einfachen Polypropylenmaterialien, bietet hohen Komfort und stützt den Körper rundum, wobei die flexible Rückenlehne gleichzeitig maximale Bewegungsfreiheit erlaubt. »Setu™«, dessen elegantes Design auf Komfort und Strapazierfähigkeit ausgelegt ist, ist ein minimalistisches Meisterwerk: leicht – so wiegt beispielsweise der Stuhl mit fünf Rollen weniger als neun Kilogramm – und benutzerfreundlich. Er besitzt zwar eine Höhenverstellung, kommt jedoch ohne Neigungsmechanismus aus, sodass die Anzahl der Komponenten gering gehalten wurde. Die neue Elastomer-Sitzflächenfederung Lyris™ macht Bewegungen in jede Richtung mit und schafft eine gleichmäßige Gewichtsverteilung. Außerdem passt sie sich der Körperform an und sorgt für ausreichende Belüftung.

Das Fußkreuz besteht aus strapazierfähigem, korrosionsgeschütztem H-Alloy™ Aluminium, das kein Finish mit toxischen Schadstoffen erfordert. »Setu™« ist zu 92 Prozent wiederverwertbar.

Jury

Sehr interessante Wipp-Konstruktion, die sich über einen Kunststoffrahmen entwickelt. Im Rückenbereich wird der Kunststoff so eingesetzt, dass er eine Federkraft ausübt. Uns gefällt auch das etwas roh wirkende Aluminium – mal nicht in Hochglanz –, das eine moderne und reizvolle Anmutung hat. Kombiniert mit dem Gewebe ist es eine zeitgemäße, leichte und interessante Aussage. Formal sehr schön gelöst: die Armlehne als Endlosband, das sich wieder in den Stuhl integriert und im Rückenbereich der Stabilisierung dient.

»Setu™« is a contemporary series of chairs that goes well in a modern office setting as well as in the home, and that sets new standards when it comes to simplicity, versatility and comfort.

It is planned to extend this series of chairs, which at present comprises chairs with four and five-pointed star base and with and without casters and armrests, as well as a lounge chair with a matching footstool. »Setu™« can be used in a variety of settings, such as team workplaces, conference rooms or cafes.

The Kinematic Spine™, a combination of two simple polypropylene materials, makes the chair extremely comfortable, and offers all-round support for the body, while the flexible backrest allows maximum freedom of movement. »Setu™«, whose elegant design is geared to comfort and hard wear, is a minimalist masterpiece. It is light – the version with five casters, for example, weighs less than nine kilograms – and user-friendly. While it is height-adjustable, it does not have any need of a tilting mechanism, and so the number of components has been kept low. Lyris™, the new elastomer that gives the seat its spring, follows every movement and ensures that weight is distributed evenly. It also adapts to body size and ensures that there is sufficient ventilation.

The base is made of hard-wearing, corrosion-resistant H-Alloy™ aluminium, which means that there is no need for any finishing with toxic materials. »Setu™« is 92 percent recyclable.

Judges panel

Very interesting rocking design derived from a plastic frame. The way the plastic is applied in the back region means that it acts like a spring. We also like the somewhat rough appearance of the aluminium – not highly polished for once – which gives it a modern and attractive air. In combination with the fabric used, it makes a contemporary, light and interesting statement. The line that is drawn like a never-ending band over the arm rest, and is then reintegrated in the chair and its back is formally very elegant, and serves to make the back of the chair stable.

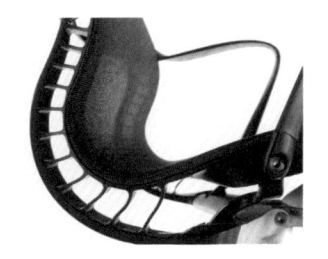

Ongo® Seat   Hocker   Stool
Objekt **Silber**   Contract furniture

Der menschliche Körper ist auf Bewegung ausgelegt; trotzdem sitzen wir einen Großteil unseres Lebens. Dem trägt »Ongo® Seat« Rechnung, indem er beides vereint: sitzen und sich bewegen.

Die innovative gewölbte Standfläche reagiert auf Gewichtsverlagerung und aktiviert die Muskulatur, die dabei nicht nur gekräftigt wird, sondern deren Verspannungen auch gelöst werden können.

Eine weitere Innovation ist die im Fuß integrierte Kugelbahn. Mitgeliefert werden drei Kugeln in unterschiedlichen Materialien und Schwierigkeitsgraden: leicht aus Stahl, mittel aus Glas und schwer aus Gummi. Die umlaufende Kugel motiviert und kontrolliert die Bewegung durch ein akustisches Feedback. Summt die Kugel, ist man auf dem richtigen Weg.

Die Sitzhöhe lässt sich mit Hilfe einer hochwertigen und verdrehsicheren Gasdruckfeder von 42 bis 64 Zentimeter verstellen. Unter dem Sitz befindet sich dafür eine umlaufende Auslösefläche, die bei Be- und Entlastung einfach gedrückt wird. Der Körper besteht aus ABS-Kunststoff in schwarz oder weiß. Die Kugelbahn gibt es passend dazu oder in silber. Beim wasch- und austauschbaren Sitzbezug aus Polyester mit etwas Elasthan hat man die Wahl zwischen zwölf verschiedenen Farben.

Durch sein zeitloses Design passt der Hocker in ganz verschiedene Umgebungen: Zuhause, im Büro, in Praxen, Studios und öffentlichen Räumen. Mit ihm lässt sich Bewegung – optional mit einem speziell entwickelten Trainingsprogramm – spielerisch in den Alltag integrieren und neben der Körperhaltung auch die Leistungsfähigkeit verbessern.

Jury

Der Name ist klasse, weil »(h)ongo« in spanisch Pilz bedeutet, aber mit stummem »h«. Einen Sitzhocker mit therapeutischen Übungen zu verbinden und mit Kugelbahn und Kugel auszustatten, ist ein ganz innovativer Produktansatz. Und das spielerisch, weil man direkt über das Geräusch und das Rollen der Kugel Rückmeldung bekommt. Eine multisensuale Kombination, man hört, sieht und spürt durch die Bewegung, was man machen sollte. Der Klang der Kugel hat wahrscheinlich auch etwas Meditatives. Formal gut integrierte Höhenverstellung.

The human body is made for movement, yet we spend a lot of our lives sitting down. »Ongo® Seat« takes account of this by combining sitting and moving.

The innovative convex base reacts to shifts in weight and activates the muscular system. It not only strengthens the muscles, but can also relieve muscular tension.

One further innovation is the ball track integrated in the base. The stool comes with three balls, made of different materials, each for a different level of difficulty: steel for easy, glass for medium difficult, and rubber for difficult. As it runs around the track, the ball motivates the user to move and monitors his movement by providing acoustic feedback. If the ball hums, the user is on the right track.

By means of a high-quality, twist-safe pneumatic spring, seating height can be adjusted from 42 to 64 centimetres. It is activated by a trigger that runs around the underside of the seat, and is simply depressed as pressure is applied and taken away. The body is made of ABS plastic, and is available in black or white. The ball track is available in black, white or silver. The washable and exchangeable seat covering, made of polyester with some added spandex, is available in 12 colours.

The stool's timeless design means it harmonizes with many different surroundings. It can be used in the home, the office, the surgery, the studio or public spaces. With a specially developed training program as an option, it allows movement to be integrated playfully into everyday routine, improving not only posture, but also performance.

Judges panel

The name is super, because »hongo« means mushroom in Spanish, but is pronounced with a silent »h«. Combining a stool with therapeutic exercises and furnishing it with a ball track and ball is a very innovative approach. It is also a playful approach, since the user receives feedback directly from the sound and movement of the ball. A multi-sensual combination. You can hear, see and feel the movement you have to make. There is probably also something meditative about the sound of the ball. Formally well integrated height adjustment.

iMove F Höhenverstellbarer Arbeitstisch
Objekt **Silber**

Height-adjustable
Contract furniture

Stundenlanges Sitzen im Büro trägt viel zur Zunahme von Rückenbeschwerden bei. Eine dynamische Arbeitsweise dagegen, bei der man spontan zwischen Sitzen und Stehen wechseln kann, verbessert nicht nur das körperliche Wohlbefinden, sondern auch die geistige Leistungsfähigkeit. Solch eine Steh-Sitz-Lösung bietet das Arbeitsplatzsystem »iMove«, das perfekte Ergonomie und Technikintegration, anspruchsvolles Design und überzeugende Funktionalität verbindet.

Benötigen marktübliche Arbeitstische mit motorischen Systemen zwischen 12 und 16 Sekunden, um von Sitz- in Stehhöhe zu wechseln, so lässt sich das hier mit einem Handgriff in nur zwei bis drei Sekunden erledigen – ein echter Vorteil gerade auch für spontane Positionswechsel; denn nur, wenn das schnell und leicht geht, wird es auch wirklich genutzt.

Das System wird in zwei Basis-Bauformen angeboten. Die eine ist geprägt durch das C-Fuß-Gestell mit Säule in gebürstetem Alu und hochglanzpolierter Fußschiene. Die andere Ausführung besitzt eine Rahmenwange, die es wahlweise auch verchromt gibt. Der leicht wirkende, rechteckige Metallrahmen des Seitenteils bietet hier eine ungewöhnliche Optik und ein prägnantes Profil.

Beide Varianten können mit Beistellmodulen kombiniert werden. Dabei wird eine Tischseite in einen Container oder ein elegantes Sideboard integriert. Beide Versionen bieten überzeugende neue Lösungen für die Unterbringung von Rechnern und Verkabelung. Der Container besitzt ein extra CPU-Fach neben den Schubladen und das Sideboard einen komfortablen CPU-Auszug unter der Arbeitsfläche.

Jury

Die überzeugende und einfach zu bedienende Höhenverstellmöglichkeit erlaubt das dynamische, und damit gesündere Arbeiten im Wechsel zwischen Stehen und Sitzen. Und das bedeutet natürlich auch eine Anpassung an die individuelle Größe des Nutzers. Sehr schöne Detaillierung auch des Sideboards. Funktional ausgezeichnet gelöst.

Sitting in an office for hours on end is one major reason for the increase in back complaints. A dynamic way of working, by contrast, which allows the worker to shift spontaneously from sitting to standing, improves not only the physical sense of well-being but also intellectual performance. Switching between sitting and standing is the idea behind »iMove«, a workplace system that combines perfect ergonomics and integrated technology with sophisticated design and impressive functionality.

While commonly available desks with motor-driven systems take between 12 and 16 seconds to move from seating to standing height, this can be done here with one hand movement in just two to three seconds. This is a true plus point when spontaneously changing position, since people will only do this if it can be done quickly and easily.

The system is available in two basic designs. The distinctive feature of the first is a C-shaped leg, with a column made of brushed aluminium and a highly polished base rail. The second design has a side frame that is also available in a chrome finish. Light in appearance, the rectangular metal side frame has an unusual look and a striking profile.

Both variants can be combined with side modules. One side of the desk is then integrated with a container or with an elegant sideboard. The two versions also come up with convincing new solutions for stowing away computers and cables. The container has a special CPU compartment next to the drawers, and the sideboard has a convenient CPU drawer below the worktop.

Judges panel

The impressive, easy-to-use height-adjusting function allows the user to work dynamically, and thus more healthily, by shifting from sitting to standing. This, of course, means adjusting to the individual height of the user. Very good attention to details, also in the sideboard. Functionally speaking, an excellent solution.

Scale® / FreeScale® Teppichfliesen
Objekt **Silber**

Carpet tiles
Contract furniture

Teppichfliesen – ein fantasieloser, zweckmäßiger Bodenbelag? Nicht bei »Scale®« und »FreeScale®«. Diese brechen bewusst mit Konventionen und eröffnen Architekten neue Horizonte bei der Gestaltung hochwertiger Raumarchitektur.

Die Kollektion umfasst Teppichfliesen mit verschiedenen Elementgrößen, Materialqualitäten, Tuft- und Webarten, Mustern und Farben, die ein Kompositionsspiel ergeben, das einem Flur ebenso gerecht wird wie einem Vorstandsbüro oder einem Konferenzraum.

Das Konzept folgt den in der Architektur üblichen Rastern und überträgt diese auf den Boden. So gibt es bei »Scale®« neben dem Standardformat (50 x 50 cm) auch Fliesen mit 60 x 60 cm, 100 x 100 cm, sowie Halb- und Viertelformate (50 x 100 cm und 25 x 100 cm), die neue, außergewöhnliche Akzente setzen und in der Kombination einen Formbaukasten für zahllose, individuelle Parkettierungen bilden.

»FreeScale®« geht mit seinen drei Freiformvarianten noch weiter. Sie lösen sich von der Verbindlichkeit des rechten Winkels. Durch eine eigens entwickelte Schnitttechnik ist dies erstmals möglich.

»Nun können wir wieder ein Bild auf dem Boden erzeugen«, erläutert Hadi Teherani. Der Boden wird zum spielerischen Unikat. Ein Design, aus dem in der Variation von Oberfläche, Farbe, Gestalt, Format und Ornamentik unzählige Bilder entstehen können – eine neue Philosophie der Raumgestaltung.

Die Teppichfliesen erfüllen zudem auch hohe Ansprüche in Bezug auf Umwelt und Gesundheit. So werden sie nicht nur ressourcenschonend und mit dem Einsatz von Recyclingmaterialien hergestellt, sondern sind auch für Allergiker geeignet.

Jury

Die Mosaikmöglichkeiten, die dieses innovative Teppichfliesensystem schafft, finden wir sehr interessant für Objekträume. Gerade auch für Architekten bieten sie großen Gestaltungsfreiraum. Sie können sozusagen mit einem vorgefertigten Modulsystem sehr individuell Räume entwerfen und ganz unterschiedliche Akzente setzen.

Carpet tiles – an unimaginative, pragmatic floor covering? Not in the case of »Scale®« and »FreeScale®«. They deliberately overthrow convention and open up new horizons for interior designers who want to create a premium look.

The collection comprises carpet tiles that differ in terms of element size, quality of materials, tuft and weave types, patterns and colours. They result in a play of compositions that is equally appropriate for a corridor, a board room or a conference room.

The concept is based on the conventional grids used in architecture, and applies them to the floor. »Scale®« carpet tiles, for example, are available in standard format (50 x 50 cm) or in 60 x 60 and 100 x 100 formats, as well as in half and quarter formats (50 x 100 cm and 25 x 100 cm). These create new and unusual accents and, when combined with other tiles, provide a repertoire for numerous individual tiling options.

»FreeScale®« goes even further, offering three free-form variants. These depart from the predictable right-angle form. A cutting technology developed in-house makes this possible for the first time.

»Now we can create an image on the floor again«, says Hadi Teherani. The floor becomes a playful, unique feature. A design whose varied surfaces, colours, structure, format and ornamentation gives rise to countless pictures – a new philosophy of interior design.

The carpet tiles also satisfy high standards with respect to health and the environment. Not only are they made in a resource-conserving way, using recycled materials, they are also suitable for allergy sufferers.

Judges panel

We think the mosaics that can be made with this innovative carpet-tile system are very interesting in a contract-furnishing setting. For architects in particular, they offer a lot of freedom of design. With a prefabricated modular system, as it were, they can design very individual spaces and set quite different accents.

Air Mü
Mu

olier

Dyson Air Multiplier Tischventilator
Ambiente, Lifestyle **Gold**

Table-top fan
Ambience, lifestyle

Dyson Ingenieure haben eine revolutionäre patentierte Technologie für einen völlig neuen Ventilator entwickelt. Zerschneiden herkömmliche Ventilatoren mit ihren Rotorflügeln die Luft und erzeugen einen stoßartigen, unregelmäßigen Luftstrom, so arbeitet der »Dyson Air Multiplier« gänzlich ohne. Dadurch entsteht ein gleichmäßiger, angenehmer, kühler Luftstrahl ohne Unterbrechungen.

Innerhalb des Luftrings befindet sich ein schmaler Schlitz, durch den die Luft beschleunigt wird. So baut sich ein ringförmiger Luftstrom auf. Dieser wird über eine Schräge geführt, die wie eine Tragfläche geformt ist, um die Richtung des Luftstrahls zu kanalisieren. Zusätzlich wird die umgebende Luft angesaugt und um das 15-fache verstärkt. Durch die Kombination von Technologien, die bei Turboladern und Düsentriebwerken genutzt werden, entsteht ein kraftvoller Luftstrom – mit bis zu 450 Litern Luft pro Sekunde.

Lässt sich die Luftgeschwindigkeit bei handelsüblichen Ventilatoren nur mit zwei oder drei Stufen regulieren, so kann sie hier stufenlos eingestellt werden. Die herkömmlichen Ventilatoren sind kopflastig, weshalb sie sich nur schwer ausrichten lassen. Anders beim »Dyson Air Multiplier«: Da der energieeffiziente, kohlenbürstenlose Motor im Standfuß sitzt, besitzt er einen niedrigen Schwerpunkt. Der Luftring lässt sich leicht kippen, um den Luftstrahl optimal auszurichten. Da der neue Ventilator aus stabilem ABS Kunststoff keine schnell rotierenden Flügel besitzt, die durch ein Gitter geschützt werden müssen, ist er sicher und lässt sich zudem einfach reinigen.

Jury

Eine technologische Innovation, formal einfach, sehr überzeugend. Es wurde eine neue Form für das Produkt gefunden, für das es keine Vorbilder gab. Einfach ein Ventilator ohne Rotorflügel, der an eine Turbine erinnert. Faszinierend. Sehr skulptural, schön für die Wohnung und den Officebereich, ein Eyecatcher. Nicht zu vergessen der Sicherheitsaspekt. Die herkömmlichen Ventilatoren waren immer auch gefährlich für Kinder. Kein Staubfänger mehr wie früher als es eine offene Struktur war. Man kann ihn leicht abwischen. Sehr einfache und intuitive Bedienerführung.

Dyson engineers have come up with a revolutionary patented technology for a completely new kind of fan. While conventional fans chop up the air with their blades, creating an irregular, buffeting flow of air, the »Dyson Air Multiplier« functions without any rotors at all. The result is a cool jet of air that is regular, pleasant and uninterrupted.

A thin slit inside the air ring accelerates the air. In this way a circular flow of air is created. This is guided over a sloping surface shaped like an aircraft wing, which directs the air jet. In addition, ambient air is drawn in and amplified 15 times. By combining technologies used in turbochargers and jet engines, a powerful jet of air is created – up to 450 litres of air per second.

While commercially available fans have two or three-stage controls to govern air speed, the Dyson fan is infinitely variable. Conventional fans are also top-heavy, which makes them difficult to direct. The »Dyson Air Multiplier« is different. As the energy-efficient, brushless motor is housed in the base, it has a low centre of gravity. The air ring can be easily tilted in order to give the air jet exactly the right direction. And as the new fan, which is made of ABS plastic, does not have any fast-turning blades that require a guard, it is both safe and easy to clean.

Judges panel

A technological innovation, formally simple, very convincing. For this product, a new, unprecedented form has been found. Simply a fan without blades, reminiscent of a turbine. Fascinating. Very sculptural, perfect for the home or the office, an eye-catcher. And the safety angle should not be forgotten. Conventional fans have always been dangerous for children. Nowhere for dust to settle anymore, compared with the old fan designs. It can simply be wiped clean. Very simple and intuitive user interface.

iBox

Schubladenbox
Ambiente, Lifestyle **Silber**

Desktop storage u
Ambience, lifestyl

»iBox« ist eine innovative Schubladenbox designed für ein repräsentatives Umfeld. Durch ihre einzigartige puristische und zeitlose Gestaltung und ihre reduzierte und klare Formensprache passt sie perfekt zu den klaren Linien moderner Schreibtischwelten und architektonisch anspruchsvoller Büros. Sie lässt sich aber ebensogut zu Hause einsetzen.

Die hochglänzende »iBox« sorgt mit ihren fünf geschlossenen Schubladen für Formate bis C4 auf dem Schreibtisch nicht nur für Ordnung, sondern ist auch ein eleganter Eyecatcher – ein stilvolles Accessoire für Ästheten.

Die qualitätvoll verarbeitete Schubladenbox besteht aus hochwertigem, schwermetallfreiem ABS-Kunststoff. Zu haben ist sie in weiß oder schwarz oder in den Kombinationen weißes Gehäuse mit schwarzen Schubladen oder umgekehrt schwarzes Gehäuse mit weißen Schubladen. Sie besitzt eine innovative Clip-Mechanik und ist mit einem patentierten und diskreten Beschriftungskonzept ausgestattet.

Jury

Eine sympathische Oberflächengeometrie. Auf Grund der Funktionalität der Clip-Mechanik, mit der die Schubladen über Fingerdruck leicht geöffnet werden, und der diskreten Beschriftungsfelder bietet sie einen spielerischen Charakter und ermöglicht andererseits eine geschlossene kubische Form. Die hohe qualitative Ausführung und das angenehme Ausgleiten der Schubladen erzeugen einen hochwertigen Charakter.

»iBox« is an innovative desktop storage unit, designed for settings where style is at a premium. Its distinctive design, which is purist and timeless, and its reduced and clear formal expression mean that it harmonizes perfectly with the clear lines of modern desks and of architecturally sophisticated offices. It can equally be used at home, however.

With its five closed drawers that offer room for formats up to C4, the highly polished »iBox« not only makes for a tidy desk, but is also an elegant eye-catcher – a stylish accessory for aesthetes.

The excellently crafted storage unit is made of high-quality ABS plastic that is free of any heavy metals. It is available in black or white. Alternatively, a black frame can be combined with white drawers, or vice versa. It features an innovative clip mechanism and has a patented, discreet labelling solution.

Judges panel

An attractive surface geometry. The clip mechanism, which allows the drawers to be opened easily with a light touch, and the discreet labelling fields give the unit a playful air, as well as allowing it to keep its closed cuboid shape. The high-quality design and pleasant way the drawers slide open give the unit its high-class character.

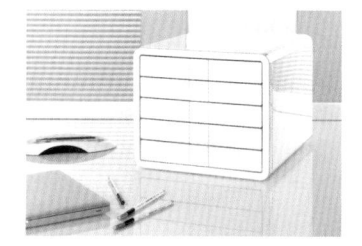

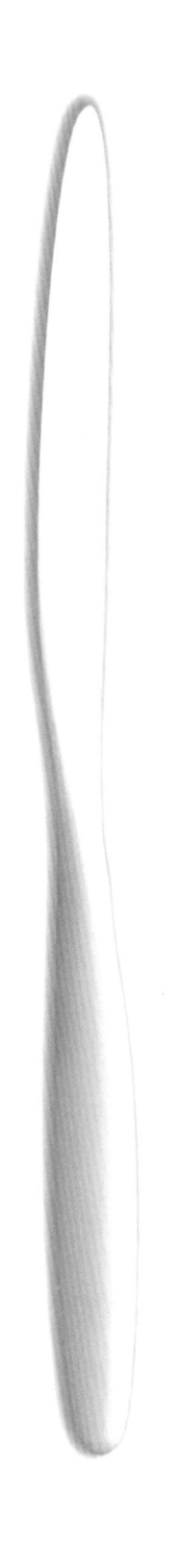

Paper & Poetry Brieföffner
Ambiente, Lifestyle **Silber**

Letter opener
Ambience, lifestyle

Die Kollektion »Paper & Poetry« verbindet Alltag und Poesie in Büro und Arbeitszimmer und bringt Produkte zum Ordnen und Sortieren, Arbeiten und Lernen, Schreiben und Malen, Erinnern und Erfreuen heraus. Diese Gegenstände machen Sinn und sind nützlich. Gleichzeitig erhellt ihr Zauber und ihre Poesie den Alltag und den Schreibtisch, auf dem sie einen schönen Blickfang bilden.

Zu dieser Kollektion gehört der Brieföffner – ein funktionaler, praktischer Gebrauchsgegenstand für Büro und Zuhause. Seine ungewöhnliche Gestaltung und sein feines Material – mattweißes Porzellan – verleihen ihm aber darüber hinaus einen kunstvollen Objektcharakter und die Qualität eines Handschmeichlers.

»Design ist für mich die Umsetzung von Lebensgefühl in Produkte«, schildert Anne Rieck ihre Arbeitsphilosophie, die sich in dem formschönen Brieföffner widerspiegelt. Durch seine in sich gedrehte, organische Form erhält er je nach Lage und Blickwinkel eine andere Gestalt und fordert nicht zuletzt auch wegen seiner angenehmen Haptik zum Berühren, Drehen, Tasten und Spielen auf.

Jury

Eine neue Materialität für einen Brieföffner, die sich auch in einer handschmeichlerischen Art und Weise zeigt. Auf Grund der Oberflächenbeschaffenheit liegt er angenehm in der Hand. Eine ungewöhnliche, schöne Form. Sehr ästhetisch und funktional. Auch die zusätzliche Verwendung als Falzbein bei diversen grafischen Anwendungen ist denkbar.

The »Paper & Poetry« collection combines poetry and the everyday in the office and the study. It includes products for tidying and sorting, for working and learning, for writing and drawing, as well as products that are simply mementos or visually attractive. These objects make sense and are useful. At the same time, their magic and poetry lighten up everyday routine and the desk, where they are attractive eye-catchers.

One of the objects in the collection is this letter opener – a functional and practical utensil for the office and the home. Moreover, its unusual form and the high-quality material – matt-white porcelain – of which it is made give it the character of an objet d'art and make it smooth to the touch.

Describing the philosophy behind her elegant letter opener, Anne Rieck says: »For me, design is putting attitude to life into product form«. Its twisted, organic form means that its shape changes depending on position and perspective, and its pleasant haptic qualities invite the user to touch, turn, feel and play.

Judges panel

A new material for a letter opener, which is also manifested in its pleasantness to the touch. Its surface qualities mean it fits pleasantly in the hand. An unusual, beautiful shape. Very aesthetic and functional. It could conceivably also be used as a folding stick in various graphics applications.

Helix   Brillenfassung   Spectacles frame
        Ambiente, Lifestyle   **Silber**   Ambience, lifestyle

»Helix« bringt einen Durchbruch beim Brillendesign. Diese neue Kollektion des jungen Brillenunternehmens besteht aus vielen Formen und Farben, aber alle Modelle besitzen ein und das gleiche geniale Scharnier – das zentrale Element der Gestaltung.

Auf der Suche, Komplexität zu reduzieren und zu vereinfachen, kamen die Designer auf die Spiralform, die auf der Helix-Geometrie basiert. Herausgekommen ist ein avantgardistisch wirkendes Scharnier, das die Blicke auf sich zieht und komplett ohne Schrauben funktioniert. Um die Bügel zu befestigen, erfordert es keine Werkzeuge. Man muss einfach nur die Spirale in Helixform durch die Löcher des Brillengestells einfädeln. Nicht mehr und nicht weniger. Dabei wird die Spitze des Spiralbügels durch das obere Loch an der Vorderseite der Brille geschoben und die Bügel dreimal gedreht. Sind die Bügel an ihrem Platz, hindert sie das spiralförmige Scharnier daran, sich um mehr als 90 Grad zu öffnen.

Das patentierte Design ist innovativ und originell, minimalistisch und puristisch. »Helix« besteht aus 1,0 Millimeter Edelstahl und ist mit einer 0,6 Millimeter-Front verbunden, die aus dem gleichen, haltbaren, leichtgewichtigen Material hergestellt ist.

Jury

Schön, dass sich die Brille zurückhält. Das Scharnier ist sehr interessant. Präzise in der Herstellung, sehr fein und elegant mit dem Zeichen der Spirale, die nach der Helix-Geometrie gestaltet ist. Ein hoher Tragekomfort ist zu erwarten durch die Leichtigkeit und das Filigrane, und die Brille passt sich gleichzeitig durch flexible Bügel gut an die Kopfform an. Außerdem bildet der Rahmen einen Bügel für den Nasenrücken.

»Helix« is a breakthrough in spectacles design. The new collection of this new spectacles company features many shapes and colours, but all models have the same ingenious hinge, which is at the same time their central design element.

In their quest to reduce complexity and simplify spectacles design, the designers hit on a spiral shape, which is based on helix geometry. The result was a hinge that is avant-garde in appearance, that is a true eye-catcher and that works without any screws at all. No tools are needed to attach the sidepieces. The spiral simply has to be threaded through the holes in the spectacles frame. No more, no less. The tip of the spiral hinge is pushed through the uppermost hole on the front of the spectacles, and the sidepiece is turned three times. Once the sidepiece is in place, the spiral hinge prevents it from opening out further than 90 degrees.

The patented design is innovative and original, minimalistic and purist. »Helix« is made of one millimetre-thick stainless steel, and is attached to an 0.6 millimetre-thick frontpiece that is made of the same long-lasting and lightweight material.

Judges panel

We like the spectacles' reserved character. The hinge is fascinating. Precisely manufactured, very fine and elegant with its spiral, which is designed on the basis of helix geometry. Its lightness and delicacy suggest that it is very comfortable to wear, and the flexible sidepiece means that the spectacles can also be adjusted to fit any size of head. The frame also forms a bridge for the nose.

Fortis Spaceleader Chronograph
Ambiente, Lifestyle **Silber**

Chronograph
Ambience, lifestyl

Die automobile Zukunft im dritten Jahrtausend wird bereits heute von Zukunftsforschern definiert. Diese Visionen sind im »Fortis Spaceleader« in Form gegossen. Ein internationales Team von Kreativen von Volkswagen Design und erfahrenen Uhrmachern und Technikern des Schweizer Traditionsunternehmens Fortis und offiziellen Ausrüsters für Luft- und Raumfahrt entwickelte gemeinsam einen zeitgemäßen Chronographen mit hochwertigem Automatikwerk in einer limitierten Auflage.

Er besticht durch seine innovative Gestaltung, seine sportliche Erscheinung und einen hohen Tragekomfort. Das mikro-mechanische Präzisionsuhrwerk liegt geschützt eingebettet im schwarzen Naturkautschuk-Armband, das mit seiner Schmetterlingsfaltschließe für sicheren Halt am Handgelenk sorgt. Der neuartige Bandverlauf ermöglicht ergonomischen Tragekomfort. Das Armband legt sich auf der einen Seite schützend um die Bedienelemente von Krone und Drücker. Auf der anderen Seite zeigt sich das hochglanzpolierte Stahlgehäuse.

Das beidseitig entspiegelte Saphirglas ermöglicht, dass die Uhr gut abzulesen ist. Die ästhetische Sprache der Automobilbauer findet sich in allen Funktionselementen der Uhr wieder und gibt ihr einen unverwechselbaren Charakter mit hohem Wiedererkennungswert.

Jury

Bei dem Chronographen überzeugt uns einerseits die gestalterisch hohe Qualität und die Integration des Armbands verschlussfrei zum Gehäuse, andererseits die Technologie des mechanischen Automatikgetriebes zum Antrieb eines elektronischen Taktgebers für die Genauigkeit der Uhr. Gutes Preis-Leistungs-Verhältnis. Die Anmutung wird höher empfunden, da sie an einem höheren Preis orientiert ist.

The automotive future in the third millennium is already being defined by futurologists. »Fortis Spaceleader« gives concrete expression to their visions. An international team made up of creative experts from Volkswagen Design and experienced watchmakers and technicians from the long-established Swiss company Fortis, which is an official supplier to the aerospace industry, have jointly developed a contemporary chronograph with outstanding automatic movement, which is now presented in a limited edition.

It is striking for its innovative design and its sporty appearance, as well as being very comfortable to wear. The micromechanical precision clockwork is embedded for protection in a black natural rubber strap, which is fitted with a butterfly buckle to keep it securely fastened to the wrist. The innovative strap makes the watch comfortable to wear. On one side, the strap wraps around and protects the crown and pusher. On the other side, the highly polished steel housing is revealed.

The sapphire glass, which is anti-reflective on both sides, ensures that the watch is easy to read. The carmaker's aesthetic expression is reflected in all the watch's functional elements, and gives the watch its unmistakable character and a high recall level.

Judges panel

We were impressed on the one hand by the chronograph's high-quality design and the way the strap has been moulded around the housing, and on the other hand by the technology of the automatic movement mechanism driving the electronic pulse generator that makes the watch accurate. Good value for money. It gives the impression of being more expensive than it actually is.

Mykii Schlüsseletui Key case
Ambiente, Lifestyle **Silber** Ambience, lifestyle

»Mykii« ist Etui und Schlüsselanhänger in einem. Das attraktive softe und flexible Gehäuse kann problemlos bis zu fünf Schlüssel beherbergen und so Hose, Handy und Handtasche vor Beschädigungen schützen. Das Gehäuse besteht aus elastischem Kunststoff.

Und das Türeöffnen klappt mit ihm wie am Schnürchen. Hat man die Hände voll mit Taschen, ermöglicht einem »Mykii«, einhändig ein Schloss zu öffnen. Dafür wird einfach der Knopf gedrückt und die Schlüssel fallen heraus. Will man sie wieder verstauen, zieht man am Stopper, bis die Schlüssel verschwunden sind.

Das Schlüsseletui ist nicht nur praktisch und funktional, sondern auch ein Eyecatcher, der für Werbezwecke bedruckt werden kann. Da es tagtäglich in Gebrauch ist, ist es ein ideales Werbemittel. Größere Nähe zum Kunden ist kaum möglich.

Jury
Eine Neuinterpretation von einem alten Schlüsselschutz, den man leicht einsetzen kann. Schön die Branding-Möglichkeit durch den Button für verschiedene Werbezwecke. Wir finden es gut, dass es die Hose schützt, wenn man den Schlüsselbund in die Hosentasche steckt. Und die Schlüssel schützt es natürlich auch. Dank dem Knopf sind sie schnell zur Hand.

»Mykii« is both a key case and a key fob. Its attractive case, which is soft and supple, has room for up to five keys, and helps to protect trousers, mobile phones and handbags from damage. The case is made of an elastic synthetic material.

Unlocking the door is easy with this key case. If your hands are full, »Mykii« allows you to unlock the door with just one hand. Simply press the push button, and the keys slide out of the case. If the keys have to be stored away again, a pull on the stopper draws them back into the case.

The key case is not only practical and functional, but is also an eye-catcher that can be customized for advertising purposes. As this is something that is in daily use, it is an excellent promotional item. It is scarcely possible to get closer to the customer than this.

Judges panel
An old way of keeping keys safe in a new interpretation that is easy to use. We like the branding possibilities, with the button that can be used for diverse advertising purposes. We also like the way it protects trousers if keys are carried in a pocket. And of course it protects the keys too. The push button means the keys are quickly at hand.

FouTavola Futtertisch für Hunde und Katzen Feeding table for
Ambiente, Lifestyle **Silber** Ambience, lifestyl

Bei dem Futtertisch für Hunde und Katzen verbindet sich attraktives Design mit hochwertigem Material und ergonomischer Funktionalität. Dazu kommt eine Farbenvielfalt, die für Futtertische ungewöhnlich ist.

»FouTavola« ist im Vergleich zu all den blechernen, rostenden oder furnierten Produkten in diesem Markt ein wohlgeformtes Möbelstück und eine Zier für jeden Haushalt oder jedes Restaurant. Die viereckigen Näpfe sind mit ihren großzügig abgerundeten Kanten für die Futteraufnahme ergonomisch optimiert – hier bleibt nichts in Ecken kleben, und kein Hund und keine Katze muss noch »im Kreis herum« fressen.

»FouTavola« ist aus hochwertigem Acrylglas hergestellt, das zu hundert Prozent lebensmittelecht und spülmaschinenfest ist. Er ist in vier unterschiedlichen Größen und sieben verschiedenen Farben zu haben, aus denen sich jeder seine ganz individuelle Kombination zusammenstellen kann.

Jury
Wir finden es gut, dass Gestaltung in einem Bereich eingesetzt wird, in dem man normalerweise keine Designprodukte erwartet. Der Futtertisch ist eine formal gute Umsetzung, praktisch mit den Schalen und den verschiedenen Höhen. Eine schlichte, aber attraktive Lösung, sehr praktikabel und gut zu reinigen.

This feeding table for dogs and cats combines attractive design with high-quality materials and ergonomic functionality. Moreover, and unusually for a product of this kind, it is available in many bright colours.

Compared with all the tinny, rusting and veneered products in this market, »FouTavola« is a well formed piece of furniture that is a stylish addition to any home or restaurant. The rectangular bowls with their generously proportioned, rounded edges have been ergonomically optimized so that pets can get at the food – nothing will remain stuck in corners, and no dog or cat will have to move around the bowl to get at the last remnants of food.

»FouTavola« is made of high-quality acrylic glass, which is completely food-safe and dishwasher-safe. It is available in four different sizes and seven different colours, which can be combined to suit individual needs and wishes.

Judges panel
We think it is good that design has been applied in an area in which you would not usually expect to find design products. The feeding table has been formally well executed, and is practical with its bowls and different heights. An unassuming yet attractive solution, very practical and easy to clean.

SL17 BasketBin   Papierkorb und Abfallbehälter
Ambiente, Lifestyle   **Silber**

Combined wastep
Ambience, lifestyle

Wohin mit Pfirsichkern, Bananenschale oder Teebeutel am Schreibtisch? »BasketBin« sorgt für eine ästhetische und saubere Lösung. Der Papierkorb bietet ein duales System fürs Büro – eine saubere und umweltfreundliche Mülltrennung zwischen Nass und Trocken, ohne den Arbeitsplatz optisch zu verschmutzen.

Nasser und klebriger Müll verschwindet ganz diskret unter dem Deckel des kleinen Abfallsammlers, der in den größeren Papierkorb eingehängt ist, und kann bequem zum Biomüll getragen werden. Anschließend lässt sich der kleine Mülleimer einfach in der Spülmaschine reinigen. Und hinter dem Zaun des großen Abfalleimers bleiben Papier und Plastik schön sauber unter sich.

Papierkorb und kleiner Abfalleimer sind aus Polypropylen hergestellt. Der große Eimer ist wahlweise in weiß oder anthrazit, der kleine in rot, grün oder schwarz erhältlich, beide können beliebig miteinander kombiniert werden.

Jury

Eine multifunktionale Lösung. Kleinere, feuchte insbesondere biologische Abfälle können in einem separaten Behälter im Bürobereich gesammelt werden. Dieser ist in einer spielerischen Art eingebunden und beim Papiermüll angesiedelt. Schön das Monomaterial und, dass Abfalleimer und Papierkorb in einer sympathischen neutralen Farbkombination nebeneinander bestehen können. Die ausgeformten Griff-Flächen ermöglichen eine leichtere Bedienbarkeit.

If you are sitting at your desk, what do you do with a peach stone, a banana skin or a tea bag? »BasketBin« offers a solution that is aesthetic and neat. The bin offers a dual waste-recycling system for the office. In an eco-friendly way, waste is neatly sorted into wet and dry, without making the workplace dirty.

Wet, sticky waste disappears discretely under the lid of the small waste receptacle, which is simply fitted onto the larger wastepaper basket, and can later be emptied into the bin for compostible waste. When it is empty, the small waste bin can simply be put into the dishwasher. In the larger wastepaper basket, meanwhile, paper and plastic stay nice and clean.

Both the wastepaper basket and the small bin are made of polypropylene. The larger wastepaper basket is available in white or anthracite, and the small bin in red, green or black. Any combination of the two is possible.

Judges panel

A multifunctional solution. Small, damp items, especially organic waste, can be collected in a separate receptacle in the office. This receptacle has been playfully combined with a wastepaper basket. We like the way a single material has been used, and that the waste bin and the wastepaper basket can coexist in an attractive neutral colour combination. The shaped grips make it easy to use.

Eva Solo® SweepUp   Handfeger und Kehrblech
                             Ambiente, Lifestyle   **Silber**

Hand-brush and d
Ambience, lifestyl

»Eva Solo® SweepUp« ist ein praktisches und zugleich ästhetisches Produkt in unverwechselbarem innovativem Design. Das Set besteht aus einem Handfeger und einem Kehrblech. Außen wie aus einem Guss, bietet es eine schöne Synergie zwischen Form, Funktion und Benutzerfreundlichkeit.

So sind Handfeger wie Kehrblech nach ergonomischen Gesichtspunkten gestaltet. Der Stiel ist 85 beziehungsweise 90 Zentimeter lang, sodass man bequem und rückenschonend den Schmutz auf das Kehrblech fegen kann, ohne sich bücken zu müssen.

Der Handfeger besitzt einen abgerundeten Kopf ohne Kanten und lange kräftige Kunststoffborsten. Das Set in stilvollem Schwarz ist hochwertig gefertigt und besteht neben Kunststoff aus Edelstahl. Der Handfegerstiel ist hohl. Dadurch lässt sich der Besen einfach auf den Stiel des Kehrblechs stecken, nachdem Böden und Ecken ausgefegt sind. So ist das Set gut aufgeräumt, nimmt wenig Platz in Anspruch und ist immer schnell zur Hand. Gleichzeitig bietet es einen eleganten Blickfang.

Das war auch die Intention des Designers Henrik Holbæk: »Es war eine interessante Aufgabe, neues Leben einem Produkt zu geben, das jeder nutzt, das man aber immer versteckt hat, weil es so plump aussieht. Deshalb haben wir dem »Eva Solo® SweepUp« ein hohes Maß an Design und Funktionalität gegeben, damit das Set in Zukunft ein integrierter Teil der Kücheneinrichtung werden kann.«

Jury

Eine ganz neue Konfiguration, da der Besen auf den Stiel des Kehrblechs gesteckt wird. Besen und Kehrblech bilden eine schöne Einheit, bestechen durch ihren Objektcharakter und funktionieren gut. Ergonomisch interessant durch die Leichtigkeit und, dass man sich nicht bücken muss. Im Grunde genommen ist es Universal Design, ohne dass man es sieht. Passt in jedes moderne Ambiente. Man muss Besen und Kehrblech nicht umständlich in einem Besenschrank unterbringen, sondern kann ihn als schönen Eyecatcher einfach hinstellen.

»Eva Solo® SweepUp« is practical and aesthetic at the same time, and its innovative design is unmistakable. The set comprises a hand-brush and a dust pan. Giving the appearance of being cast from a single mould, it is an attractive synergy of form, function and user-friendliness.

Ergonomic considerations were taken into account when designing the hand-brush and the dust pan. The handles are 85 and 90 centimetres long, allowing dirt to be swept comfortably into the dust pan without bending and putting any strain on the back.

The hand-brush has a rounded, smooth head and long, powerful plastic bristles. With its stylish black finish, the set is manufactured to a high quality standard, and is made of plastic and stainless steel. The hand-brush handle is hollow. This means that the brush can simply be stuck on to the dust pan handle once cleaning has been done. This keeps the set neatly together, so that it does not use up much space. But when it is needed, it is quickly at hand. At the same time, it is an elegant eye-catcher.

This was also the intention of Henrik Holbaek, the designer: »It was an interesting task to give new life to a product that everyone uses, but that is always kept hidden because it looks so ugly. This was why we made »Eva Solo® SweepUp« so well designed and so functional. In the future, a set like this can be an integral part of the kitchen furniture.«

Judges panel

A completely new configuration, as the brush is stuck onto the dust pan handle. The brush and pan form an attractive entity, have a striking objet d'art quality, and work well. Ergonomically interesting because of their lightness, and because they can be used without having to bend. At root, this is universal design, even though this is not immediately apparent. Looks good in any modern setting. The brush and pan do not have to be stored away in a broom cupboard, but can simply be positioned in the room as an eye-catcher.

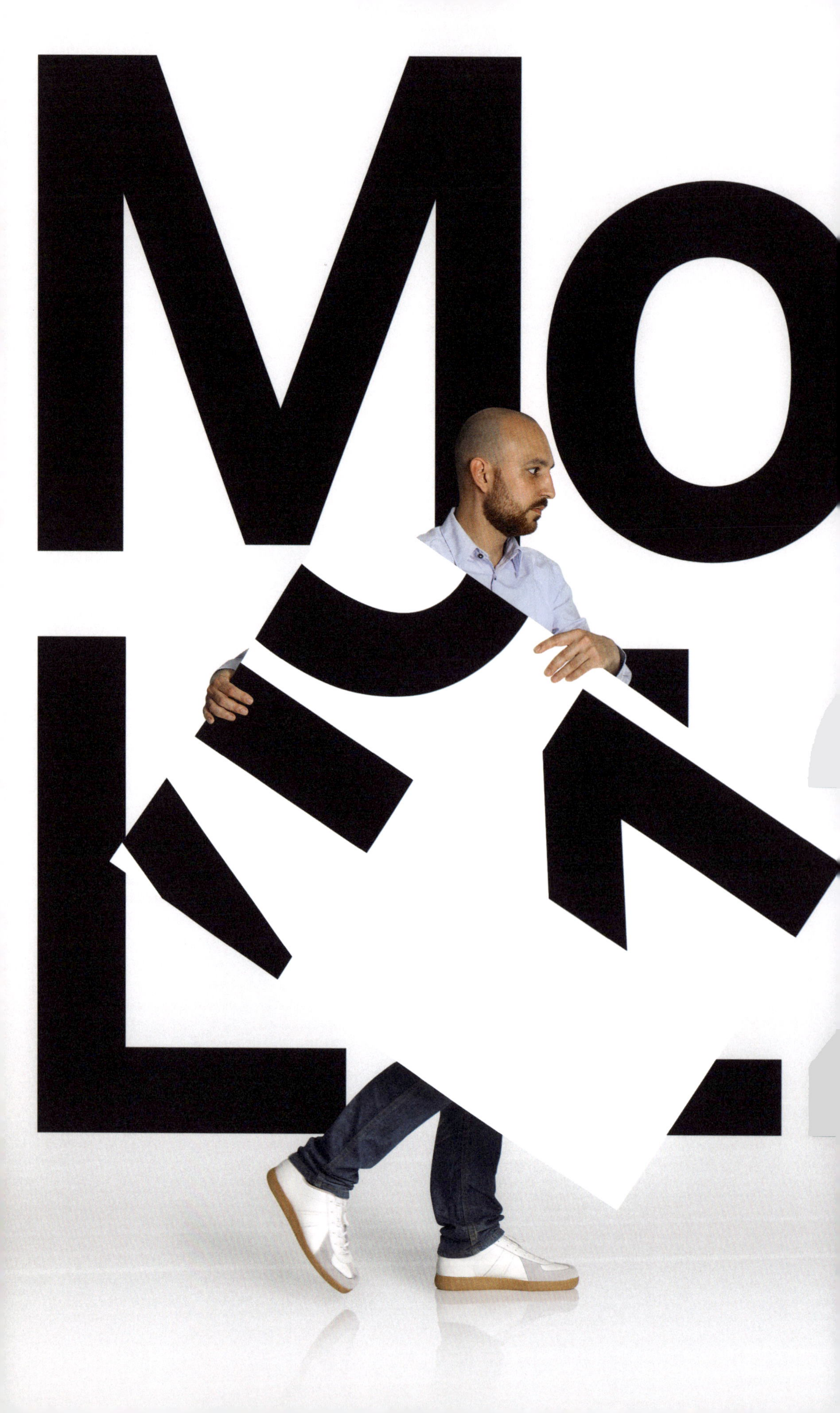
Mo

ul
a
o

| Modul L 120 | Pendelleuchte
Beleuchtung **Gold** | Pendant lamp
Lighting **Gold** |

»Modul L 120« ist eine sehr flache, höhenverstellbare LED.next Pendelleuchte, die sowohl für den Office- als auch für den Homebereich eingesetzt werden kann. Klare, strenge Gestaltung und aufs Wesentliche reduzierte, puristische Formensprache vereinen sich bei ihr mit Lichttechnik auf höchstem Niveau.

Die Diffusorfläche ist mit Kegelbohrungen mit integrierter Linsentechnik zur Lichtlenkung und Ausblendung versehen. Das Licht tritt eng abstrahlend nach unten aus. Optische Linsen definieren einen stärker gerichteten Austrittswinkel. Die Kegelsenkungen lenken das Licht blendfrei und effizient genau dorthin, wo es benötigt wird und sorgen somit für eine wirkungsvolle Ausleuchtung von Arbeitsflächen.

Die elegante Leuchte ist auch bei geringen Pendellängen für verschiedene Beleuchtungsaufgaben bestens geeignet. Sie wird mit einer Edelstahlseilabhängung geliefert, die nach Bedarf von 30 bis 180 Zentimeter eingestellt werden kann. »Modul L 120« besteht aus verchromtem oder silber-eloxalfarbenem Aluminium mit einer Diffusorfläche aus mattiertem Acrylglas.

Jury
Klar, schön, streng und doch poetisch. Die Leuchte ist so minimalisiert, dass man eigentlich kaum noch Gestaltung hat und trotzdem sieht man da eine gut überlegte Ecke, dort wie das Material schön herumgezogen ist und das Profil offen bleibt. Das ist Minimalismus at its best. Wunderbar, wie das Logo »Nimbus« in Weiß auf Silber ganz dezent aber trotzdem gebrandet angebracht ist. Die Lichtstärke ist für eine LED-Leuchte sehr hoch. So funktioniert sie gut als Tischbeleuchtung, was bei anderen Leuchten ähnlicher Bauart noch nicht ganz eingelöst ist.

»Modul L 120« is a very flat, height-adjustable LED.next pendant lamp that can be used both in the home and in the office. In this lamp, clear, strict design and a purist formal expression that has been reduced to the essentials combine with the highest level of lighting technology.

The diffusor surface is furnished with dimples with integrated lenses that direct light and reduce glare. Down light is emitted in a narrow beam. Optic lenses create a more strictly defined angle of light. The dimples efficiently direct the light without glare to exactly where it is needed, and thus ensure that work surfaces are effectively illuminated.

Even when it is not suspended far from the ceiling, the elegant lamp is excellently suited for a variety of lighting tasks. It comes complete with stainless-steel suspension cords, which can be adjusted to any length between 30 and 180 centimetres. »Modul L 120« is available either in chrome-plated or silver-anodized aluminium, with a diffuser surface of matt acrylic glass.

Judges panel
Clear, beautiful, unadorned, and yet poetic. The lamp is so minimalistic that you can scarcely see any design. Nonetheless, you can see a carefully considered corner here, where the material has been beautifully shaped and the profile remains open. Minimalism at its best. The way the Nimbus logo has been applied in white on silver is wonderful: unassuming, but branded nonetheless. For an LED lamp, luminosity is very high. This means it works well as a table lamp, which is something that cannot yet be said of other lamps of similar design.

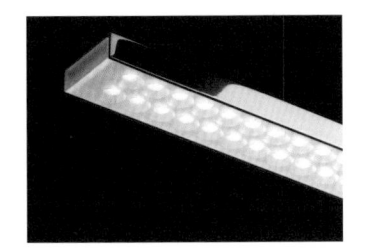

LEDy   LED Tischpendelleuchte   LED pendant tab
    Beleuchtung **Silber**   Lighting **Silver**

Die elegante Tischpendelleuchte »LEDy« besticht durch ihren filigranen Körper, ihre zurückhaltende Form und ihren minimalistischen Purismus. Scheinbar schwerelos schwebt sie über dem Tisch.

Aber auch ihre zukunftsweisende Technik und hohe Funktionalität zeichnen diese energieeffiziente Tischpendelleuchte aus. Sie wird auf Präzisionsmaschinen aus dem vollen Material eines Aluminiumkörpers gefräst und die Oberfläche anschließend hochwertig veredelt: in Nickel-Hochglanz poliert oder Nickel satiniert gebürstet. Diese Materialkonstruktion gibt der schlanken Leuchte – sie ist nur 35 Millimeter breit – Stabilität.

»LEDy« ist in zwei Versionen erhältlich: eine kürzere Leuchte (ein Meter), die sich für Tische bis ein Meter sechzig empfiehlt, und eine lange Variante (ein Meter vierzig), die in ihren Proportionen und ihrer Lichttechnik mit Tischen bis zwei Meter Länge am besten harmoniert. Die kürzere Leuchte ist mit 60, die längere mit 84 hocheffizienten Power-LEDs bestückt, die für eine gleichmäßige, angenehme Ausleuchtung des Tisches sorgen. Dabei benötigt die kürzere nur eine Anschlussleistung von 13 und die längere von 19 Watt. Durch die exzellente Wärmeableitung – trotz des schlanken Körpers ist reichlich Kühlvolumen vorhanden – garantiert der Hersteller eine Lebensdauer der LEDs von circa 50 000 Stunden.

Die Tischpendelleuchte wird an zwei dünnen, zwei Meter langen Silberdrähten abgehängt, die am oberflächenidentischen Metallbaldachin eingestellt werden können.

Jury

Sehr elegant, leicht, minimalistisch, ja vor allem beeindruckt uns so eine puristische Gestaltung. Ungewöhnliche, auffallende Form. Hier geht es um das Maximieren des Schlanken und Zurückgenommenen. Licht als Wahrzeichen im Raum.

The striking features of this elegant table pendant lamp are its delicate body, its unassuming form and its minimalistic purity. It appears to float weightlessly above the table.

But »LEDy« is more than this. This energy-efficient table pendant lamp also features pioneering technology and a high level of functionality. Using precision machinery, it is carved from a single piece of aluminium, and its surface is then given a high-quality finish: either highly polished or satin-brushed. This construction material gives the slim lamp (which is only 35 millimetres wide) its stability.

»LEDy« is available in two versions: a shorter lamp (one metre long), which is recommended for tables up to 1.60 metres in length and a longer lamp (1.40 metres long), whose proportions and lighting technology harmonize best with a table up to two metres long. The shorter version is furnished with 60 highly efficient power LEDs, and the longer version with 84. They ensure that the table is evenly and pleasantly lit. Yet the shorter version consumes only 13 watts, and the longer one 19 watts. The lamp's excellent heat-conducting properties – there is plenty of cooling volume despite the slim shape – allow the manufacturer to guarantee a service life of roughly 50,000 hours for the LEDs.

The pendant lamp is suspended on two silver wires, two metres long. Their length can be adjusted at the metal canopy, whose surface is identical.

Judges panel

Very elegant, light, minimalistic: what impresses us most is the purist design. Unusual, striking shape. It's about maximizing slim, unassuming properties. Light as a distinguishing feature in the room.

Sattler Acousticlight Deckenleuchten mit Schallabsorption
Beleuchtung **Silber**

Sound-absorbing
Lighting **Silver**

Lärmbelästigung und schlechte Akustik sind zunehmende Probleme am Arbeitsplatz und im Alltag. Vermehrter Stress und Ermüdungserscheinungen sind die Folgen. Daher wird es immer wichtiger, die Akustik in Räumen zu verbessern, in denen Kommunikation eine wichtige Rolle spielt und der Geräuschpegel hoch ist.

Die neu entwickelten »Sattler Acousticlight« Deckenleuchten bieten hierfür Lösungen und verbinden großflächige Beleuchtung mit zukunftsweisender Schallabsorptionstechnologie. Sie erfüllen damit zwei Aufgabenstellungen in einem Produkt. Erstens gleichmäßiges homogenes, weiches Licht im Raum und zweitens die spürbare Reduktion der Nachhallzeit.

Die innovativen Leuchten überzeugen durch ihre hohe Funktionalität und ihre zeitgemäße, elegante, reduzierte Gestaltung, die sich harmonisch in moderne Architektur einfügt. Zur Serie gehören sowohl Einbau-, Anbau- und Pendelleuchten als auch komplette Lichtdecken. Das großflächige Einbaugehäuse besteht aus verzinktem, pulverbeschichtetem Stahlblech. Die Leuchten sind mit energiesparenden Leuchtstofflampen bestückt.

Mit dem neuen Lichtkonzept werden völlig neuartige Lösungen im Innenausbau und der Gestaltung von Raumdecken und -wänden möglich. Es erlaubt kreativen Gestaltungsspielraum und perfekte Akustik selbst in großen Räumen.

Jury

Uns hat einerseits die große, regelmäßige Lichtfläche und andererseits auch die Kombination mit einer innovativen schallabsorbierenden Technologie überzeugt. Dadurch werden sowohl Licht- als auch Akustikprobleme gelöst. Sehr schön, dass verschiedene Funktionen in einem Leuchtelement integriert sind. Die Leuchten bieten so gute Raumlösungen.

Noise pollution and poor acoustics are becoming more and more of a problem – at work and in everyday life. The consequences are increased stress and symptoms of fatigue. This is why it is becoming increasingly important to improve acoustics in rooms in which communication plays an important role and the level of noise is high.

The newly developed »Sattler Acousticlight« ceiling lamps offer a solution for this, combining extensive lighting with pioneering sound-absorbing technology. One product thus fulfils two tasks. First, it fills the room with even, homogeneous, soft light, and second, it noticeably reduces reverberation.

The innovative lamps are highly functional and feature a contemporary, elegant, reduced design that harmonizes well with modern architecture. The series includes flush-mounted, surface-mounted and pendant lamps, as well as complete light ceilings. The large-surface housing is made of zinc-plated, powder-coated sheet steel. The lights are fitted with energy-saving fluorescent lamps.

This new lighting concept allows completely new solutions to be applied in interior design and the design of ceilings and walls, and gives scope for creative design and perfect acoustics, even in large rooms.

Judges panel

We were impressed on the one hand by the large, regular lighting surface and, on the other, by the combination with an innovative noise-absorbing technology. This solves both lighting and acoustic problems. Very good to see different functions integrated in one lighting element. In this way, the lamps offer good possibilities for designing rooms.

LED LENSER® P5R und M7R   Aufladbare LED-Taschenlampen
Beleuchtung **Silber**

Rechargeable LED Lighting **Silver**

»P5R« ist nicht einmal zwölf Zentimeter lang und wiegt nur 80 Gramm, erbringt aber eine Lichtleistung, die an Scheinwerfer erinnert: bis zu 200 Lumen mit einer Leuchtweite von 175 Metern. Ermöglicht wird das durch die hochpräzise Reflektorlinse des innovativen patentierten Advanced Focus System® AFS.

Ist die »P5R« für den Privatbereich, so wird die größere und leistungsstärkere »M7R« (220 Lumen und 255 Meter Leuchtweite) im professionellen Bereich eingesetzt, wie etwa beim Technischen Hilfswerk oder der Polizei.

Die akkubetriebenen Taschenlampen sind besonders einfach aufzuladen dank dem Floating Charge System. Durch einen Magnetkontakt verbinden sich Lampe und Adapter bei Berührung. Das bringt Vorteile gegenüber herkömmlichen Ladetechniken. So müssen Akkus nicht mehr entnommen werden, die Magnetkontakte sind verschleißfrei – keine Probleme mehr mit unzuverlässigen und filigranen Ladesteckern. Vielfältige Anschlussmöglichkeiten, wie zum Beispiel USB- und Autoadapter, runden das neue Ladekonzept ab.

Für unterschiedliche Situationen entwickelten Lichtdesigner die Microcontroller gesteuerte Smart Light Technology. Damit stehen bei Bedarf verschiedene Lichtfunktionen, die über einen einzigen Tast-Schalter bedient werden, zur Verfügung, wie Power für hohe Lichtleistung, Low Power zum blendfreien Lesen und Arbeiten oder Defence Strobe mit hochfrequenten Lichtblitzen, die eine schnelle und wirkungsvolle Methode zur Verteidigung sind. »M7R« bietet noch weitere Funktionen, wie etwa Dimmen, S.O.S oder Boost, mit der man auch morsen kann.

Die Lampen bestehen aus einem robusten mattschwarzen Metallgehäuse mit unterschiedlichen Oberflächenstrukturen. Durch den bis zu 1000 mal aufladbaren Akku sind sie im Betrieb kostengünstig und umweltfreundlich.

Jury
Klein, lichtstark, aufladbar. Die Akkufunktionalität ist überzeugend gelöst, auch die Fokussierung der Lichtmenge. Uns gefällt die haptische Qualität, die Lampe liegt gut in der Hand. Grundsätzlich eine sehr hohe Verarbeitungsqualität. Die kleine Taschenlampe kann man auch sehr gut überallhin mitnehmen.

Less than 12 centimetres long and weighing just 80 grams, the »P5R« torch emits a powerful light reminiscent of a searchlight: up to 200 lumen, with a lighting distance of 175 metres. This is possible thanks to the extremely precise reflector lens of the innovative and patented AFS Advanced Focus System®.

While »P5R« is for the private sphere, the larger and more powerful »M7R« (220 lumen and a lighting distance of 255 metres) is for use in the professional sphere, such as the emergency services or the police.

Powered by rechargeable batteries, the torches are especially simple to charge thanks to the Floating Charge System. A magnetic contact means that the torch and the adapter link up on contact. Compared with conventional charging techniques, this has the advantage that rechargeable batteries no longer have to be removed, and the magnetic contacts are wear-free. There are no longer any problems with unreliable, fragile adapter plugs. The torch can also be recharged via a USB connection or from the car battery.

For different situations, the light designers have developed Smart Light Technology, which is governed by a microcontroller. Here, various lighting functions are available as required, which can be operated using a single pushbutton switch. There is »Power« for powerful lighting, »Low Power« for dazzle-free reading and working, or »Defence Strobe« with its rapidly flashing light, which is a fast and effective means of self-defence. »M7R« has even more functions, such as dimming, S.O.S. or boost, which can also be used for sending morse-code messages.

The torches have a robust matt-black metal housing with diverse surface structures. As their rechargeable batteries can be recharged up to 1,000 times, they are cost-effective to use and eco-friendly.

Judges panel
Small, extremely bright, rechargeable. The recharging issue has been convincingly solved, as has the way the light can be focused. We like their haptic qualities, the torches sit well in the hand. The finishing is generally of very high quality. These small torches can be taken anywhere without any difficulty.

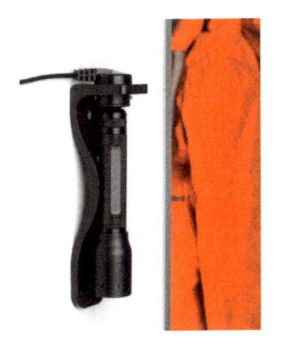

Portax 150   Gartenwagen   Garden cart
Freizeit, Outdoor **Silber**   Leisure, outdoor

Mussten große Laubhaufen, Ast- oder Rasenschnitt bisher mit Rechen und Schaufel in die Schubkarre geschafft und dann in die Tonne oder auf den Komposthaufen gefahren werden, lassen sich mit dem »Portax 150« nun Grün- und Gartenabfälle schnell und komfortabel beseitigen; denn der praktische Gartenwagen lässt sich einfach kippen. So können, ganz ohne Bücken, Schnittgut oder Laub bequem hineingefegt werden.

Der Gartenwagen wiegt nur zwölf Kilogramm, befördert aber 150 Liter Gartenabfälle aller Art, Obst, Gemüse oder auch Kaminholz. Das Transportgut kann dabei bis zu 50 Kilo schwer sein. Möglich machen das der stabile Korpus sowie die extragroßen, luftbereiften Räder mit einem Durchmesser von 26 Zentimeter, die dafür sorgen, dass »Portax 150« sehr wendig ist, leicht geschoben und mühelos mit einer Hand manövriert werden kann.

Die beiden stabilen Kunststoffschalen sind mit hochfestem Gewebe miteinander verbunden. Zwei Griffe – einer oben, einer unten – sorgen für eine komfortable Handhabung ebenso wie die integrierten Aussparungen, in die Spaten und Harke oder Rechen und Besen sicher verstaut und mittransportiert werden können. Wird der Gartenwagen nicht gebraucht, lässt er sich bequem zusammenklappen und Platz sparend aufbewahren.

Jury

Simple, clevere Lösung. Der Gartenwagen lässt sich leicht verstauen, ist schmal in der Garage oder im Gartenschuppen und dann aber sehr großzügig mit seiner Öffnung nach vorne hin, sodass man ihn leicht be- und entladen kann. Sieht gut aus, rot und gelb auf grüner Rasenfläche. Schönes Branding.

While large piles of leaves, pruned branches and grass cuttings used to have to be placed in a wheelbarrow using a rake and a shovel, and then transported to the bin or compost heap, »Portax 150« now allows garden waste to be removed quickly and conveniently, since the practical garden cart can simply be tipped. Prunings, cut grass and leaves can then simply be swept in, without any need to stoop.

The garden cart weighs just 12 kilograms, but can transport 150 litres of garden waste of all kinds, as well as fruit, vegetables or firewood. The load itself can be as heavy as 50 kilograms. This is possible thanks to the robust bodywork and the extra-large pneumatic wheels measuring 26 centimetres in diameter. These wheels ensure that »Portax 150« turns on a sixpence, can be pushed effortlessly, and easily manoeuvred using just one hand.

The two robust plastic shells are connected by a rigid fabric. Two handles, one on top and one beneath, ensure that the cart is easy to handle, as do the integrated recesses, in which a spade, hoe, rake or broom can be safely stowed away or brought along. If the garden cart is not in use, it can easily be folded up and stowed away without taking up much space.

Judges panel

Simple, clever solution. The garden cart is easy to stow away, takes up little space in the garage or shed, but is generously proportioned when opened out, with the large opening making it easy to load and unload. Looks good, red and yellow on a green lawn. Elegant branding.

**Rechteckregner
OS 5.320 SV**

Gartensprinkler
Freizeit, Outdoor **Silber**

Garden sprinkler
Leisure, outdoor

Der Gartensprinkler, der für die Bewässerung großer und mittelgroßer Gärten und Flächen bis zu 320 Quadratmeter eingesetzt wird, überzeugt nicht nur durch seine technische Kompetenz und Hochwertigkeit, seine Prägnanz und Eigenständigkeit, sondern bietet dem Nutzer jede Menge praktische Details und Lösungen.

Beispielsweise lässt sich der bereits laufende Regner verstellen oder noch ausrichten, ohne dass man dabei nass wird. Dank dem integrierten Spritzschutz SplashGuard – eine drehbare Hülse – lässt sich ein Teil der Düsen abdecken, sodass man sich am Regner in einem trockenen Bereich aufhalten und das Gerät neu platzieren oder weitere Einstellungen vornehmen kann. Die Bedienelemente hierfür sind eindeutig und selbsterklärend.

So kann die Größe der Beregnungsfläche mit Schiebern am Düsenkörper variiert werden, zum Beispiel, wenn schmale Rasenstreifen oder große Gärten bewässert werden sollen. Ebenso lässt sich die Wassermenge nach Bedarf von null bis Maximum einstellen und die Reichweite der Beregnung stufenlos regulieren. Damit ist ein sehr effizienter Wassereinsatz möglich.

Die nötige Standfestigkeit während der Beregnung garantieren ausklappbare Spieße, die im Standfuß des Sprühregners untergebracht sind. Der Rechteckregner ist mit dem bewährten Klicksystem ausgestattet und lässt sich damit spielend leicht an den Gartenschlauch anschließen. Wird er nicht benötigt, kann er bequem am Fuß aufgehängt und aufbewahrt werden. So läuft auch das Restwasser heraus, was Frostschäden im Winter verhindert. Verstopfte Düsen sind mit herausnehmbarem Pin schnell wieder frei gemacht.

Jury

Eine sehr schöne Lösung für die zahlreichen Funktionen, die rein auf mechanischer Basis integriert sind: die Einstellung der Sprinklerbreite, das Ein- und Ausstellen der verschiedenen Sprühköpfe, die Funktion der Verankerung im Rasen, die Sprühintensität, also der Druck ist verstellbar, und auch die Veränderungsmöglichkeit der Reichweite inklusive eines gut untergebrachten, aber nützlichen Accessoires, mit dem die Düsen gereinigt werden können. Dafür wurde eine einfache logische Form, die sich daraus ergibt, gefunden. Sehr überzeugend.

This garden sprinkler, which is used to irrigate large and medium-sized gardens and surfaces up to 320 square meters in area, is impressive not only for its technical competence and high quality, clarity and distinctiveness. It also offers the user many practical details and solutions.

For example, when it is in operation, the sprinkler can be adjusted or set without the user getting wet. Thanks to an integrated, rotatable sleeve – the SplashGuard – some of the nozzles can be covered, allowing the user to stay dry while close to the sprinkler. He can then move it to a new position or make other adjustments. The operating elements needed to do this are clear and self-explanatory.

Slide controls on the nozzle holders allow the size of the area to be irrigated to be varied, depending on whether a narrow strip of lawn or a large garden has to be watered. The water quantity can also be varied as needed, from zero to maximum, and the sprinkler range can be infinitely varied. This allows a very efficient use of water.

Spikes stowed in the sprinkler base are folded out to give the appliance the grip it needs while in operation. The sprinkler is fitted with the tried and tested click system, which makes it child's play to connect it to a garden hose. If it is not in use, it can simply be hung up and stored. Any residual water can then drip out, thus avoiding any frost damage in the winter. A removable pin is provided to unblock any clogged nozzles.

Judges panel

A very elegant solution for the many functions that are integrated in a purely mechanical way: adjusting sprinkler width, turning the individual nozzles on and off, anchoring the sprinkler in the lawn, stray intensity or pressure can be adjusted, and even the range of the sprinkler can be set. Not to forget a well concealed but useful accessory for cleaning the nozzles. A simple logical form has been found that satisfies all these criteria. Very impressive.

MW56 Magnesit Drei-Wege-Kopf Magnesit 3-way he
Freizeit, Outdoor **Silber** Leisure, outdoor

Der Magnesit Drei-Wege-Kopf verbindet technisches Knowhow mit funktionaler Ästhetik und erfüllt hohe Ansprüche an Qualität, Vielseitigkeit und Design. Funktionstransparenz und optimale ergonomische Eigenschaften werden durch klare Formen und strukturierte Volumen bestärkt.

Der »MW56« besticht durch seine extrem weiche und präzise Handhabung. Für komfortablen Horizontal- und Vertikalschwenk sorgen die Fluid-gelagerten Achsen. Der Magnesit Drei-Wege-Kopf besitzt zudem eine integrierte Wasserwaage. Mit seinen ergonomisch geformten und gummierten – und damit rutschfesten – Griffen kann der leichtgängige Stativkopf exakt positioniert werden. Er bietet präzise Skalierung für alle drei Ebenen.

Weitere Vorteile sind die zuschaltbare Dämpfung und die kurzen Funktionswege der Griffklemmung. Es gibt kein Spiel auch bei gelöstem Griff. Der Drei-Wege-Kopf besteht vorwiegend aus hochwertigem Aluminium. Zum »MW56« gehört die Magnesit Schnellkupplungseinheit »MX 465«, die in drei Positionen montierbar ist.

Das klare, kompakte und zeitgemäße Design des Magnesit Drei-Wege-Kopfes steht für Qualität und Präzision.

Jury

Speziell diese Kopfsituation mit den Verstellmechanismen in drei Richtungen ist formal sehr schön und in sich schlüssig. Der Drei-Wege-Kopf hat eine große ergonomische Qualität. Die angenehme Haptik der Griffe ist über die Formveränderung vom Rund zum Oval sehr überzeugend gelöst. Und auch das Preis-Leistungsverhältnis überzeugt uns.

The Magnesit tripod head combines technical know-how with functional aesthetics, and meets high standards when it comes to quality, versatility and design. It is immediately clear how it works, and this quality, as well as its perfect ergonomic properties, are emphasized by its clear forms and structured shape.

The »MW56« stands out by virtue of its extremely soft, precise handling. The fluid bearings in the axles ensure smooth horizontal and vertical panning. The Magnesit also features an integrated spirit level. Its grips are ergonomically formed and rubber-coated, and thus anti-slip. They allow the smooth-running tripod head to be positioned exactly. It can be set precisely on all three planes.

Other benefits include the switchable damper and the quick release function. Even when the grip is unlocked, there is no play. The 3-way head is mainly made of high-quality aluminium. To complement the »MW56«, there is also the MX 465 quick connect unit, which can be mounted in three positions.

The clear, compact and contemporary design of the Magnesit 3-way head stands for quality and precision.

Judges panel

This head in particular, with the mechanism for adjusting in three directions, is formally very elegant and logical. Ergonomically, the quality of the 3-way head is very good. The pleasant tactile quality of the grips is very well done, with a transition from a round to an oval shape. The head is also good value for money.

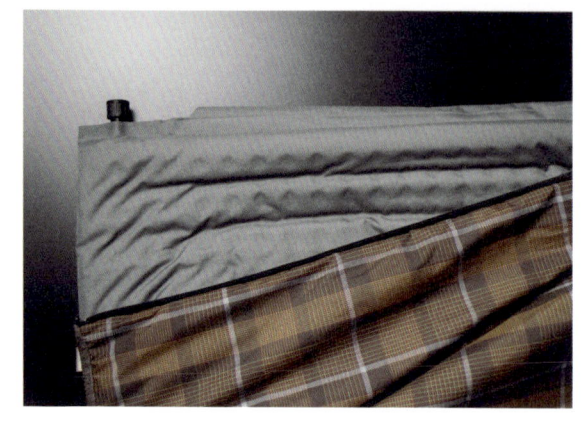

One Night Stand Schlafsack mit integrierter Isomatte Sleeping bag with
Freizeit, Outdoor **Silber** Leisure, outdoor

»One Night Stand« eignet sich optimal für einen kurzen Übernachtungsaufenthalt. Der ungewöhnliche Schlafsack ist mit einer Isomatte ausgestattet, die sich selbst aufpumpt. Somit ist er ein idealer Begleiter auf kurzen Städtereisen und spontanen Wochenendtrips ebenso wie für komfortable Langzeitausflüge.

Die innovative Verbindung aus warmem Schlafsack und bequemer Isomatte ist dabei flexibel und vielseitig einsetzbar in Kombination, ohne Isomatte oder der Schlafsack als Decke. Wird »One Night Stand« nicht gebraucht, können Isomatte und Schlafsack in kleinem Packmaß zusammen Platz sparend verstaut werden. In eingerollter Form lässt er sich am praktischen Trägerband über die Schulter hängen und leicht in Zug, Bus oder Auto mitnehmen.

»One Night Stand« besteht aus hochwertigen Materialien, die sich in der modischen Urban Kollektion wiederfinden. Die technisch funktionale Schlafsackgestaltung hat sich hier in ein junges urbanes und trendiges Design gewandelt. Die sechs Zentimeter dicke selbstaufblasende Isomatte im Inneren bietet höchsten Schlafkomfort. Das Innenmaterial des Schlafsackes besteht aus einer Mischung aus organischer Baumwolle mit recyceltem Polyester und ist somit nicht nur besonders hautfreundlich, sondern auch ökologisch. Die Liegefläche ist zusätzlich mit einer Lage Wattierung gefüttert, sodass der Schlafsack auch ohne Isomatte genutzt werden kann. Gefüllt ist sie mit hochwertiger 70/30 Graue Entendaune aus Europa. Außerdem ist eine praktische Tasche für Schlüssel und Dokumente integriert.

Jury

Eine komfortable Schlafgelegenheit für individuelle Situationen, universell einsetzbar für innen und außen, auch für Gäste. Man kann nur die Matratze verwenden und aus dem Schlafsack eine Bettdecke machen. Es ist keine Isomatte, sondern eher eine sehr bequeme Luftmatratze in den Schlafsack integriert. So kann man auch nicht von der Matratze rutschen. Sehr gut gemacht. Das haben wir so noch nicht gesehen. Man kann ihn kompakt einrollen und schultern. Farblich schöne Applikationen, ein attraktives Produkt auch für den Wohnbereich.

»One Night Stand« is perfect for a brief overnight stay. This unusual sleeping bag is equipped with its own insulated mat, which self-inflates. This makes it an ideal companion, for short city trips and spur-of-the-moment weekend trips just as much as for long holidays.

This innovative combination of warm sleeping bag and comfortable insulated mat is also flexible in use. It can be used either in combination, without the insulated mat, or with the sleeping bag as a duvet. When not in use, »One Night Stand« can be stored away in a small package. When rolled up, its practical carrying strap means it can be slung from the shoulder and easily transported by train, bus or car.

»One Night Stand« is made of high-quality materials, which are also to be found in Vaude's fashionable »Urban« collection. The usual functional sleeping-bag design has been transformed into a youthful, urban and trendy design. The self-inflating insulated mat on the inside of the bag is six centimetres thick, and thus extremely comfortable. The sleeping-bag lining is made of a mixture of organic cotton and recycled polyester, which makes it not only kind to the skin, but also eco-friendly. The sleeping surface is lined with an additional layer of wadding, which means that the sleeping bag can also be used without the mat. It is filled with high-quality 70-30 grey duck down from Europe. There is also an integrated, practical pouch for keys and documents.

Judges panel

A comfortable place to sleep for individual situations. Can be used anywhere, inside or out, also for guests. You can just use the mattress and turn the sleeping bag into a duvet. It's not so much an insulated mat as an extremely comfortable airbed that has been integrated into the sleeping bag. As a result, you cannot slide off the mattress. Excellently done. It's like nothing we have ever seen before. It can be rolled up into a compact bundle and slung from the shoulder. Elegant applications colour-wise, an attractive product also for the living area.

PickUp Einkaufskorb Shopping basket
Freizeit, Outdoor **Silber** Leisure, outdoor

»PickUp« ist flexibel und clever. Im Handumdrehen entfaltet er sich zu seiner vollen Größe und macht sich ebenso schnell wieder klein. Der praktische Einkaufskorb ist ein idealer Einkaufsbegleiter. Ganz klein passt er zu Hause oder im Auto in jede Lücke. Gibt es aber etwas zu transportieren, zeigt er seine wahre Größe.

Er wird in nur drei Schritten einfach aufgeklappt, bietet dann mit seinen Maßen von 21 mal 21 mal 46 Zentimetern viel Stauraum und ist so stabil, dass er Einkäufe bis zu 20 Kilogramm trägt. Die rechteckige Form des Einkaufskorbes garantiert dabei optimale Raumnutzung. Nach Gebrauch kann er wieder Platz sparend zusammengeklappt werden. Dann misst er 33,5 mal 23 Zentimeter bei einer Breite von nur 3 Zentimetern.

»PickUp« überzeugt nicht nur durch seine elegantsachliche Gestaltung, sondern auch durch seine hochwertige Verarbeitung. So ist der stabile Bügel aus mattiertem Cromargan® Edelstahl Rostfrei 18/10 mit einer Kunststoffeinlage ausgestattet, die für ein angenehmes Tragegefühl sorgt. Der Bezug aus strapazierfähigem Polyester ist reißfest und abwaschbar. Er besitzt eine Innentasche mit Reißverschluss für Geldbörse oder Autoschlüssel. »PickUp« ist in zwei Farben – schwarz oder rot – zu erhalten.

Jury

Er nimmt die formale Ästhetik des alten Spankorbes auf. Der Griff ist ergonomisch, so trägt sich der Korb sowohl mit einer Hand als auch über dem Arm sehr gut. Man hat ihn zusammengeklappt im Auto oder zu Hause. Braucht man ihn, klappt man ihn auseinander. Dank seiner Proportionen lässt er sich auch bestückt gut tragen, ohne dass man sich an den Kleidern etwas aufreißt oder schwere Teile gegen die Oberschenkel stoßen und man blaue Flecken bekommt. Er ist kein Blümchen-Einkaufskorb, sondern hat etwas Modern-Sachliches und steht auch Männern gut.

»PickUp« is flexible and clever. It unfolds to its full size in a thrice, and folds back up again just as quickly. This practical shopping basket is an ideal shopper's companion. Since it is so small, it fits into any small space, at home or in the car. But if there is something to be carried, it reveals its true size.

In just three simple steps, it is unfolded to its full size of 21 by 21 by 46 centimetres. It therefore offers plenty of space, and can carry up to 20 kilograms of shopping. The shopping basket's rectangular form guarantees that every bit of space is used. After use, it can be folded up again, and takes up little space. In its folded state it measures just 33.5 by 23 centimetres, and is just 3 centimetres deep.

»PickUp« is impressive not just for its elegantly sober design, but also for its high-quality workmanship. The robust handle is made of Cromargan® 18/10 stainless steel with a matt finish and a plastic insert that makes it pleasant to carry. The basket's polyester fabric is tear-proof and washable. There is also a zip pocket on the inside for storing away a purse or car keys. »PickUp« is available in two colours – black or red.

Judges panel

It alludes to the formal aesthetic of the chip basket. The grip is ergonomic, allowing the basket to be carried comfortably in the hand and over the arm. Folded up, it can be kept in the house or in the car. If you need it, you simply unfold it. Thanks to its proportions, it is also easy to carry when full. It does not brush against your clothes, and you won't get any bruises as a result of heavy parts bumping against your thigh. It's not a feminine basket. There's something modern and sober about it. It's a basket men can carry.

Hook Träger für Getränkekästen
Freizeit, Outdoor **Silber**

Carrier for bottle
Leisure, outdoor

Wer kennt das nicht: man muss sperrige Getränkekisten tragen, hat keine Hand frei für eine zusätzliche Einkaufstasche oder um die Tür aufzumachen. Das ist anstrengend und unbequem.

Hier schafft »Hook« Abhilfe. Dieses innovative Trägersystem ist leicht, schnell und sicher in der Handhabung. Die Haken werden an den Griffen des Kastens eingehängt und der breite Träger über die Schultern gelegt. »Hook« verhindert damit Druckstellen an Händen, lange Arme oder Kreuzschmerzen.

So lässt sich das Gewicht, das nun gleichmäßig verteilt ist, komfortabel schultern und die Kästen bequem auch auf größere Distanz transportieren, zum Beispiel zur Strandparty, oder beim Treppensteigen; denn man kommt damit mühelos durch enge Treppenhäuser und Türen. Es lassen sich zudem mehrere Kästen – auch zwei übereinander – tragen.

»Hook« transportiert nicht nur Getränkekisten, PET-Flaschen-Pakete und Six-Packs, sondern auch andere Gegenstände bis 20 Kilogramm. Die Haken bestehen aus verstärktem Polypropylen und das strapazierfähige Gurtband aus Nylon. Das universelle Hakensystem ist in vier verschiedenen Farben zu haben: blau, grün, gelb und weiß.

Jury

Ein bestehendes Problem, das jeder kennt, das Tragen von Getränkekisten. Dafür ist dieser Kastenträger eine einfache und kostengünstige Lösung, die unterschiedliche Möglichkeiten des Einsatzes, wie Tragen über der Schulter oder über beide Schultern, von einer Kiste oder von zwei erlaubt und dadurch eine wirkliche Unterstützung bietet. Schöne Verpackungslösung und Produktgrafik.

We all know the problem: bulky bottle crates have to be carried, and you haven't got a free hand for an additional shopping bag or to open the door. This is tiresome and uncomfortable.

This is where »Hook« can help. This innovative carrier system is light, fast and safe to use. The hooks are placed under the grips of the crate, and the broad carrying band is placed over the shoulder. In this way, »Hook« prevents pressure marks on the hands, a load on the arms, and back pain.

Instead, weight is now evenly distributed, and can be comfortably shouldered. Crates can easily be carried even over longer distances – to a beach party for example, or when climbing stairs, for »Hook« makes it easy to manoeuvre narrow stairs and doors. Moreover, several crates can be carried at once, or one on top of the other.

»Hook« can be used to carry not only bottle crates, packs of PET bottles and six packs, but also other objects weighing up to 20 kilograms. The hooks are made of polypropylene, and the hard-wearing shoulder strap of nylon. The universal hook system is available in a choice of four different colours: blue, green, yellow and white.

Judges panel

A problem all of us are familiar with – carrying bottle crates. This carrier is a simple and cost-effective solution, which can be used in different ways, such as slung over one shoulder or both shoulders. One or even two crates can be carried. It is a real help. Elegant packaging solution and product graphics.

Trailbanger Hydro XT Enduro Bike
Sport **Silber**

Enduro bike
Sport **Silver**

Enduro ist zusammengesetzt aus dem spanischen »duro« für hart und aus dem englischen »endurance« für Ausdauer. Enduro Bikes sind für Fahrer, die wilde Strecken in den Bergen hinunterfahren auch über grenzwertige Trails, besondere Kicks suchen und nur wenn notwendig auch mal den Berg hinauffahren.

Deshalb ist das Enduro Bike »Trailbanger Hydro XT« vor allem für die Abfahrt und extreme Fahrsituationen gebaut. Es ist so konstruiert, dass es sogar im Grenzbereich noch sicher zu kontrollieren ist.

So mildert der gewaltige 160 Millimeter-Federweg selbst Stöße von ausgewachsenem Wurzelwerk ab. Konstruktiv wesentlich aufwändiger als übliche Systeme mit nur zwei Lagerpunkten ist die VPP-Federung – der Virtual Pivot Point, der »imaginärer Drehpunkt« bedeutet. Der Hinterbau dreht sich hier beim Einfedern nicht wie üblich um einen fixen Punkt, sondern beschreibt gleichsam eine Kurve. Die Federung agiert damit weitestgehend entkoppelt vom Antrieb.

Das Enduro Bike besitzt einen »starken Knochenbau«. Mit Verstrebungen und zusätzlichen Profilsträngen wurde der Rahmen verwindungssteif gemacht – und das bei vertretbarem Gewicht.

Der Hinterbau des »Trailbanger« bildet ein eigenes stabiles Dreieck, das auch abrupten, äußerst heftigen Stoß-Impulsen standhält, wenn auf den Trails die 160 Millimeter gefordert werden.

Die X 12-Steckachse von Syntace trägt viel zur Stabilität des Hinterbaus bei und sorgt außerdem dafür, dass die Bremsscheibe stets perfekt ausgerichtet ist. Der Tapered Steerer – das konische Steuerrohr – leitet die Kräfte der Gabel harmonisch in den Rahmen ein.

Jury

Ein auf den Einsatzbereich als Enduro-Bike exzellent abgestimmtes Fahrrad, das sich insbesondere durch die stabile Konstruktion der Hintergabel auszeichnet und ein extrem gutes, leichtes Gewichtsverhältnis hat.

Enduro is an allusion to »endurance« and »duro«, the Spanish word for »hard«. Enduro bikes are designed for riders who take their bikes down rugged downhill tracks or along trails »at the limit«, who are looking for special kicks and only ride up a mountain if they have to.

This is why the »Trailbanger Hydro XT« enduro bike has been constructed above all for downhill and extreme rides. It has been designed so that it can still be safely controlled even when pushed to the limit.

The huge spring deflection of 160 millimetres can cushion the shocks caused by fully grown tree roots. With just two bearing points, its VPP (virtual pivot point) suspension is far more complex in design than conventional systems. In this system, when the spring is compressed, the rear fork does not turn about a fixed point, as is usual, but describes a curve, as it were. As a result, the suspension acts practically independently of the pedals.

The enduro bike has a strong »skeleton«. By means of struts and additional profile strands, the frame has been made torsion-resistant, yet the bike's weight does not suffer unreasonably.

The Trailbanger's rear fork is a self-contained, robust triangle that can handle even abrupt and extremely violent shocks – when riding a trail calls for the full 160-millimetre spring deflection.

The Syntace X-12 through-axle helps considerably to improve the stability of the rear fork, and also ensures that the brake disc is perfectly aligned at all times. The tapered steerer efficiently diverts forces from the fork into the frame.

Judges panel

A bicycle that has been excellently trimmed for use as an enduro bike. The robust design of the rear fork is especially outstanding, and its weight ratio is excellent.

Tech Pack Wasserdichter Alpinrucksack   Watertight alpine r
Sport **Silber**   Sport **Silver**

Dieser Prototyp entstammt einer Konzeptstudie über die Outdoor-Ausrüstung von morgen. Das Ergebnis ist ein Alpinrucksack, in dem bewährte Materialien und Hightech Equipment fusionieren. Das Material ist ein hochwertiger, robuster Stoff (300D), der beidseitig mit einer TPU-Folie (Thermoplastisches Polyurethan) laminiert ist.

Dadurch lässt er sich komplett wasserdicht verschweißen. Außerdem sind die Nähte versiegelt, der Rollverschluss und die Reißverschlüsse sind ebenfalls wasserdicht. »Tech Pack« bietet somit Hightech für die Berge, besonders auch für widrige Wetterbedingungen.

Da der Rucksack als Toploader mit Wickelverschluss konzipiert ist, wird er bequem und praktisch von oben beladen. Auf seiner Rückseite ist eine wasserdichte iPhone-Tasche für mobile Endgeräte integriert, die dazu dient, GPS Tracks aufzuzeichnen und das Gerät direkt zu bedienen ohne es herausnehmen zu müssen. Personen, die hinter dem Rucksackträger sind, können so immer besonders leicht mitverfolgen, wo gerade gewandert oder geklettert wird. Oder es können dort auch topografische Karten, Lawinenlageberichte, Panoramakarten oder ein Kompass eingesteckt werden. Ein weiterer großer Vorteil sind die in den Rucksack integrierten Solarpanels, die elektronische Geräte mit Energie versorgen.

Der Rucksack fasst ein Volumen von 45 Litern, nimmt man das Deckfach dazu, das komplett abnehmbar ist, sind es 55 Liter. Außerdem besitzt er externe Kompressionsriemen.

Die Kombination von wasserdichtem, sehr strapazierfähigem Material mit stabilen Metallschnallen und der Integration von mobilen Endgeräten mit GPS macht den Rucksack zu einem hochfunktionellen Transportsystem für Speedbegehungen.

Jury

Der Prototyp geht in die richtige Richtung. Innovative Verknüpfung von einem leichten Rucksack mit neuen technologischen Vernetzungen, wie Solarpanels oder die wasserdichte Tasche für iPhone oder andere Geräte. Spannende Mischung von verschiedenen Stilen: wir haben sowohl eine Art LKW-Plane als auch ein ganz leichtes Material, wasserdichte Reißverschlüsse aus dem Bekleidungsbereich, ein schnelles Navigationssystem zum Einhaken der einzelnen Elemente, ein Fixierungselement, das universal eingesetzt werden kann, und die Verbindung von Rucksack und Tasche.

This prototype is the result of a design study addressing the outdoor equipment of the future. The upshot is an alpine rucksack that brings together tried and tested materials and high-tech equipment. It is made of a high-quality, tough material (300D), coated on both sides with a thermoplastic polyurethane (TPU) film.

This means it can be welded and made completely watertight. In addition, the seams are sealed, and the roll-up seal and zip fasteners are also watertight. »Tech Pack« thus offers high-tech for the mountains, and especially for inclement weather conditions.

Since the rucksack is designed as a top-loader with a wraparound seal, it is convenient and practical to pack. A watertight iPhone pouch for mobile terminals has been integrated into its front panel. GPS tracks can be recorded and the instrument operated without having to remove it from the pouch. This means that anyone behind the rucksack-wearer can always easily see where exactly they are walking or climbing. Alternatively, topographic maps, avalanche reports, panorama maps or a compass can be kept in the pouch. One further benefit is the solar panels integrated into the rucksack. These provide electronic devices with power.

The rucksack has a volume of 45 litres, or 55 litres if the removable top compartment is counted. It is also furnished with external compression straps.

This combination of watertight, extremely tough material and sturdy metal buckles, as well as the integration of mobile GPS terminals, makes the rucksack a highly functional transport system when climbing against the clock.

Judges panel

This prototype points in the right direction. An innovative combination of a light rucksack with connections to technical devices, such as the solar panels or the watertight pouch for an iPhone or other device. Exciting mixture of different styles: we have a kind of tarpaulin as well as an extremely light fabric, watertight zips from the clothing segment, a fast navigation system for plugging in the individual elements, a universal fixing element, and the combination of rucksack and holdall.

Waikiki Zehenstegsandale Flip-flops
Kids, Familie **Silber** Children, family

Flip-Flops sind beliebt und im sommerlichen Straßenbild nicht mehr wegzudenken; denn sie werden schon lange nicht mehr nur am Strand getragen.

Aber die meisten bestehen aus einem EVA-Plattenmaterial und ihre Riemen aus PVC, die immer noch mit Weichmachern versetzt sind. Durch Schweiß gelöst gelangen diese in die Haut und schwächen das Immunsystem. Außerdem bieten diese Modelle kaum Halt beim Laufen. Somit sind sie nicht kindgerecht.

Anders bei »Waikiki«. Hier wurde erstmalig eine Zehenstegsandale entwickelt, die komplett aus sehr leichtem, umweltfreundlichen Polyurethan (PU) hergestellt wird. PU ist nicht nur frei von Weichmachern und kann später rückstandslos entsorgt oder sogar zu 100 Prozent recycelt werden, sondern ist zusätzlich um 40 Prozent leichter als PVC und Gummi.

Die Zehenstegsandale wird aus einem Stück hergestellt, was sie robust macht, ohne ihre Elastizität einzuschränken. Sie garantiert hervorragende Passform und optimalen Halt dank der dreidimensionalen Gestaltung der Riemen, die vom Zehensteg bis zur Ferse in einer Schale auslaufen. Die geschlossene Spitze verleiht »Waikiki« nicht nur ein eigenständiges, funktionales Design, sondern schützt auch vor dem Umknicken des Vorderfußbereiches. Gerade für Kinderfüße im Wachstum ist es wichtig, dass sie Halt haben. Der Zehensteg ist deshalb besonders stabil, um ein Ausfädeln zu verhindern.

Die Sandalen sind in verschiedenen Farben zu haben. Sind sie ausgetragen oder zu klein, können sie kostenfrei an den Hersteller zurückgegeben werden, der sie weiterverwertet und zugleich 50 Cent pro Paar an eine Einrichtung für krebskranke Kinder spendet.

Jury

Das Produkt bietet gegenüber vielen herkömmlichen Badesandalen große Vorteile: Ein Material ohne Weichmacher. Ein Verzichten auf den üblichen Steg, stattdessen eine andere Ausformung der Verbindung von Riemen zu Schuhsohle über einen schmalen Zehensteg und ein Halten der Sandale über den Verlauf des Fußrückens. Dadurch eine verbesserte, innovative Ergonomie. Einzigartig. Es ist wirklich etwas Neues in dem Bereich.

Flip-flops are popular and an integral part of the summer scene. The days are long gone when they would only be worn at the beach.

However, most of them are made using EVA for the base and PVS for the strap, and both materials are still made using plasticizers. Dissolved by sweat, these can find their way into the skin and weaken the immune system. Moreover, shoes like these offer little support when walking. This makes them unsuitable for children.

With »Waikiki«, it is a different story. For the first time, a flip-flop has been developed that is made completely out of very light, eco-friendly polyurethane. Not only is polyurethane plasticizer-free, it can also be disposed of completely or completely recycled later. Moreover, it is 40 percent lighter than PVC or rubber.

The flip-flops are made from one piece, which makes them sturdy without restricting their elasticity. The three-dimensional design of the straps, which run from the toe to the heel in one piece, guarantees an excellent fit and optimum support. The closed toe end not only gives Waikiki its special functional design but also provides protection against twisting the front part of the foot. Especially when children are growing, it is important that their feet are given support. The toe divider is therefore especially sturdy, so that the sandal cannot slip off unintentionally.

The sandals are available in different colours. Once they have worn out or become too small, they can be returned free of charge to the manufacturer, who will recycle them, as well as donating 50 cents for each pair to an institution for children with cancer.

Judges panel

Compared with many conventional bathing sandals, this product offers great benefits. A material without plasticizers. Instead of the usual thong, a new design for joining the strap to the sole via a narrow toe piece, and a sandal that is held in place along the entire length of the foot. The result is enhanced, innovative ergonomics. A class of its own. Really something new in this area.

Ypso   Treppenhochstuhl   Stepped high chair
            Kids, Familie   **Silber**   Children, family

Der zeitgemäße Treppenhochstuhl erinnert in seiner Form an ein auf dem Kopf stehendes »Y«, daher sein Name »Ypso«. Neben seinem modernen Design besticht er durch sehr gute Funktionalität und hohe Flexibilität.

Dank seiner Rollen und der Griffstange ist er leicht transportierbar. Er passt sich dem Alter, der Größe und den Bedürfnissen der Kinder an. Die vierzehn Verstellmöglichkeiten von Sitz- und Fußplatten garantieren das Mitwachsen des Stuhles. Ab circa sechs Monaten können Babys hier Platz finden, gefüttert werden, auf der optionalen Spiel- und Essplatte, die nur angeklemmt wird, selbst erste Essversuche machen oder spielen. Für sicheren Halt der Kleinsten sorgt der optionale Sicherheitsbügel mit Schrittgurt. Kindergarten- und Schulkinder sitzen dann ergonomisch richtig und in der optimalen Höhe am Tisch. Und auch Mama und Opa können auf dem Stuhl Platz nehmen; denn er ist bis circa 100 Kilo belastbar. Ein Stuhl für alle Generationen. Damit alle bequem sitzen, dafür sorgen auch die vorne abgerundeten Kanten der ergonomisch geformten Sitzflächen.

Ein praktisches Detail ist eine Schlüsselgarage – ein Kunststoffmäppchen, das unter dem Sitz versteckt ist. Dort wird der Inbus-Schlüssel versorgt, mit dem man die Rollen arretiert und die Sitz- und Fußposition einstellt: Das heißt, nie mehr suchen müssen.

»Ypso« besitzt stabile Rahmenteile aus schichtverleimter massiver Buche, seine Rückenlehne, Sitz- und Fußplatten bestehen aus Buche Formsperrholz. Man kann passend zur Wohnungseinrichtung unter drei Farbkombinationen wählen: weiß, Buche in Nussbaumfarbton oder klassische Buche.

Jury

Eine eigenständige Lösung, die funktional einige Verbesserungen bringt, wie die leichte Verschiebemöglichkeit oder die interessante Verstellbarkeit von Sitz- und Fußplatte. Besonders attraktiv zum Mitwachsen. Sauber in allen Details gelöst, langlebig und auch Holz als Material ist unter ökologischen Gesichtspunkten sehr überzeugend. Clever ist, dass der Inbus-Schlüssel in einer Extra-Tasche unterm Sitz verstaut wird, so hat man ihn immer parat, wenn man etwas verstellen möchte. Eine echte Alternative für einen Markt, der nicht so viele Lösungen bietet.

The form of this contemporary high chair is reminiscent of an upside-down »Y«, which is why it is called »Ypso«. Apart from its modern design, it is also remarkable for its excellent functions and great flexibility.

Thanks to the casters and grip, it is easy to transport. It adapts to the age, size and needs of the child. As the seat and footrest can be adjusted to 14 different positions, the chair grows with the child. From about the age of six months, babies can sit here, be fed and even play or make their first attempts at feeding themselves on the optional playing and feeding tray, which is simply clamped into place. An optional safety bar with a crotch strap keeps the little ones safely in place. And kindergarten or school-age children can sit ergonomically correctly at the table, at just the right height. Even parents or grandparents can sit on the chair, which can take a load of up to roughly 100 kilos. A chair for every generation. The rounded front edges of the ergonomically shaped seat surfaces ensure that everyone can sit comfortably.

One practical detail is the key compartment – a plastic pouch hidden under the seat. This is where the Allen key is kept, which is used to block the casters and set the height of the seat and footrest. No more searching frantically for the key.

»Ypso« is made of robust frame elements of solid, glue-laminated beech, and its back rest, seat and footrests are made of beech plywood. Three colour combinations are available to suit furnishing style: white, walnut-coloured beech or classic beech.

Judges panel

A self-contained solution that comes up with a number of functional improvements, such as the ease with which it can be moved or the interesting way seat and footrest can be adjusted. The way it grows with the child is especially attractive. The details are cleverly done. The use of wood as material is also very convincing from an ecological perspective. Clever the way the Allen key is kept in an extra pouch under the seat. In this way, it is always to hand when something needs adjusting. A real alternative for a market that does not offer many solutions.

Vit
30

cal

Vitocal 300-G Wärmepumpe
Architektur **Gold**

Heat pump
Architecture **Gol**

»Weniger ist mehr« heißt das Gestaltungsprinzip der neuen Wärmepumpe. Entsprechend ihrer wesentlichen Funktion, wirtschaftlich und umweltverträglich Wärme emissionsfrei und ohne Abwärme zu erzeugen, hat die »Vitocal 300-G« mit modernster Wärmepumpentechnologie das Aussehen eines leistungsstarken Wärmetresors. Mit ihrem klar gegliederten Korpus und der einteiligen Front fügt sie sich gut in das Umfeld moderner Architektur.

Die intelligente Bedienung befindet sich geschützt in dem aufklappbaren Regelungsgehäuse, und ihre Neigung kann individuell eingestellt werden. Alle Bedienvorgänge werden mit der zentralen Cursorsteuerung der neu entwickelten Vitotronic vorgenommen und auf dem großen kontrastreichen Display grafikunterstützt dargestellt. Durch die Fokussierung auf die wichtigsten Funktionen und die klare Hierarchisierung der Informationen und Bedienebenen steigt die Bedienfreundlichkeit vor allem auch für unerfahrene Anwender.

Die Farbe Silber des Korpus spiegelt Klarheit, Hochwertigkeit und Fortschrittlichkeit wider. In Kombination mit der Akzentfarbe Orange, dem Symbol für Wärme, verbindet sie Innovation mit Tradition. Die Durchgängigkeit der Designsprache und Gleichbehandlung des Markenauftritts über das gesamte Programm lässt eine formale Identität entstehen, die Orientierung und Vertrauen schafft.

Jury
Viessmann schafft es wieder, ein Stück Innovation in diese Produktwelt zu bringen, indem das Gehäuse sehr schlicht belassen, das Bedienelement aber als ein hochwertiges und schönes orangefarbenes Beauty-Case ausgeführt wird. Eine neue Ästhetik für so ein klassisches Produkt. Konsequente und erfolgreiche Umsetzung des Corporate Design mit hohem Wiedererkennungswert und schöner Bildung der Markenfamilie, gute Positionierung des Logos in hoher Wertigkeit. Betonung nur der wirklich aufwendigen Bedienelemente, ansonsten eine einfache geometrische Form in einer kraftvoll soliden Ausführung.

»Less is more« is the design principle behind this new heat pump. By analogy to its main function, which is to generate heat economically and in an eco-friendly way, without emissions and waste heat, »Vitocal 300-G« with its cutting-edge heat pump technology looks like a high-end safe for storing heat. With its clearly structured contours and one-part front panel, this heat pump harmonizes with any modern architectural setting.

Its intelligent controls are hidden away in a hinged control housing. The angle of opening can be set to suit the user. The newly developed Vitotronic with its central cursor control is used to operate all functions, which are also shown graphically on the large, high-contrast display screen. Because it focuses on the main functions and arranges information and user levels according to a clear hierarchy, user-friendliness is increased, especially for inexperienced users.

The silver colour of the body is an expression of clarity, high quality and progressiveness. Combined with highlights in orange, to symbolize warmth, it combines innovation and tradition. The uniform design language and consistent way brand identity is maintained across the entire range gives rise to a formal identity that creates orientation and trust.

Judges panel
Viessmann has done it again. It has brought innovation to this product world by leaving the housing very plain but designing the control element as a high-quality, attractive vanity case in orange. A new aesthetics for such a classic product. Consistent and successful application of corporate design with high recognition value and attractive creation of the brand family. The logo is nicely positioned, giving an impression of high quality. Only the really complex control elements are emphasized. For the rest, a simple geometric shape in a powerful, solid design.

EcoVent KWL EC 60 Lüftungsgerät mit Wärmerückgewinnung
Architektur **Silber**

Fan with heat reco
Architecture **Silv**

Mangelnde Feuchtigkeitsabfuhr in Räumen fördert das Entstehen von Staubmilben und Schimmelpilz und führt zu gesundheitlichen Beeinträchtigungen. Eine überzeugende Lösung bietet hier »EcoVent«. Es ist ein äußerst kompaktes Unterputz-Wandeinbaugerät für die Be- und Entlüftung mit Wärmerückgewinnung für Einzelräume. Da ein Luftverteilsystem nicht erforderlich ist, eignet es sich vor allem für die Sanierung eines bestehenden Gebäudes, das auf den gesetzlich geforderten Standard der Energie-Einsparverordnung (EnEV) zu bringen ist.

Das Design der eleganten Innenfassade ist auf das Wesentliche reduziert und neutral gestaltet, auf herkömmliche Frontöffnungen wurde verzichtet. Dadurch fügt sich »EcoVent« dezent in jedes Raumambiente ein, und lästige Schmutzablagerungen am Lüftungsgitter gehören der Vergangenheit an. Die Schlitze für Lufteintritt und Luftaustritt sind unauffällig seitlich angeordnet. Das erlaubt eine einfache Reinigung der Blende und hinterlässt im Raum immer einen optisch sauberen Eindruck. Die Öffnung an der Außenwand wird durch eine formschöne Edelstahlfassade verdeckt, die sich architektonisch in den gegenwärtigen Trend von Fassadenrenovierungen gut einfügt.

»EcoVent« sorgt für steten Luftaustausch bei minimalem Stromverbrauch. Gerüche und feuchte Luft werden nach außen abgeführt. Die frische Außenluft nimmt im Wärmetauscher die Abluftwärme auf und strömt vorgewärmt ein. Damit wird ein Wärmerückgewinnungsgrad von über 70 Prozent erreicht und Heizenergie eingespart. Das Gerät sorgt so für ein gesundes, behagliches Raumklima und verhindert Feuchteschäden und Schimmelbildung wirkungsvoll.

Jury

Ein kleines Lüftungsgerät für die Wärmerückgewinnung speziell für den Einsatz in nachträglich sanierten Häusern. Eine sehr kompakte Bauweise und eine überzeugende Anmutung der beiden Öffnungsabdeckungen im Innenraum und in der Außenfassade. Leichter Zugang für Wartungsarbeiten und durch die Gestaltung auch ein Vermeiden von unschönen Schmutzablagerungen.

The failure to de-humidify rooms encourages dust mites and mould, and poses a risk to health. »EcoVent« offers a convincing solution to this problem. It is an extremely compact, flush-mounted wall-installed unit for ventilating individual rooms, combined with a heat-recovery function. As there is no need for an air distribution system, it is especially suitable when renovating an existing building that has to be brought up to legally required energy-saving standards.

The design of the elegant interior facia has been reduced to the essentials and kept neutral in style. Unlike conventional fan units, there are no front apertures. »EcoVent« thus harmonizes well with any kind of room, and irksome deposits of dust on the ventilation grille are a thing of the past. The slits for air intake and discharge are arranged inconspicuously at the sides. This allows simple cleaning of the panel, and creates a visually neat impression in the room at all times. On the exterior wall, the aperture is covered by an elegant stainless steel facia, which blends well with the current architectural trends for façade renovation.

»EcoVent« ensures a constant exchange of air, while consuming a minimum of electricity. Smells and humidity are directed out of the room. In the heat exchanger, the fresh air from outside is warmed by the exhaust air, and streams into the room in a pre-heated state. More than 70 percent of this waste heat is recovered, and heating energy is saved. The appliance ensures a healthy, cosy room climate, and effectively prevents mould and damage due to damp.

Judges panel

A small fan for heat recovery, especially for use in houses that are being renovated. Very compact design and a convincing solution for the aperture covers, both exterior and interior. Easy access for maintenance work, and the design also prevents any unsightly dust settling.

C100

Stegrost
Architektur **Silber**

Grating
Architecture **Sil**

Abdeckungen für Bodenablaufrinnen sind Alltagsprodukte ohne besonderen Aufmerksamkeitswert und werden traditionell aus Stahlguss produziert. Ganz anders dagegen »C100« – eine Neuerfindung des Stegrosts.

»C100« ist der weltweit erste Stegrost aus Fibretec. Durch diesen hochwertigen glasfaserverstärkten Kunststoff sind die Abdeckungen korrosionsfrei, weniger diebstahlgefährdet, leichter und somit günstiger im Transport. Und er garantiert extreme Langlebigkeit.

Das neue Material ermöglicht zudem eine innovative Formensprache, die dem Produkt im Markt Eigenständigkeit verleiht. So orientiert sich das Design nicht an der bekannten Gussoptik, sondern definiert die visuell dominanten Durchbrüche neu: als weich geformte, elliptische Öffnungen, die das Erscheinungsbild eleganter und auch wertiger machen. Die Stege sind nach oben leicht überspannt ausgebildet, um die Belastungen besser aufnehmen zu können. Vom Rand einlaufende, ebenfalls elliptische sowie erhabene Zungen optimieren die Schwallwasserführung und sorgen zusammen mit der rauen Oberfläche für normgerechte, fest integrierte Rutschhemmung.

Die Stegroste werden im Spritzgussverfahren in Deutschland hergestellt.

Jury

Das ist eine völlig neuartige Abdeckung für Bodenablaufrinnen, die traditionell aus Gusseisen gefertigt werden und damit sehr schwer sind. Hier wurde erstmalig ein Kunststoff eingesetzt, der auch gestalterisch neue Möglichkeiten bietet, die konsequent umgesetzt und genutzt wurden. Gute Lösung auch für den Rutschschutz, und durch die Leichtigkeit gewinnt das Produkt auch eine höhere Nachhaltigkeit.

Gratings for drainage channels are everyday products. Little attention is paid to them. Generally, they are made of cast steel. »C100« is completely different, a reinvention of the grating.

It is the world's first grating to be made of Fibretec. This high-quality, glass fibre-reinforced plastic means that the gratings are rust-free and less likely to be stolen. In addition, they are lighter, and thus less expensive to transport. This material also guarantees a long service life.

Moreover, the new material allows a new formal expression that sets the product apart in the market. The design does not takes its lead from the appearance of conventional cast steel gratings, but re-defines the visually dominant openings: these are now soft and elliptic, creating a more elegant and more high-quality appearance. The stays are slightly overstretched towards the top, which improves their load-bearing properties. Elliptic, raised tongues pointing in from the sides optimize the channelling of splash water. Together with the rough surface, they ensure that the grating meets anti-slip requirements.

The gratings are made in Germany, using injection-moulding techniques.

Judges panel

This is a completely new cover for drainage channels that are traditionally made of cast iron and are thus very heavy. For the first time in this area, plastic has been used. This also opens up possibilities for design, which have been consistently applied and used here. Good solution also for preventing slipping. The product's lightness also means that it is more sustainable.

ECO by Cosentino® Recycelte Oberflächen Recycled surface
Architektur **Silber** Architecture Sil

»ECO by Cosentino®« schafft einen neuen Standard für Architektur und Design. Es ist ein high-performance Recyclingmaterial, das Materialien nutzt, die sonst keine weitere Verwendung mehr haben. Die Oberfläche besteht aus 75 Prozent recycelten Materialien wie Spiegel-, Glas- und Porzellanstückchen, Porzellanfliesen und verglaster Asche, und aus 25 Prozent Natursteinresten und ökologischem Harz.

Neben den verwendeten Rohstoffen ist aber für ein umweltfreundliches Produkt ebenso wichtig der Herstellungsprozess. Dieser ist hier ein sauberes Verfahren, in welchem fast keine Emissionen freigesetzt werden, der Einsatz an Energie stetig minimiert und bis zu 94 Prozent des verwendeten Wassers wiederaufbereitet wird. Das garantiert auch das »Cradle to Cradle«-Zertifikat, das »ECO by Cosentino®« unter anderem erhalten hat. Die »Cradle to Cradle«-Philosophie verfolgt die Idee, dass kein Endverbraucherprodukt geschaffen werden sollte, wenn es nach Vollendung seines Lebenszyklus unbrauchbar oder ein potentieller Müllieferant wird.

»ECO by Cosentino®«, das in verschiedenen Variationen und Farben erhältlich ist, ist aber nicht nur ökologisch sinnvoll, sondern auch sehr widerstandsfähig, kratzfest, fleckenbeständig und wärmeunempfindlich. Und es sieht optisch ansprechend und nicht wie ein recyceltes Produkt aus. Seine Einsatzgebiete sind vielfältig, sowohl in Küchen und Badezimmern als auch als Bodenbelag, Wandverkleidung und in anderen Anwendungen in privaten und öffentlichen Bauten, wie Krankenhäusern, Schulen, Hotels und Restaurants.

Jury

Ein Werkstoff aus recycelten Materialien, der eine sehr hohe Wertigkeit erreicht. Er stellt ein überzeugendes Konzept, das »Cradle to Cradle«-Prinzip, dar: vom Einsatz der Materialien, von der Herstellung bis hin zur Verwertung und Wiederverwertung. Zudem sind es sehr attraktive Oberflächen, die nicht wie recycelte Produkte aussehen.

»ECO by Cosentino®« sets a new standard for architecture and design. It is a high-performance recycled material that uses materials that would otherwise have no further use. The surface comprises 75 percent recycled materials, such as pieces of mirrors, glass and china, porcelain tiles and ash, and 25 percent left-over natural stone and ecological resin.

If a product is to be an ecological one, the manufacturing process is just as important as the raw materials used. The process used here is clean, giving rise to practically no emissions, constantly minimizing the amount of energy used, and retreating up to 94 percent of the water used. This is also guaranteed by its Cradle to Cradle certification, one of many that »ECO by Cosentino®« has received. The Cradle to Cradle philosophy believes that a consumer product should not be created if, when it reaches the end of its life cycle, it can no longer be used or is a candidate for the rubbish tip.

»Eco by Cosentino®«, which is available in many variants and colours, not only makes ecological sense, but is also very tough, scratch-resistant, stain-resistant and heat-resistant. It is also visually attractive, and does not look like a recycled product. It can be used in many areas, in kitchens and in bathrooms, as a floor covering, wall panelling and in other applications in the private and public sphere, such as hospitals, schools, hotels and restaurants.

Judges panel

A material made from recycled materials, which gives an impression of very high quality. It is a convincing embodiment of the Cradle to Cradle principle: from the way materials are used, to its manufacture, to its use and recycling. In addition, these are very attractive surfaces that don't look like they are recycled.

Ruhr Museum
Zeche Zollverein Essen   Museumsgestaltung   Public Design   **Silber**

Museum design
Public design   Si

Die Gestaltung des neuen Ruhrmuseums in der ehemaligen Kohlenwäsche auf Zeche Zollverein in Essen stellte aufgrund der kulturhistorischen Bedeutung des Gebäudes und des Maschinenbestandes eine besondere Herausforderung dar. Der Ausstellung wurde eine eigenständige Erscheinung verliehen, die sich deutlich von der Gebäudearchitektur abhebt und darum leicht zu identifizieren ist.

Sie tritt jedoch nicht mit dem Gebäude in Konkurrenz, die Bestandteile der Kohlenwäsche fungieren als stumme Zeugen. Formale Zurückhaltung der Ausstellungsarchitektur, Einfachheit der Raumstrukturen und eine klare, schnell verständliche Besucherführung stehen im Zentrum des Konzepts. Die Ausstellungsgestaltung basiert auf wenigen Grundideen: Jeder Bereich ist inhaltlich eindeutig belegt, folgt einem klaren gestalterischen Ansatz und orientiert sich zudem an den früheren Nutzungen der Ebenen.

Auf der Empfangsebene, wo einst die Trennung und Sortierung von Kohle und Gestein stattfand, »sortieren« sich die Besucher auf die Angebote des Hauses. Die erste der drei musealen Ebenen, ursprünglich Ort der Fördergutverteilung, widmet sich der Gegenwart. Die offene Struktur und die helle Erscheinung der Einbauten fängt gestalterisch das Licht ein. Einen schönen Kontrast bilden die vierzehn mächtigen Becherwerke. Der ehemalige Kohlebunker speichert heute das Gedächtnis des Ruhrgebiets. So werden beispielsweise in den zwölf Bunkerräumen Exponate von besonders hohem ästhetischen Wert zum Thema »Traditionen« präsentiert. Wo früher Kohle verteilt und verladen wurde, ist heute die Geschichte der Industrieregion zusammengetragen, die narrativ in Form eines inszenierten Schaudepots dargestellt wird.

Jury

Eine Museumsgestaltung in einem faszinierenden Umfeld, die die Exponate und die Geschichte strukturiert darstellt, aber innerhalb der Struktur Highlights bildet wie Perlen an einer Kette mit hoher Informationsdichte und Liebe zum Detail. Aber nicht langweilig, sondern immer wieder mit visuellen Höhenpunkten, sodass das industrielle Umfeld, das ja keine ruhige Ausstellungsstruktur ist, einen passenden Gegenpol bildet: parallel zum Schwarz der Umgebung und der Kohle wird mit weiß und hell kontrastiert und der Blick auf Exponate und Informationen gelenkt.

Because of the cultural and historical importance of the building and the machinery it contains, designing the new Ruhr Museum in the former coal-washing plant of the Zollverein colliery in Essen was a special challenge. The exhibition was given an independent identity that sets it significantly apart from the architecture of the building, making it easily recognizable.

However, it does not compete with the building – the coal-washing plant's machinery looks on as a silent witness. The formal reserve of the exhibition architecture, the simplicity of the room structures and the clear, easily understandable viewing route are the core elements of the concept. The exhibition is based on just a few central ideas. The content of each area is clearly defined, and each area follows a clear design concept, as well as orienting to the different levels' former use.

At the reception level, where once coal was separated from rock and then washed, the visitors »sort themselves out«, and find out what there is to see. The first of the three museum levels, originally the place where the material was conveyed in different directions, is dedicated to the present. Its light, with its open structures and the bright appearance of the fixtures is captured by the design. The 14 huge bucket conveyors form a striking contrast. The former coal bunker is now the site of the Ruhr's memory. In the 12 bunker rooms, for example, aesthetically very valuable exhibits are presented, dealing with the theme of traditions. And where once coal was distributed and loaded, the history of this industrial region is now brought together, presented as a narrative in the form of a show depot.

Judges panel

A museum design in a fascinating environment. It presents the exhibits and history in structured fashion, but within this structure creates highlights like pearls on a chain, with a great depth of information and great attention to detail. It isn't boring, though, but constantly comes up with visual highlights, with the result that the industrial setting, which is not a static exhibition structure, forms a fitting counterpoint. Against the black of the surroundings and the coal, white and brightness are used as a contrast, directing the visitor's gaze to the exhibits and information.

Turbostream TS 10 000   Hochleistungs-Schneeräummaschine
Transport, Verkehr   **Silber**

High-performance
Transport, traffic

Die Schneeräummaschine für Flughäfen räumt dank intelligenter Technik schnell, unkompliziert und professionell große Schneemengen. Sie ist mit einem Powerpaket aus Hochleistungsräumkopf und einer Antriebsleistung von 681 Kilowatt ausgestattet, die das Räumen von 8 000 Tonnen Schnee pro Stunde garantiert. Der »Turbostream TS 10 000« schafft spielend eine Schneeauswurfsweite bis zu 60 Metern sowie eine Räumgeschwindigkeit von bis zu 50 Kilometern die Stunde. Der Hochleistungsräumkopf mit einer Räumbreite von drei Metern wird frontseitig am Trägerfahrzeug angebaut. Dennoch sorgt die optimale Anordnung der Komponenten für ausgezeichnete Sicht und ermöglicht damit die präzise Räumung.

Der »Turbostream TS 10 000« ist einfach und logisch zu bedienen. Mit einem ergonomischen Joystick werden Räumkopf und Schleuderradgehäuse gehoben, gesenkt und verstellt. Alle wichtigen Steuerfunktionen und Einstellungen sind einfach und bequem am großen Display in der Fahrerkabine ablesbar.

Ein weiterer Vorteil ist die Multifunktionalität, die den »Turbostream TS 10 000« ausgesprochen ökonomisch macht. Das gesamte Schneeräumgerät ist schnell wechselbar. Somit kann das Trägerfahrzeug das ganze Jahr über eingesetzt werden. Der leistungsstarke Traktor lässt sich dann für andere Instandhaltungsarbeiten nutzen wie etwa Wiesen mähen. Zur Wirtschaftlichkeit tragen auch der Einsatz von Standardkomponenten beim Schneeräumgerät sowie hochwertiger Materialien, die gegen alle Enteisungsmittel korrosionsbeständig sind, und die Wartungsplattform oder Verschleißteile aus Hardox bei. Sie alle sorgen für einen geringen Wartungsaufwand und reduzieren damit Zeit und Kosten für die Instandhaltung.

Jury

Wir finden es spannend, dass man sich bei Investitionsgütern in dieser Größenordnung einerseits ergonomisch viele Gedanken über die Ausbildung der Steuerkanzel gemacht hat. Andererseits ist man aufgrund der großen Dimensionen auch in die Formgebung der abnehmbaren Bauteile gegangen und hat dadurch eine Dynamik in einer Maschine erzeugt, die ja per se genau das nicht auslöst. Die Modularität durch eine Antriebseinheit und ein austauschbares Frontaggregat ermöglicht, die Maschine, die auf den ersten Blick nur für den Winter geeignet scheint, das ganze Jahr über zu nutzen.

This snow plough for airports uses intelligent technology to clear huge volumes of snow – quickly, uncomplicatedly and professionally. It is equipped with a power package comprising a high-performance clearing head and a powerful engine developing 681 kilowatts, with a guaranteed snow-clearing performance of 8,000 metric tons per hour. »Turbostream TS 10 000« easily manages a snow ejection distance of up to 60 metres, and allows clearing work to be done at speeds of up to 50 kilometres per hour. The high performance clearing head, with a total clearing width of three metres, is mounted on the front of the carrying vehicle. Nonetheless, thanks to the optimum arrangement of the clearing components, visibility is excellent, and so precise clearing is possible.

Operation of the »Turbostream TS 10 000« is simple and logical. With the aid of the ergonomically designed joy stick, the clearing head and the blower wheel housing can be lifted, lowered and displaced. All important control functions and settings can be simply and conveniently read from the large display in the driver's cab.

The machine's multi-functionality is a further benefit, and makes the »Turbostream TS 10 000« very economical. The complete snow clearing unit is quickly removable. As a result, the carrying vehicle can be used throughout the year. The high-performance tractor can then be used for other maintenance tasks, such as grass-cutting. This value for money is further enhanced by the use of standard components with the snow clearing unit, by high quality materials that are corrosion resistant to all de-icing agents, by the maintenance platform, and by wear parts made of Hardox steel. All these details ensure low maintenance and hence reduce the time and cost required for keeping the vehicle in readiness.

Judges panel

In capital goods of this size, it is exciting for us to see so much thought being given to ergonomics and the design of the driver's cab. Because of the large size, thought has also been given to the design of the main removable parts, and the result is dynamism of a kind you would not expect to see in a machine like this. The modular design of the drive unit and the snow-clearing unit means that a machine which at first glance appears to be suitable only for winter operation can be used all year round.

**Mercedes-Benz
SLS AMG**

Sportwagen
Transport, Verkehr **Silber**

Sports car
Transport, traffic

Der Flügeltürer – ein Begriff, bei dem Autofans ins Schwärmen kommen und an die automobile Ikone, den legendären 300 SL aus den 1950er Jahren, denken. Kein anderer Sportwagen konnte dieses Konzept faszinierenden Designs, fortschrittlicher Technologie und rennsporttauglicher Fahrdynamik adäquat fortführen.

Nun ist mit dem neuen »SLS AMG« ein Supersportwagen herausgekommen, der den außergewöhnlichen und einzigartigen Charakter des Flügeltürers ins 21. Jahrhundert transformiert. In ihm integrieren sich Erfahrung und Wissen aus dem Bau von Renntourenwagen und technologische Spitzenleistung mit Anklängen aus dem Flugzeugbau.

Mit seinem Design spiegelt er die Prinzipien des modernen Sportwagenbaus wider: Die knapp zwei Meter lange Motorhaube, das flache, weit hinten positionierte Greenhouse und das kurze Heck mit dem ausfahrbaren Heckflügel stehen ebenso für Dynamik wie der lange Radstand, die breite Spur und die großen Räder. Nicht nur die spektakulären Flügeltüren erinnern an die Sportwagen-Legende, sondern auch der breite Kühlergrill mit der flügelförmigen Querfinne und dem exponierten Mercedes-Stern, bei dessen Tubus im Profil auch der Lufteinlass eines Jet-Triebwerks anklingt.

Im Interieur werden Assoziationen an ein Fluzeugcockpit geweckt. Prägendes Stilelement ist die Instrumententafel, die in Form eines kraftvoll gespannten Flügelprofils für optische Breite sorgt.

Die Karosserie und das extrem verwindungssteife Chassis bestehen weitgehend aus Aluminium. Geringes Gewicht, niedriger Schwerpunkt und eine optimale Gewichtsverteilung auf Vorder- und Hinterachse sorgen für beeindruckende Agilität. Der hubraumstarke V8-Motor garantiert höchste Fahrleistungen.

Jury

Dieses Auto weckt alle Träume von Automobilität und Freude an der Bewegung. Für Mercedes ist es eine Fortführung und Weiterentwicklung eines Klassikers, der in eine neue Dimension und Ära geführt wird. Wir unterstützen den Drang, weiter an diesem Kult zu arbeiten. Das ist spannend. Der Kult der Flügeltüren. Eine emotionenweckende Analogie zu den damaligen Flügeltürenautos von Mercedes aber mit einer harmonischen Integration der allerneuesten Technologien, die ja weitestgehend rennsporterprobt in dieses Modell eingeflossen sind.

The gull-wing coupé – for car fans, a name that brings back fond memories of an automotive icon, the legendary 300 SL of the 1950s. No other sports car was able to take up and properly continue this concept of fascinating design, advanced technology and racing-car dynamics.

Now, with the new »SLS AMG«, a super sports car has been presented that transposes the unusual and distinctive character of the gull-wing coupé into the 21st century. It marries experience and know-how in the building of touring cars with technological prowess, with a few nods in the direction of aircraft construction.

Its design reflects the principles of modern sports car construction. The engine hood, just under two metres long, the flat greenhouse positioned well to the rear, and the short tail with its extendable spoiler stand for dynamism, as do the long wheelbase, the wide track width and the large wheels. Not only the spectacular gull-wing doors are reminiscent of the sports car legend, but also the broad radiator grille with its wing-shaped cross-fin and the prominent Mercedes star, which from the side alludes to the air intake of a jet engine.

The interior brings associations with an aircraft cockpit to life. The dominant stylistic element is the instrument panel. Its shape, like a powerfully stretched profile of a wing, creates optical width.

The bodywork and the extremely torsion-resistant chassis are made mainly of aluminium. Low weight, a low centre of gravity and optimum distribution of weight between the front and rear axle make the car impressively agile. The beefy V8 engine guarantees peak performance.

Judges panel

This car awakens dreams of automobility and the joy of motion. For Mercedes, it is the continuation and further development of a classic, which is being led into a new dimension and a new era. We support the drive to work further on this cult. This is exciting. The cult of gull-wing doors. An emotion-arousing analogy to the gull-wing Mercedes of days gone by, but harmoniously integrating the very latest technologies, most of which find their way into this car after having been tested on the race track.

VW Polo　　　Kleinwagen　　　　　　　　　　　　　　　　　　　　　　　　　　　　Subcompact car
　　　　　　　Transport, Verkehr　**Silber**　　　　　　　　　　　　　　　　　　Transport, traffic

Der »Polo« setzt neue Maßstäbe in der Kleinwagenklasse. Er tritt mit einer markanten, dynamischen Formensprache, kraftvollen Proportionen und hohen Qualitätsansprüchen auf. Und er besitzt ungewöhnliche, innovative Details, wie beispielsweise die in die Außenspiegel integrierten Blinker, schwarze Kühlerschutzlamellen, prägnante Linien in der Karosserie oder auffällig geschnittene Frontscheinwerfer, die eine optische Einheit mit dem flachen Grill bilden.

Wie sein Exterieur- so ist auch sein Interieurdesign gelungen. Unter der vollverzinkten Schale befinden sich optisch und haptisch hochwertige Oberflächen mit hoher Anmutungsqualität, ein sportliches Drei-Speichen-Lenkrad und viel Ablagefläche für all die Dinge, die man im Auto dabei hat: Handy, Getränke, CDs et cetera. Zudem punktet er mit hervorragendem Sitz- und Raumkomfort sowie mit Übersichtlichkeit und guter Funktionalität, aber auch mit Sicherheit. Er ist dabei zudem sparsam und umweltbewusst.

Mit serienmäßigem Stabilitätssystem wird er hohen Sicherheitsmaßstäben gerecht und verbraucht dank dem neuen emissionsarmen 1,2-Liter TSI-Motor durchschnittlich lediglich 5,3 Liter auf 100 Kilometer, bringt es aber auf noch mehr Dynamik mit 105 PS und auf eine Höchstgeschwindigkeit von 190 Stundenkilometern bei einem reduzierten CO_2-Ausstoß von nur 124 Gramm pro Kilometer. Neben vier verschiedenen Benzin- gibt es auch drei Dieselmotoren. Einer davon – im Polo BlueMotion – ist der 1,2 Liter TDI, der mit einem Durchschnittsverbrauch von 3,3 Litern pro 100 Kilometern und 87 Gramm CO_2 pro Kilometer der derzeit sparsamste und emissionsärmste Fünfsitzer ist.

Jury

Ein Kleinwagen, der von der Verarbeitungsqualität, dem Komfort und der Funktionalität die Ansprüche einer höheren Fahrzeugklasse bereits erfüllt und einlöst. Er hebt sich in dem Segment, in dem viele Kleinwagen jetzt gerade auf den Markt kommen, als sehr wertig ab. Die Gestaltung fügt sich einerseits gut in die Markenstrategie von VW ein und besitzt trotzdem eine Eigenständigkeit gegenüber den anderen Fahrzeugen. Außerdem ist er sehr sparsam.

This VW »Polo« sets new standards in the subcompact class. Its appearance is characterized by a striking, dynamic formal expression, powerful proportions and high quality standards. And it has unusual, innovative details, such as the blinker integrated in the wing mirror, black radiator grille ribs, striking lines in the bodywork and unconventionally shaped front headlights that form an optical unity with the flat grille.

Its interior is just as well designed as its exterior. On the inside of the fully galvanized shell, its surfaces are high quality and appealing, in both a tactile and a visual sense. It has a sporty three-spoke steering wheel and plenty of surfaces for depositing all the things that a driver and passengers need, such as a mobile phone, drinks, CDs, etc. It also offers excellent seating comfort and plenty of room, clear all-round vision and good functions, as well as good safety features. It is also economical and eco-friendly.

With a stability system as standard equipment, it satisfies high safety standards. Its new, low-emission, 1.2-litre TSI engine consumes just 5.3 litres for every 100 kilometres driven, and develops a dynamic 105 horsepower. It reaches a top speed of 190 kilometres per hour, but emits just 124 grams of CO_2 per kilometre. Apart from four different petrol engines, there are three diesel engines to choose from. One of these, in the Polo BlueMotion, is a 1.2-litre TDI engine that consumes an average of 3.3 litres per 100 kilometres. At 87 grams of CO_2 per kilometre, it is currently the most economical and lowest-emission five-seater in the market.

Judges panel

A subcompact whose finishing, comfort and functions satisfy the standards expected of a higher vehicle class. It stands out as a beacon of quality in a market which is seeing the launch of many subcompacts. Its design is consistent with the VW brand strategy, yet it also has a certain quality that sets it apart from other vehicles. Moreover, it is very economical.

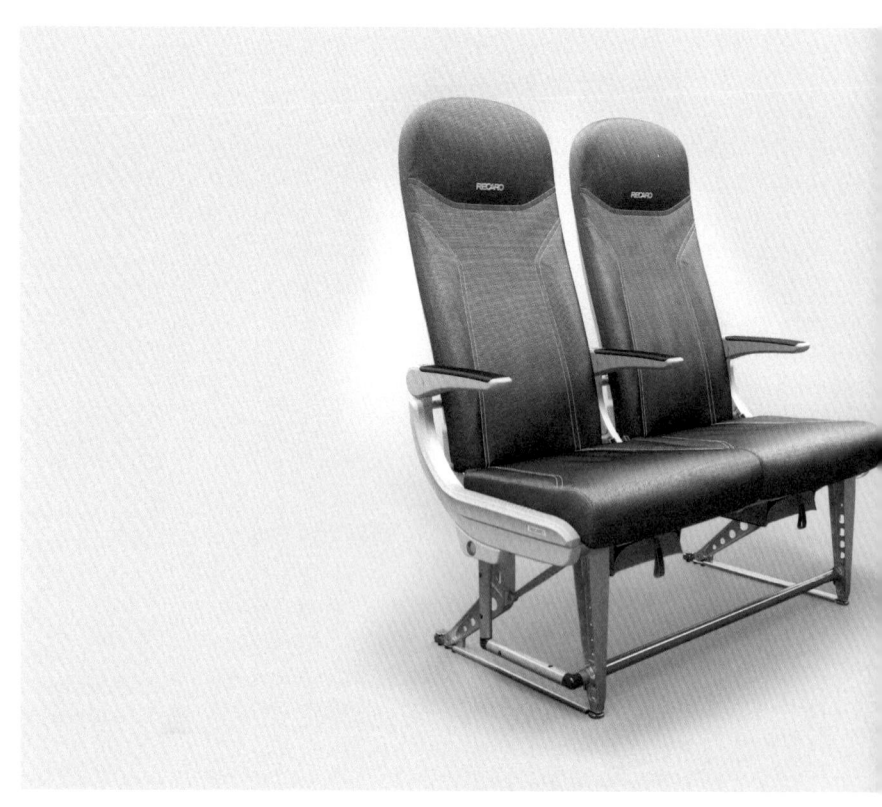

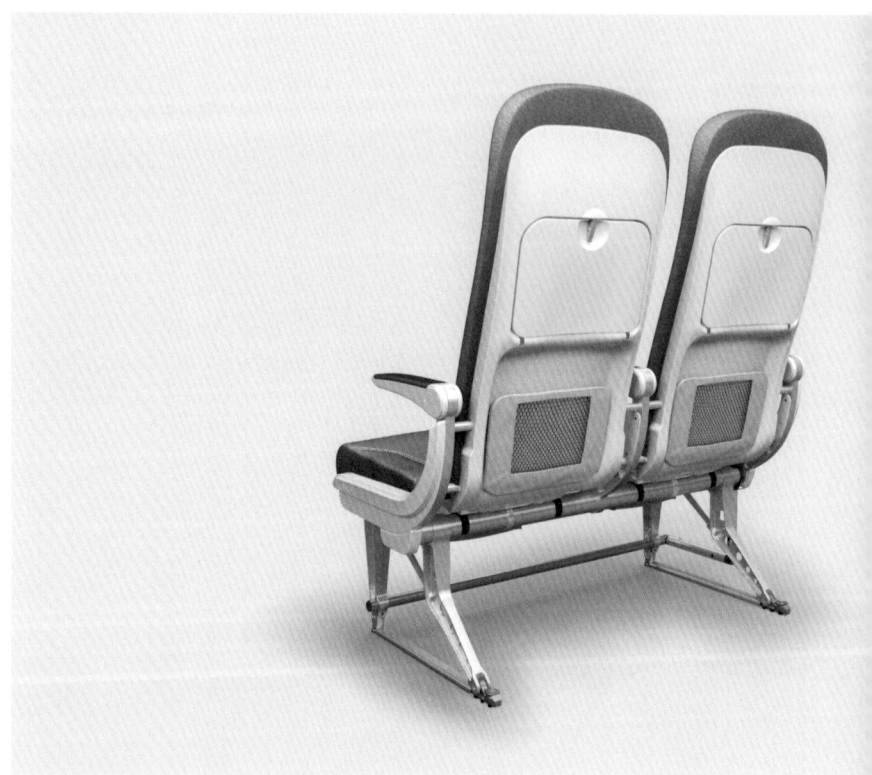

Smart Line 3510 Fluggastsitz
Transport, Verkehr **Silber**

Aircraft passenger
Transport, traffic

Die Entwicklung des neuen Fluggastsitzes ist eine Antwort auf hohe Treibstoffkosten und Einsparungsprogramme der Fluggesellschaften. »Smart Line 3510« ist der zur Zeit leichteste, am Markt erhältliche Economy-Class-Sitz für Kurzstreckenflüge bis zu vier Stunden. Er kombiniert auf einzigartige Weise ein Gewicht von gerade mal 9,1 Kilogramm mit Haltbarkeit, Materialqualität und einem Maximum an Komfort.

Erreicht wurde das, indem alle technischen Einrichtungen, die zusätzliches Gewicht und eine schwierige Handhabung bedeuten, entfallen. Gleichzeitig wurden seine ergonomischen Eigenschaften optimiert. So ist die Rückenlehnenstruktur auf entspanntes Sitzen ausgerichtet. Sie besteht aus einem Aluminiumrahmen mit einer speziellen, flexiblen Netzstruktur, die sich individuell der Wirbelsäule anpasst und Druckpunkte des Rückens entlastet. Weiteren Komfort bieten der optimierte Kopfstützenbereich und die weichen Armlehnen aus einem speziellen Polycarbonat, das ebenfalls Gewicht einspart. Die nicht verstellbare Rückenlehne ist zudem so dünn, dass sie dem Passagier ein Maximum an Beinfreiheit ermöglicht. Der Tisch ist direkt an der Rückenlehnenstruktur angebracht.

Herausgekommen ist ein eleganter Sitz mit schlanker Silhouette. Sein modernes und gleichzeitig zeitloses Design macht den »Smart Line 3510« zu einer perfekten Synthese aus umweltfreundlicher Gewichtseinsparung und optischer Eleganz, die dem Passagier ein Maximum an Bequemlichkeit bietet. Durch das geringe Gewicht verbraucht Air France, die den »Smart Line 3510« bereits eingesetzt haben, laut eigenen Angaben jährlich 1 700 Tonnen weniger Kerosin und senkt damit den CO_2-Ausstoß um rund 5 200 Tonnen.

Jury

Der Sitz ist gedacht für Kurzstreckenflüge von bis zu vier Stunden in der Economy-Class. Entsprechend ist er auch mit beschränkter Variabilität unter dem Aspekt der Kosten- und Platzersparnis sowie der Leichtigkeit gestaltet, aber ohne am Design zu sparen. Das Ergebnis ist eine formal sehr überzeugende, hochwertige Lösung mit ausreichendem Komfort und vor allen Dingen eine Erhöhung der Beinfreiheit durch die leichte und schmale Bauweise. Eine elegante, platzeffiziente Lösung.

This new aircraft passenger seat has been developed in response to high fuel costs and airlines' cost-cutting programmes. »Smart Line 3510« is the lightest economy-class seat currently available in the market. It is designed for short-range flights lasting up to four hours. It is a unique combination of light weight – weighing just 9.1 kilograms – and durability, high-quality materials and a maximum of comfort.

This was achieved by doing away with all the technical trappings that cause extra weight and make seats difficult to use. At the same time, its ergonomic properties were optimized. The back rest, for example, has been designed to allow relaxed seating. It is made of an aluminium frame with a special flexible mesh that adapts individually to the spine and relieves pressure points on the back. Further comfort is provided by the optimized headrest and the soft armrests made of a specially designed polycarbonate, which also reduces weight. In addition, the non-adjustable backrest is so thin that passengers gain a maximum of leg room. The table is directly attached to the backrest structure.

The result is an elegant seat with a slim outline. Modern and at the same time timeless design makes »Smart Line 3510« a perfect synthesis of eco-friendly weight-reduction and elegant appearance, which offers the passenger a maximum of comfort. The »Smart Line 3510« seat is already used by Air France, and the airline reports that its light weight helps save 1,700 metric tons of jet fuel annually, which is equivalent to some 5,200 metric tons of CO_2.

Judges panel

The seat is designed for short-range flights lasting up to four hours. Accordingly, it has been designed so that it cannot be adjusted as much, and also to save space, cost and weight. Nonetheless, there have been no savings on design. The result is a formally very convincing and high-quality solution that offers sufficient comfort, and above all greater leg room due to the light and slim design. An elegant solution that uses space efficiently.

Mia Seeger, 1927 — Mia Seeger Preis 2010 — Mia Seeger Prize 2

entlich meine Idee – beim Nachdenken
is: in die ›Lücken‹ gehen, die noch
chtet worden sind.«
er, 1987

he idea of a prize, what really concerned
ognize work done in areas that have tended
ed up to now.«
er, 1987

Jährlicher Wettbewerb der Mia Seeger Stiftung für junge Designerinnen und Designer – Absolventen der Studiengänge Industriedesign / Produktgestaltung, Innenarchitektur / Möbeldesign, Architektur, Investitionsgüter- oder Transportation Design an deutschen Hochschulen

Preissumme 8.000 Euro

Ausgezeichnet werden Abschlussarbeiten aus den Jahren 2008 bis 2010. Bei der Bewertung der eingereichten Arbeiten ist neben den üblichen Designkriterien der soziale Nutzen entscheidend.

Jury
Prof. Karin Kirsch, Stuttgart
Adelheid Maier, Siemens AG, München
Prof. Ulrich Hirsch, Design & Identität, Brügge
Peter Keilbach, keilbach design and products,
    Dörzbach – Mia Seeger Preis
    und Stipendium 1991
Gerrit Terstiege, Chefredakteur »form«, Basel

Annual competition organized by the Mia Seeger Stiftung für young designers – graduates from courses in Industrial Design / Product Design, Interior Design / Furniture Design, Architecture, Capital Goods Design or Transportation Design at German institutes of higher education

Total prize money: 8,000 euros

Undergraduate dissertations from 2008 to 2010 are eligible for entry. Apart from the usual criteria, the decisive benchmark when accessing the studies submitted is their social utility.

Juges panel
Prof. Karin Kirsch, Stuttgart, DE
Adelheid Maier, Siemens AG, Munich, DE
Prof. Ulrich Hirsch, Design & Identität,
    Brügge, DE
Peter Keilbach, keilbach design and products,
    Dörzbach, DE – Mia Seeger Prize
    and Scholarship 1991
Gerrit Terstiege, Editor-in-chief »form«,
    Basel, CH

Mia Seeger
Stiftung

Boje System zur effektiven Ölteppichbekämpfung
Mia Seeger Preis 2010   **1. Preis**

System for effectiv[e]
Mia Seeger Prize 2[010]

Netzteppich kontra Ölteppich. Vom Flugzeug aus im 50m-Abstand abgeworfene Bojen spannen fast flächendeckend radiale Netze auf, die sich von unten her an die Ölschicht legen. Die fraktale Feinstruktur der Netze bindet das Öl. Schiffe schleppen die vollgesogenen Netze an Land. Dort lassen sich Öl, Netz und Bojen trennen und wiederverwerten. Auf See sind die Bojen über Radar, Licht und GPS einfach zu orten. Ultraschallerzeuger halten Seevögel fern.

Jury
Mit Bedacht sind hier zwei bionische Prinzipien miteinander verbunden. Einzeln tut jede Boje ihre Arbeit mit einem Netz, das wie das Haarkleid eines Tieres wirkt; gegen die Ölpest als ganze aber kommen die Bojen erst an, indem sie sich zum Schwarm zusammenschließen. Dass mit dem Einsatz aus der Luft her ein besonders schneller Weg der Hilfe gefunden ist, macht das Konzept vollends schlüssig. Zudem ist es überaus überzeugend durchgestaltet und vorgestellt.

Meshwork for ensnaring oil slicks. Buoys dropped from a plane at 50-meter intervals span radial nets which capture the oil slick from below. The way the nets are designed means that they cover practically the entire area of the spill. The fractal, fine mesh of the nets binds the oil. Ships drag the saturated nets to the shore, where the oil is removed from the nets and buoys, so that they can be used again. At sea, the buoys can be located by radar, light and GPS. Ultrasound generators keep sea birds away.

Judges panel
Two bionic principles have deliberately been combined here. Individually, each buoy does its work with a net that functions like an animal's coat. However, the buoys can only effectively combat the oil slick if they act together like a swarm. It is only logical to deploy them from the air, since this allows relief to be especially fast. Moreover, the design and presentation of this concept are extremely convincing.

Pivomed   Umlagerungshilfe für   Aid for repositioni
übergewichtige Patienten in Narkose   patients under na
Mia Seeger Preis 2010   **1. Preis**   Mia Seeger Prize 2

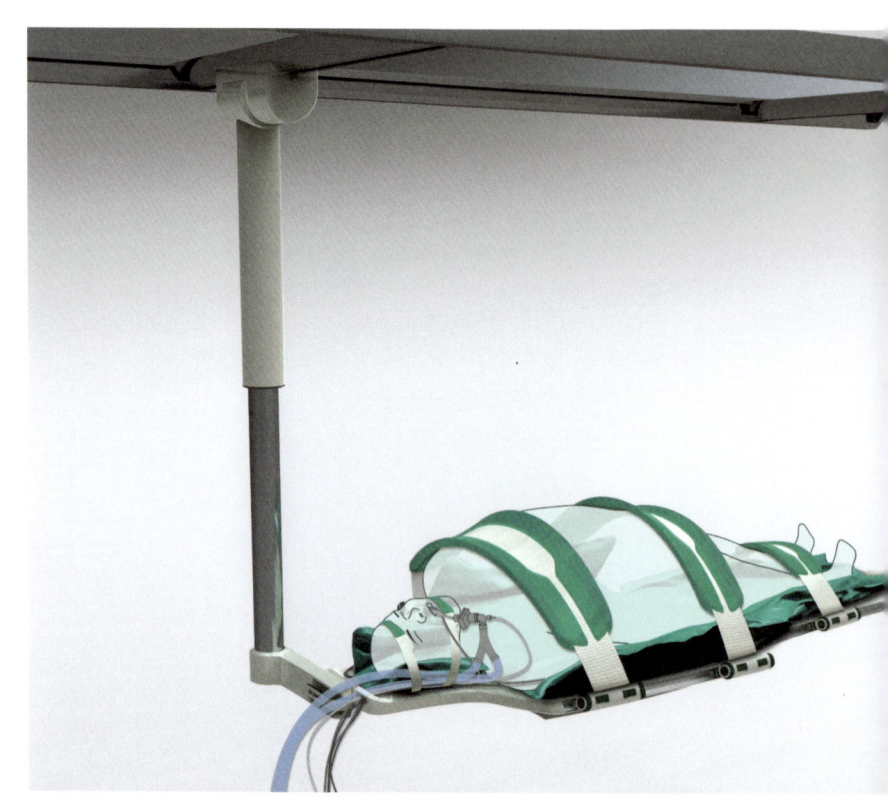

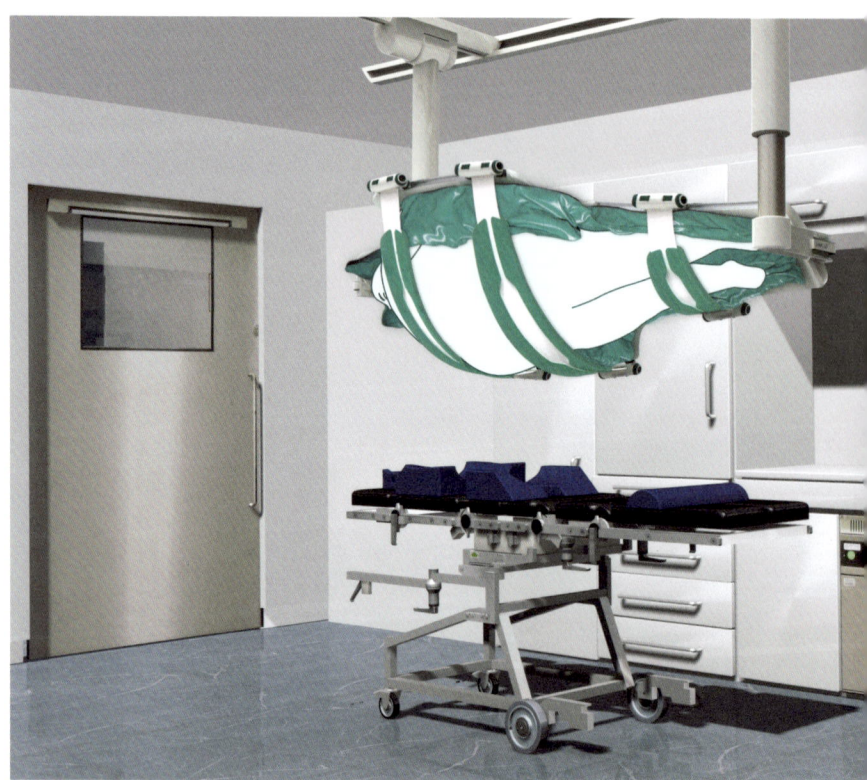

Übergewichtige, krankhaft übergewichtige Patienten in Narkose manuell umzulagern, ist für alle Beteiligten ein riskanter Kraftakt. Vorhandene Hilfsmittel sind wenig hilfreich oder noch riskanter. Abhilfe schafft ein Hebewerk, das im Vorraum des OP-Saals an der Decke montiert wird. Eingebettet in eine Vakuummatratze auf biegesteifer Liege und gehalten von breit gepolsterten Gurten, lässt sich der Patient anheben, drehen und in Bauchlage auf dem OP-Tisch ablegen.

Jury

Aus einem problembeladenen wird ein behutsamer, für Patient und Personal schonender Vorgang ohne Überwachungslücken, der sich zudem mit Zeitgewinn in den Ablauf der OP-Vorbereitungen einfügt. Mit großer Sorgfalt sind für alle Komponenten geeignete Technologien, Materialien und formale Ausprägungen bestimmt. Besonderes Augenmerk liegt auf dem rein mechanischen Gurtaufroller, der in sich so unterschiedliche Aufgaben wie Auf- und Nachspannen, Verlängerung unter Last, verschiebbare Befestigung an der Liege oder Tragegrifffunktion vereint – intelligent gelöst, überzeugend gestaltet.

Manually repositioning overweight or obese patients under narcosis is a strenuous and risky business for all involved. The aids available offer little help, or make the procedure even riskier. Relief is available in the form of a hoist that is fixed to the ceiling in the vestibule to the operating theatre. Embedded in a vacuum mattress on a rigid trolley, and supported by wide, padded belts, the patient can be lifted, turned, and placed in a prone position on the operating table.

Judges panel

A problematic procedure has been turned into a gentle one that reduces stress for patient and medical personnel. The patient is under observation at all times, and when incorporated into preparations for surgery, the procedure can also help save time. When designing the components, great care has been taken to find the right components, materials and formal expression. Special mention should be made of the purely mechanical belt winder, which unites a wide variety of functions: spanning and relaxing, giving under strain, and adjustable attachment to the trolley, as well as functioning as a handle. An intelligent solution, convincingly designed.

DropNet Autonome Trinkwasserversorgung
durch Nebelkollektoren
Mia Seeger Preis 2010   **Anerkennung**

Autonomous drink
using fog collecto
Mia Seeger Prize 2

Es gibt Gegenden, Höhenlagen zwischen 400 und 1200 m, küstennah und trocken, da könnte wenigstens der Nebel eine Trinkwasserquelle sein – wenn es eine Vorrichtung gäbe, die Nebeltröpfchen einzusammeln. Also bedarf es einer Konstruktion, leicht zu transportieren, einfach zu bauen auf verschiedenerlei Grund, unaufwendig zu warten, die ein UV-beständiges Polypropylene-Netz dreidimensional aufspannt. Eine doppelte Sattelfläche hat sich als günstig erwiesen. Mittel des Zeltbaus machen es möglich. Auffangrinnen, Leitungen, Filter und Kanister komplettieren die Anlage.

Jury

Der Entwurf des Nebelkollektors setzt das ursprünglich statische Konzept der kanadischen Organisation FogQuest in ein mobiles, folglich in Leichtbau um. Konsequent ist alle Konstruktion darauf angelegt, dass die Natur mit ihrem ganzen Vermögen – Schwerkraft, Adhäsion und Hydraulik – das Einsammeln autonom besorgt. Spannmechanik und Minimalflächen treten in Gegensatz zur oft kargen Landschaft. Im lebendigen Spiel von Farbe und rhythmisch wiederholten Bögen aber mildert sich die Spannung. Und das Sinnfällige der auffangbereiten Trichterform spielt mit hinein.

In certain arid areas near the coast, at an altitude between 400 and 1200 metres, fog might at least be one source of drinking water – if there were some way of collecting the droplets of fog. What is needed is a structure that is easy to transport, simple to assemble on all types of terrain, and easy to maintain, and which spans a UV-resistant polypropylene net three-dimensionally. A double saddle surface proved to be a convenient solution. It can be achieved using materials from tent construction. Gutters, pipes, filters and canisters round off the system.

Judges panel

The fog collector design adapts the original static concept presented by the Canadian organization FogQuest to make it mobile and light. The entire design is consistently geared to allowing nature to work independently to collect water – using gravity, adhesion, and hydraulics. The spanning mechanism and minimal surfaces contrast with the frequently bare landscape. However, this contrast is mitigated by the lively play of colour and rhythmic repetition of curved forms. A role is also played by the purpose of the funnel form, which is ready to collect water.

Sipurion Mobile Trinkwasseraufbereitungsanlage Mobile drinking wa
Mia Seeger Preis 2010 **Anerkennung** Mia Seeger Prize 2

Nach Katastrophen, wenn trinkbares Wasser nur aus einer verunreinigten Quelle zu gewinnen ist, wäre für ein betroffenes Dorf oder Notlager ein gemeinsam nutzbares Gerät das beste. Die dazu nötigen Komponenten – Pumpmodul, Membran- und Aktivkohlefilter – sind in einem Zylinder angeordnet. Die dreigeteilte Umhüllung ist mit Griffleisten armiert; beim Transport ist sie schützende Verpackung; bei Inbetriebnahme wird sie zum standfesten (fast mannshohen) Stativ. Dann sind nur noch unten die Zu-, oben die Ableitung anzuschließen, und die Wasseraufbereitung kann beginnen.

Jury

Von Menschen, die einem großen Unglück entronnen sind, kann keiner Höchstleistungen an Geduld, Sorgfalt und Geschick im Umgang mit ungewohnter Gerätschaft erwarten. Einfach und von jedermann zu bedienen muss so eine Anlage sein, leicht zu verstehen, zu reinigen und zu warten; Stöße, Fehler und unsanften Transport darf sie nicht übel nehmen – das alles ist bedacht. Und gut, dass sie wie ein trigonometrischer Punkt den lebenswichtigen Ort markiert, wo gereinigtes Wasser zu gewinnen ist.

Following catastrophes, when potable water can only be drawn from a polluted source, an appliance that can be used by the entire community would be the best solution for a village or emergency camp. The components that are needed – pump module, membrane and activated carbon filter – are arranged in a cylinder: the three-part casing is furnished with handles. During transport, the casing protects against damage, when the plant goes into operation it functions as a robust tripod (almost head-high). All that then has to be done is attach the feed pipe at the bottom and the out-pipe at the top, and water treatment can begin.

Judges panel

People who have just escaped a disaster cannot be expected to show extreme patience, care and skill in dealing with unusual appliances. A piece of equipment such as this has to be simple and easy for anyone to use. It has to be easy to understand, clean and maintain, and must be able to take operating errors and rough transport in its stride – all these points have been considered. We also like the way it acts as a kind of orientation point, marking the vital spot where clean water can be obtained.

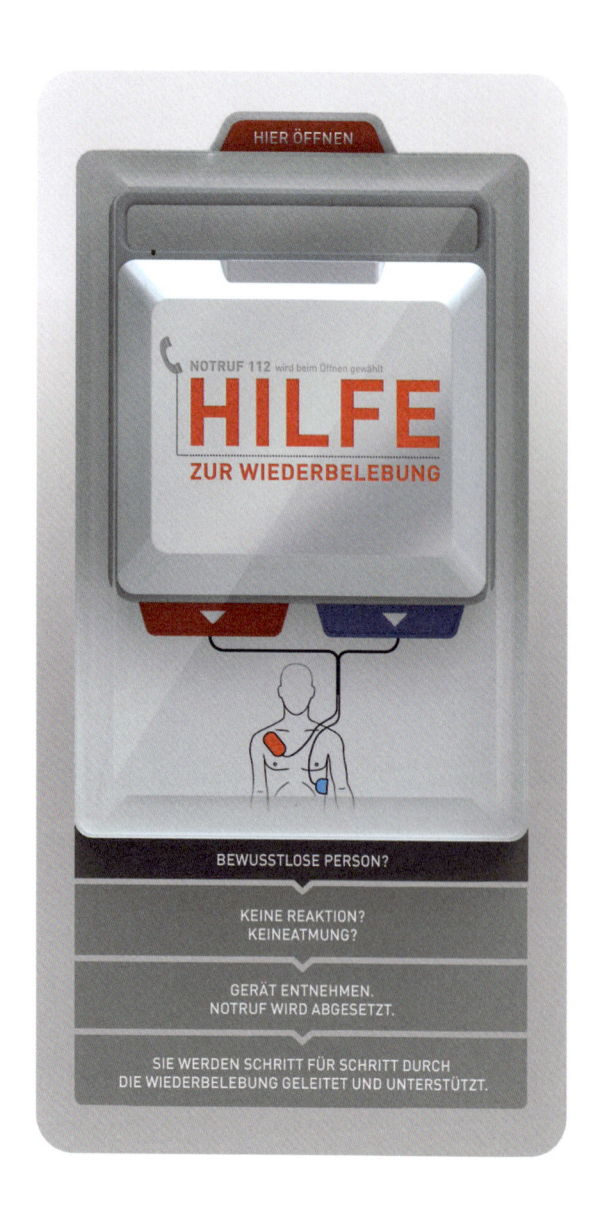

30 / 2 Assist Defibrillator für den öffentlichen Raum
Mia Seeger Preis 2010 **Anerkennung**

Defibrillator for pu
Mia Seeger Prize 2(

Eigentlich geht es darum, ein aus dem Takt geratenes Herz neu zu starten. Sobald der Helfer das Gerät aus der Wandhalterung nimmt, ist er mit einer Leitstelle verbunden, die ihn berät. Danach dann zeigt der Bildschirm ihm Schritt für Schritt, was er zu tun hat: Anlegen der Elektroden, Abgabe des Schocks, ggf. Herzmassage, evtl. Mund-zu-Mund-Beatmung. Immer kommen Informationen und Anweisungen unmittelbar, bevor sie gebraucht werden. So wird der Helfer durchs Notfallprogramm geführt.

Jury

Bevor einer etwas falsch macht, macht er lieber gar nichts – und ruft nur 112. Diese Hemmschwelle schwindet, wenn die Technik unmittelbar nachvollziehbar und die Anleitung unmissverständlich ist. Lenkt jetzt auch noch das Gerät die Aufmerksamkeit des Helfers im richtigen Augenblick auf den richtigen Handgriff, so kann das dem Selbstvertrauen nur gut tun. Unterstützend wirkt, dass äußerste Ruhe, strikte Beschränkung auf das Notwendige und unbedingte Klarheit Form und Funktionen des Defibrillators bestimmen.

The idea behind this apparatus is to restart a heart that has lost its rhythm. As soon as the helper removes the apparatus from its wall mounting, he is connected with a command centre that provides him with advice. The screen then shows him step by step what he has to do: Positioning the electrodes, administering the shock, and if necessary cardiac massage and mouth-to-mouth resuscitation. Information and instructions are always delivered just before they are needed. In this way, the helper is guided through the first-aid procedure.

Judges panel

Rather than do something wrong, people prefer to do nothing – and simply dial 999. This inhibition disappears if the technology is immediately clear and instructions cannot be misunderstood. And if the apparatus shows the helper the right move at exactly the right time, this can only boost his confidence. These qualities are backed up by the form and function of the defibrillator, which is characterized by a calm exterior, strict reduction to the essentials and absolute clarity.

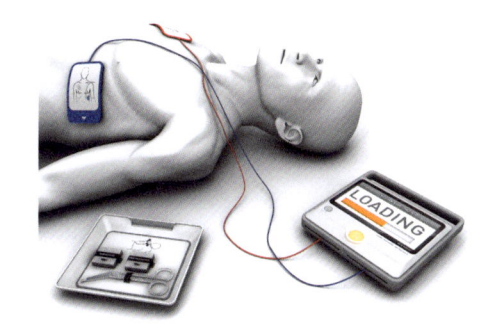

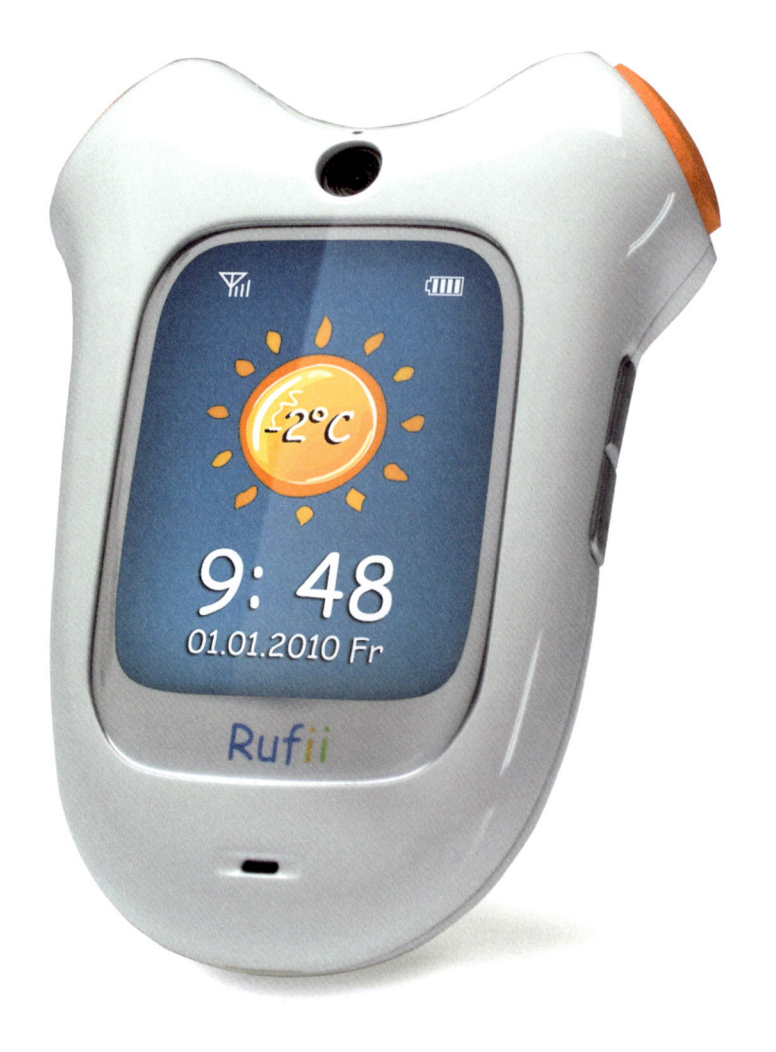

Rufii Notrufsystem für Kinder   Alarm system for c
Mia Seeger Preis 2010 **Anerkennung** Mia Seeger Prize 2

In der Not reicht ein Tastendruck, und Mutter oder Vater melden sich auf dem kleinen Bildschirm. Über GPS wissen sie, wo ihr Kind ist. Auf ihrem Handy sehen sie, was los ist, können mit dem Kind sprechen und sich um Hilfe kümmern. Wenn die Eltern nicht erreichbar sind, geht der Ruf direkt zum Rettungsdienst, der dabei gleich die persönlichen und medizinischen Grunddaten des Kindes übermittelt erhält. Das System, das Hand- und Aufladegerät sowie CD-ROM zur Programmierung des elterlichen Handys umfasst, soll Kindern zwischen 4 bis 10 Jahren zugute kommen.

Jury

Sinnvollerweise ist das Gerät nur für Belange der Gesundheit und Sicherheit des Kindes ausgelegt. Anhand von Szenarios, in denen das Kind als verletzt, von Unfall oder Anfall betroffen, als verirrt, verwirrt oder verängstigt angenommen wird, ist der Kommunikationsbedarf ermittelt und die Funktionsvielfalt entsprechend spezifiziert worden. Zur Bedienung genügen dann wenige markante Tasten an einer eigenständigen Gehäuseform, die sich in die Kinderhand schmiegt.

All a child has to do in an emergency is press a button, and mother or father appear on the small screen. Via GPS, they know where their child is. On their mobile phone, they can see what the matter is, speak with their child, and arrange for help. If the parents cannot be reached, the call is diverted direct to the emergency services, which receive the child's personal and medical data at the same time. The system, comprising a handset and charger, as well as a CD-ROM for programming the parents' mobile phones, is intended for children between 4 and 10.

Judges panel

Sensibly, the device is designed solely for matters of the child's health and safety. On the basis of scenarios which assume a child who is injured, involved in an accident, or suffering from a fit, and is lost, confused or frightened as a result, communication needs have been ascertained and the variety of functions specified accordingly. All that is needed for operation is a few prominent buttons positioned on a self-contained housing which fits neatly into a child's hand.

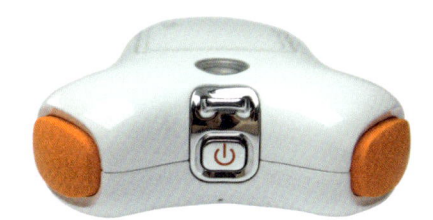

Mia Seeger Stiftung

Mia Seeger Stiftung
c/o Design Center Stuttgart
im Haus der Wirtschaft
Willi-Bleicher-Straße 19
D-70174 Stuttgart
T +49 711 123 2686
F +49 711 123 2771
E-mail tiziana.zamponi@rps.bwl.de

Mia Seeger war die »Grande Dame« des Design. Vor dem Zweiten Weltkrieg wirkte sie an großen Ausstellungsprojekten des Deutschen Werkbundes mit, 1927 z.B. an der Weißenhofsiedlung in Stuttgart. Nach dem Krieg führte sie als Präsidialmitglied zwölf Jahre lang den Rat für Formgebung in Darmstadt. 1986 rief sie die nach ihr benannte Stiftung ins Leben, deren Zweck die Bildung im Bereich Gestaltung ist. Namhafte Sponsoren aus der Wirtschaft haben sich ihren Zielen angeschlossen.

Mit der Absicht, besonders den Nachwuchs im Design zu fördern und ihn dabei zur Auseinandersetzung mit sozialen Fragen herauszufordern, schreibt die Stiftung jährlich den Mia Seeger Preis bundesweit aus, zusätzlich den Mia Seeger Förderpreis zur Unterstützung von Projekten.

Ausführliche Informationen zur Stiftung über Internet www.mia-seeger.de oder bei der Geschäftsstelle.

Mia Seeger (1903 – 1991)

Impressum
Herausgeber: Mia S
Redaktion: Wolfgan
Grafikdesign:
Stapelberg & Fritz,
Ausstellungsgestal
Sandy Tsiris, sitibi
Kommunikation Gm
Fotos: Preisträger
und Ausgezeichnete

Publishing details
Published by: Mia S
Editor: Wolfgang Be
Graphic design:
Stapelberg & Fritz,
Exhibition design:
Sandy Tsiris, sitibi
Kommunikation Gm
Photographs: prize-
and commended en

Stuttgart 2010

Adressen
Hersteller, Designer und Vertriebe

Namenregister

Fotonachweis

Addresses
Manufacturers, designers and distributors

Index of names

Photographs
(acknowledgements)

Adressen
Addresses

Hersteller,
Designer
und Vertriebe

Manufacturers,
designers
and distributors

A

ADS-Tec GmbH
Raiffeisenstraße 14
D-70771 Leinfelden-Echterdingen
T +49 711 45 89 46 00
F +49 711 45 89 49 92
mailbox@ads-tec.de
www.ads-tec.de
Seite / Page 25

Werksdesign / In-house design
Matthias Bohner, Axel Fett
Seite / Page 25

Jan Armgardt Design
Sonnenleite 14
D-86938 Schondorf
T +49 81 92 99 80 17
janarmgardt.design@t-online.de
Seite / Page 99

Auerhahn Bestecke GmbH
Im oberen Tal 9
D-72213 Altensteig
T +49 74 53 9 46 80
F +49 74 53 9 46 8 90
info@auerhahn-bestecke.de
www.auerhahn-bestecke.de
Seite / Page 93

B

Martin Ballendat
Maximilianstraße 15
D-84359 Simbach am Inn
T +49 85 71 60 56 60
F +49 85 71 60 56 66
office@ballendat.de
www.ballendat.de
Seite / Page 187

Bene AG
Schwarzwiesenstraße 3
A-3340 Waidhofen a. d. Ybbs
T +43 74 42 5 00 32 50
F +43 74 42 5 00 99 32 50
peter.handlgruber@bene.com
www.bene.com
Seite / Page 123

Bene Stuttgart GmbH
Breitwiesenstraße 19
D-70565 Stuttgart
T +49 711 3 41 81 80
F +49 711 34 18 18 99
katrin.lorenz@bene.com
www.bene.com
Seite / Page 123

Christoph Böhler
Benno-Strauß-Straße 5
D-90763 Fürth
T +49 911 43 07 04 72
F +49 911 43 07 04 79
c.boehler@boehler-design.de
www.boehler-design.de
Seite / Page 29, 31, 171

Jens Borstelmann
Hansinckstraße 14A
D-30655 Hannover
jens.borstelmann@gmx.de
Seite / Page 93

Robert Bosch Hausgeräte GmbH
Carl-Wery-Straße 34
D-81739 München
T +49 89 45 90 02
F +49 89 45 90 23 47
www.bosch-hausgeräte.com
Seite / Page 79

Werksdesign / In-house design
Thomas Ott, Robert Sachon
Seite / Page 79

Budde Industrie Design GmbH
Dülmener Straße 67
D-48163 Münster
T +49 25 36 33 06 21
F +49 25 36 33 06 33
r.borchers@budde-design.de
www.budde-design.de
Seite / Page 201

C

Antonio Citterio and Partners S.r.l.
Via Cerva 4
I-20122 Milano
T +39 02 7 63 88 01
F +39 02 76 38 80 80
www.antoniocitterioandpartners.it
Seite / Page 63

Constructa
Carl-Wery-S
D-81739 Mü
T +49 89 45
F +49 89 45
ulrike.burck
www.neff.d
www.const
Seite / Page

Werksdesig
Elena Leinn
Gerhard Nü
Seite / Page

Werksdesig
Ralf Groble
Seite / Page

Werksdesig
Thomas Kn
Seite / Page

Werksdesig
Tobias Schr
Seite / Page

Cosentino
Birkerfeld 4
D-83627 W
T +49 80 24
F +49 80 24
info.de@co
www.coser
www.ecoby
Seite / Page

Cosentino
Ctra. Baza
E-04850 Ca
T +34 9 50
F +34 9 50
vtijeras@c
www.coser
www.ecoby
Seite / Page

Crosscreat
Manuel Ayd
Lameystra
D-75173 Pf
T +49 72 31
F +49 72 31
aydt@cros
www.cross
Seite / Page

Cullmann P
Waldstraße
D-90579 La
T +49 91 02
F +49 91 02
j.sonntag@
www.cullm
Seite / Pag

D

Daimler AG
HPC X 800
D-71063 Sindelfingen
T +49 70 31 9 04 42 34
F +49 70 31 90 36 99
hansharald.hanson@daimler.com
www.daimler.com
Seite / Page 203

Matthias Demacker
Richelstraße 4
D-80634 München
T +49 89 13 95 87 93
F +49 89 13 95 87 93
md@demacker-design.de
www.demacker-design.de
Seite / Page 101

Diakonisches Werk Baden e.V.
Projekt Loony
Vorholzstraße 3
D-76137 Karlsruhe
T +49 7 21 9 34 92 70
F +49 7 21 93 49 62 70
kl@diakonie-baden.de
www.diakonie-baden.de
Seite / Page 125

Ding 3000
Carsten Schelling, Sven Rudolph,
Ralf Webermann
Ratswiese 18
D-30453 Hannover
T +49 5 11 3 53 93 76
F +49 5 11 3 53 93 76
info@ding3000.com
www.ding3000.com
Seite / Page 155

DNS Designteam Neth Schäflein
Erkelenzdamm 59, Portal 2a
D-10999 Berlin
T +49 30 78 71 33 88
F +49 30 78 71 33 89
berlin@dns-design.de
www.dns-design.de
Seite / Page 151

Dogtor Mia
Im Öschle 9
D-89134 Blaustein
T +49 73 04 92 88 88
F +49 73 04 92 88 81
dogtor-mia@email.de
www.dogtor-mia.de
Seite / Page 153

Werksdesign / In-house design
Malou Huberle
Seite / Page 153

Dovo
Stahlwaren Bracht GmbH & Co. KG
Böcklinstraße 10
D-42719 Solingen
T +49 2 12 23 00 10
F +49 2 12 2 30 01 42
www.dovo.com
Seite / Page 57

Dyson GmbH
Lichtstraße 43b
D-50825 Köln
T +49 2 21 50 60 00
F +49 2 21 50 60 01 90
infoline@dyson.de
www.dyson.de
Seite / Page 141

Dyson Ltd.
James Dyson und RDD Team
Tetbury Hill
Malmesbury, Wiltshire SN 16 ORP UK
T +44 16 66 82 7 20 00
askdyson@dyson.co.uk
www.dyson.co.uk
Seite / Page 141

E

Eisfink Max Maier GmbH & Co. KG
Rheinlandstraße 10
D-71636 Ludwigsburg
T +49 71 41 47 90
F +49 71 41 47 92 99
ralph.martin@eisfink.de
www.eisfink.de
Seite / Page 75

Emporia Telecom
Industriezeile 36
A-4020 Linz
T +43 7 32 7 77 71 70
F +43 7 32 7 77 71 78
marketing@emporia.at
www.emporia.at
Seite / Page 49

EOOS Design GmbH
Zelinkagasse 2/6
A-1010 Wien
T +43 1 4 05 39 87
F +43 1 4 05 39 87 80
design@eoos.com
www.eoos.com
Seite / Page 103, 105

Eva Solo A/S
Malov Teknikerby 18-20
DK-2760 Måløv
T +45 36 73 20 60
F +45 36 70 74 11
mail@evadenmark.com
www.evadenmark.com
www.evasolo.com
Seite / Page 91, 157

F

Festo AG & Co. KG
Ruiter Straße 82
D-73734 Esslingen
T +49 7 11 34 70
www.festo.com
Seite / Page 41

Werksdesign / In-house design
Karoline von Häfen
Seite / Page 41

Fortis Peter Peter Team GmbH
Wellweg 98
D-31157 Sarstedt
T +49 50 66 90 21 80
F +49 50 66 9 02 18 29
info@de.fortis-watches.com
www.fortis-watches.com
Seite / Page 149

Fortis Uhren AG
Lindenstraße 45
CH-2540 Grenchen
T +41 32 6 53 33 61
F +41 32 6 52 59 42
l.peter@fortis-watches.com
www.fortis-watches.com
Seite / Page 149

G

Gallus Druckmaschinen GmbH
Steinbruchstraße 5
D-35428 Langgöns-Oberkleen
T +49 64 47 92 50
F +49 64 47 60 64
www.gallus-group.com
Seite / Page 27

Gallus Ferd. Rüesch AG
Harzbüchelstraße 34
CH-9016 St. Gallen
T +41 71 2 42 83 21
F +41 71 2 42 89 89
www.gallus-group.com
Seite / Page 27

H

HAN Bürogeräte GmbH & Co. KG
Daimlerstraße 2
D-32051 Herford
T +49 52 21 93 37 18
F +49 52 21 93 37 50
simon@han-online.com
www.han-online.com
Seite / Page 143

Hansgrohe AG
Auestraße 5-9
D-77761 Schiltach
T +49 78 36 5 10
F +49 78 36 51 13 00
info@hansgrohe.de
www.hansgrohe.de
Seite / Page 63

Hansgrohe Deutschland Vertriebs GmbH
Auestraße 5-9
D-77761 Schiltach
T +49 78 36 5 10
F +49 78 36 51 13 00
info@hansgrohe.de
www.hansgrohe.de
Seite / Page 63

Hauraton GmbH & Co. KG
Werkstraße 13
D-76437 Rastatt
T +49 72 22 95 81 99
F +49 72 22 95 82 81 99
bernd.schiller@hauraton.com
www.hauraton.com
Seite / Page 195

Vertrieb / Distributor
F +49 72 22 95 81 10
Seite / Page 195

Helios Ventilatoren
Lupfenstraße 8
D-78056 Villingen-Schwenningen
T +49 77 20 60 60
F +49 77 20 60 61 66
info@heliosventilatoren.de
www.heliosventilatoren.de
Seite / Page 193

Herman Miller Ltd.
Methuen Park
Chippenham, Wiltshire SN14 0GF UK
T +44 12 49 70 74 00
chloe_richardson@hermanmiller.com
www.hermanmiller.com
Seite / Page 131

Herman Miller Ltd. Deutschland
Niederlassung Deutschland
Heßlingsweg 71
D-44309 Dortmund
T +49 80 31 3 52 23 68
F +49 80 31 3 52 23 76
kristin_stelling@hermanmiller.com
www.hermanmiller.com
Seite / Page 131

HG Merz Architekten Museumsgestalter
Ostendstraße 110
D-70188 Stuttgart
T +49 7 11 7 07 12 80
F +49 7 11 70 71 28 60
stuttgart@hgmerz.com
www.hgmerz.com
Seite / Page 199

Imke Höhler
Lotzestraße 38
D-37083 Göttingen
M +31 6 27 59 21 11
imke@muthesius.de
Seite / Page 215

Hoffmann GmbH
Haberlandstraße 55
D-81241 München
T +49 89 8 39 12 92
F +49 89 83 91 52 92
t.walther@hoffmann-group.com
www.hoffmann-group.com
Seite / Page 31

Vertrieb / Distributor:
T +49 89 8 39 13 13
F +49 89 8 39 13 13
c.freitag@hoffmann-group.com
Seite / Page 31

Humanelektronik GmbH
Binger Straße 52
D-67549 Worms
T +49 62 41 95 54 89
F +49 62 41 95 54 87
info@humanelektronik.de
www.humanelektronik.de
Seite / Page 53

I

Boris Innecken
Hoffmannstraße 28
D-64285 Darmstadt
M +49 176 23 94 73 69
forg@gmx.net
Seite / Page 211

IPDD GmbH & Co. KG
Calwer Straße 11
D-70173 Stuttgart
T +49 7 11 3 26 54 60
F +49 7 11 3 26 54 61
info@ipdd.com
www.ipdd.com
Seite / Page 21

J

jp designs
Julia Pfizen
Reeßweg 21
D-70565 Stu
T +49 7 11 7
julia.pfizenr
Seite / Page

Just Mobile
Fronhoferst
D-12165 Be
T +49 30 85
F +49 30 2 0
nils@just-m
www.just-m
Seite / Page

Werksdesig
Erich Huang
Seite / Page

K

Alfred Kärc
Alfred-Kärc
D-71364 Wir
T +49 71 95
F +49 71 95
m.meyer@c
www.kaerch
Seite / Page

W. F. Kaiser
Werner-von
D-65582 Die
T +49 64 32
sonja.hanke
www.kaiser
Seite / Page

Keilbach de
Friedhofstra
D-74677 Dö
T +49 79 37
F +49 79 37
mail@keilba
www.keilba
Seite / Page

Werksdesig
Peter Keilba
Seite / Page

Kettnaker G
Möbel Manu
Bussenstra
D-88525 Dü
T +49 73 71
F +49 73 71
info@kettna
www.kettna
Seite / Page

Sonja Kind
Reiner-Hütten-Straße 34
D-51519 Odenthal
M +49 1 76 21 23 15 85
sonjakind@web.de
Seite / Page 213

KLS Martin GmbH & Co. KG
Am Gansacker 1B
D-79224 Umkirch
T +49 74 61 70 60
F +49 74 61 70 61 93
info@klsmartin.com
www.klsmartin.com
Seite / Page 51

Walter Knoll AG & Co. KG
Bahnhofstraße 25
D-71083 Herrenberg
T +49 70 32 20 80
F +49 70 32 20 82 50
info@walterknoll.de
www.walterknoll.de
Seite / Page 103, 105

L
Leuwico GmbH & Co. KG
Hauptstraße 2-4
D-96484 Wiesenfeld
T +49 95 66 8 82 04
F +49 95 66 8 81 14
info@leuwico.com
www.leuwico.com
Seite / Page 135

Werksdesign / In-house design
Michael Wirsing
T +49 95 66 8 81 70
F +49 95 66 8 81 70
Seite / Page 135

Liebherr-Werk Biberach GmbH
Hans-Liebherr-Straße 45
D-88400 Biberach
T +49 73 51 41 23 26
F +49 73 51 41 22 23
info.lbc@liebherr.com
www.liebherr.com
Seite / Page 21

Loony-Design operated by Integra e.V.
Josef-Reiert-Straße 24
D-69190 Walldorf
T +49 62 27 38 39 69 01
F +49 62 27 3 83 96 99
schmidt@loony-design.de
www.loony-design.de
Seite / Page 125

M
Magazin GmbH
Lautenschlagerstraße 16
D-70173 Stuttgart
T +49 7 11 22 87 00
F +49 7 11 2 28 70 33
stuttgart@magazin.com
www.magazin.com
Seite / Page 117

Mango Design
Nussbergstraße 17
D-38102 Braunschweig
T +49 5 31 34 57 44
F +49 5 31 34 58 97
marcus@mangodesign.de
www.mangodesign.de
Seite / Page 49

Gebrüder Martin GmbH & Co. KG
Ludwigstalerstraße 132
D-78501 Tuttlingen
T +49 74 61 70 60
F +49 74 61 70 61 93
info@klsmartin.com
www.klsmartin.com
Seite / Page 51

Mercedes-Benz AG
www.mercedes-benz.de
Seite / Page 203

Merida & Centurion Germany GmbH
Blumenstraße 49-51
D-71106 Magstadt
T +49 71 59 9 45 96 00
F +49 71 59 9 45 95 00
simon.oppold@merida-centurion.com
www.centurion.de
Seite / Page 181

Meyer-Hayoz Design Engineering Group
Zollernstraße 26
D-78462 Konstanz
T +49 75 31 9 09 30
F +49 75 31 90 93 90
info.de@meyer-hayoz.com
www.meyer-hayoz.com
Seite / Page 27, 55

Molinari S.r.l.
Zona Ind. Loc. VAT
I-38079 Tione di Trento
T +39 04 65 32 28 37
F +39 04 65 32 28 47
info@molinarisrl.com
www.molinarisrl.com
Seite / Page 107

Monoqool
Kratbjeg 212
DK-3400 Fredensborg
T +45 31 50 44 94
F +45 28 17 43 43
nko@monoqool.com
www.monoqool.com
Seite / Page 147

MTD Products AG
Geschäftsbereich Wolf-Garten
Industriestraße 83-85
D-57518 Betzdorf
T +49 27 41 28 10
F +49 27 41 28 12 10
info@wolf-garten.com
www.wolf-garten.com
Seite / Page 169

N
Nedo GmbH & Co. KG
Hochgerichtsstraße 39/43
D-72280 Dornstetten
T +49 74 43 2 40 10
F +49 74 43 24 01 45
info@nedo.com
www.nedo.com
Seite / Page 35, 37

Nimbus Group GmbH
Sieglestraße 41
D-70469 Stuttgart
T +49 7 11 63 30 14 30
F +49 7 11 63 30 14 14
info@nimbus-group.com
www.nimbus-group.com
Seite / Page 161

Nishimura JIG
4-11-32, Kitayasue
Kanazawa 920-00 22, Japan
T +81 7 62 23 27 27
F +81 7 62 65 53 36
Seite / Page 39

O
Ongo® GmbH
Klopstockstraße 51
D-70193 Stuttgart
T +49 7 11 1 20 03 98
F +49 7 11 1 20 04 45
e.lenz@ongo.eu
www.ongo.eu
Seite / Page 133

Werksdesign / In-house design
Eberhard Lenz
Seite / Page 133

P
Paidi Möbel GmbH
Hauptstraße 87
D-97840 Hafenlohr
T +49 93 91 50 10
F +49 93 91 50 11 15
info@paidi.de
www.paidi.de
Seite / Page 187

PearsonLloyd
117 Drysdale Street
London N1 6ND UK
T +44 20 70 33 44 40
F +44 20 70 33 44 40
tom.lloyd@pearsonlloyd.com
www.pearsonlloyd.com
Seite / Page 123, 129

Performa®
Möbel und Design GmbH
Dieselstraße 9
D-74076 Heilbronn
T +49 71 31 3 90 34 35
F +49 71 31 3 90 34 36
welcome@performa.de
www.performa.de
Seite / Page 109

Phoenix Design GmbH & Co. KG
Kölner Straße 16
D-70376 Stuttgart
T +49 7 11 9 55 97 60
F +49 7 11 95 59 76 99
info@phoenixdesign.com
www.phoenixdesign.com
Seite / Page 191

Piltz Design
Henrich Piltz
Himmelreichallee 51
D-48149 Münster
T +49 2 51 9 82 97 07
M +49 1 71 6 90 78 80
info@piltz-design.de
www.piltz-design.de
Seite / Page 143

Michael Plewka
Helgoländer Ufer 6
D-10557 Berlin
T +49 30 39 49 39 12
F +49 30 39 49 46 48
michaelplewka@t-online.de
Seite / Page 107

R
Thomas Radschuweit Handelsagentur
Elsdorfergasse 27
D-51143 Köln
T +49 1 77 3 55 73 23
tomradschuweit@aol.com
Seite / Page 147

Hartmut Räder Wohnzubehör GmbH & Co.KG
Kornharpener Straße 126
D-44791 Bochum
T +49 2 34 95 98 70
F +49 2 34 59 45 19
info@raeder.de
www.raeder.de
Seite / Page 95, 145

Werksdesign / In-house design
Tobias Langner, Sarah Baumann
Seite / Page 95, 145

Recaro Aircraft Seating GmbH
Daimlerstraße 21
D-74523 Schwäbisch Hall
T +49 7 91 5 03 70 00
F +49 7 91 5 03 71 63
info@recaro-as.com
www.recaro-as.com
Seite / Page 207

Reform Design Produkt
Kotulla & Wagner & Winkler GbR
Industriestraße 25
D-70565 Stuttgart
T +49 7 11 7 82 95 35 24
F +49 7 11 7 82 95 35 25
christoph.winkler@reform-design.de
www.reform-design.de
Seite / Page 195

Ricosta Schuhfabriken GmbH
Dürrheimerstraße 43
D-78166 Donaueschingen
T +49 7 71 80 51 20
F +49 7 71 8 05 41 80
kai.moewes@ricosta.de
www.ricosta.de
Seite / Page 185

Anne Rieck Produktdesign
35 Rue Francastel
F-84740 Velleron
T +33 4 90 90 99 72
a.rieck@annerieck-design.com
www.annerieck-design.com
Seite / Page 145

Rohde & Grahl GmbH
Voigtei 84
D-31595 Steyerberg
T +49 57 69 70
F +49 57 69 3 33
info@rohde-grahl.de
www.rohde-grahl.com
Seite / Page 127

S
Sattler Objektlicht
Untere Weingartenstraße 2
D-73092 Heiningen
T +49 71 61 9 20 19 30
F +49 71 61 92 01 93 40
info@sattler-objektlicht.de
www.sattler-objektlicht.de
Seite / Page 165

Werksdesign / In-house design
Ulrich Sattler
Seite / Page 165

Scala Desig
Technische
Wolf-Hirth-
D-71034 Bö
T +49 70 31
F +49 70 31
scala@sca
www.scala
Seite / Page

Schell Gmb
Raiffeisens
D-57462 Ol
T +49 27 61
F +49 27 61
klaus.held@
www.schel
Seite / Page

Scherfdes
Dillenburge
D-51105 Kö
T +49 2 21
F +49 2 21
scherf@sc
www.scher
Seite / Page

Udo Schill
Herdweg 10
D-70193 St
T +49 7 11
us@udosch
www.udosc
Seite / Page

Georg Schl
Kapellenwe
D-88525 Dü
T +49 73 71
F +49 73 71
info@schle
www.schle
Seite / Page

Stephan Sc
Urbanstraß
D-70190 St
T +49 1 73
F +49 7 11
schmidt@k
www.kleine
Seite / Page

Schmidt W
und Komm
Albtalstraß
D-79837 St
T +49 76 72
emil.wasm
www.aebi-
Seite / Page

Vertrieb / D
T +49 76 72
thomas.po
Seite / Page

Alexander Schmied
Dreimühlenstraße 13
D-80469 München
M +49 172 8 13 07 24
alex_schmied@gmx.de
www.siebenpunkt-design.de
Seite / Page 117

Klaus Schneider Produktdesign
Daimlerstraße 22
D-70736 Fellbach-Oeffingen
T +49 7 11 51 30 03
F +49 7 11 51 66 95
schneider@der-ideenschreiner.de
www.moebelschreiner.de
Seite / Page 113

Seefelder Möbelwerkstätten
Bahnhofstraße 17
D-82229 Seefeld
T +49 81 52 9 90 00
F +49 81 52 99 00 99
gabi.meyer-bruehl@seefelder.com
www.seefelder.com
Seite / Page 99, 101

Sick AG
Erwin-Sick-Straße 1
D-79183 Waldkirch
T +49 76 81 20 20
F +49 76 81 2 02 39 26
info@sick.de
www.sick.de
Seite / Page 33

Sick Vertriebs GmbH
Willstätterstraße 30
D-40549 Düsseldorf
T +49 2 11 5 30 13 01
F +49 2 11 5 36 13 02
kundenservice@sick.de
www.sick.de
Seite / Page 33

Ute Sickinger
Greifenhagener Straße 39
D-10437 Berlin
M +49 1 79 1 26 53 02
mail@utesi.de
www.utesickinger.de
Seite / Page 87

Signce Design GmbH
Oskar-Schlemmer-Straße 15
D-80807 München
T +49 89 3 66 67 90
F +49 89 36 66 79 10
info@signce.eu
www.signce.eu
Seite / Page 177

Konstantin Slawinski
Housewarming Objects
Wilhelm-Mauser-Straße 49c
D-50827 Köln
T +49 2 21 28 55 39 00
F +49 2 21 28 55 39 09
tk@konstantinslawinski.com
www.konstantinslawinski.com
Seite / Page 155

Slogdesign
Jürgen Hinderhofer
Waldseer Straße 13
D-88400 Biberach
T +49 73 51 1 79 33
F +49 73 51 1 79 37
hinderhofer@slogdesign.de
www.slogdesign.de
Seite / Page 181

Spek Design GbR
Schopenhauerstraße 39
D-70565 Stuttgart
T +49 7 11 74 54 31 30
F +49 7 11 74 54 31 40
info@spek-design.de
www.spek-design.de
Seite / Page 53

Stadtnomaden®
Schreinerei Krapf
Andernacherweg 8
D-70376 Stuttgart
T +49 7 11 9 35 29 18
F +49 7 11 9 35 29 19
info@stadtnomaden.com
www.stadtnomaden.com
Seite / Page 81

Werksdesign / In-house design
Oliver Krapf, Linda Altmann
Seite / Page 81

Steelcase S.A.
Z. I. rue A. Lumière
F-57400 Sarrebourg
pbraeu@steelcase.com
www.steelcase.fr
Seite / Page 129

Werksdesign / In-house design
Steelcase Design Studio
Seite / Page 129

Steelcase Werndl AG
Georg-Aicher-Straße 7
D-83026 Rosenheim
T +49 80 31 40 55 61
M +49 15 20 92 22 87 13
F +49 80 31 40 53 30
pbraeu@steelcase.com
www.steelcase.de
Seite / Page 129

Steng Licht AG
Hedelfinger Straße 103
D-70327 Stuttgart
T +49 7 11 23 88 00
F +49 7 11 2 38 80 88
mail@steng.de
www.steng.de
Seite / Page 163

Werksdesign / In-house design
Peter & Andreas Steng
andreas.steng@steng.de
Seite / Page 163

Stotz-Design.com GmbH & Co. KG
Besenbruchstraße 6
D-42285 Wuppertal
T +49 2 02 30 06 67
F +49 2 02 30 06 68
info@stotz-design.com
www.stotz-design.com
Seite / Page 57

Henning Strobel
Dietramszeller Straße 29
D-83624 Otterfing
M +49 1 76 24 25 36 27
henning.strobel@gmx.net
Seite / Page 217

Studio 7.5
Nithackstraße 7
D-10585 Berlin
T +49 30 3 41 70 34
F +49 30 3 42 70 63
contact@seven5.com
www.seven5.com
Seite / Page 131

SVG Medizinsysteme GmbH & Co. KG
Schlattstraße 59
D-75443 Ötisheim
T +49 7 41 9 61 50
F +49 7 41 96 15 15
info@premion-line.de
www.premion-line.de
Seite / Page 55

Synapsis Design GmbH
Teckstraße 56
D-70190 Stuttgart
T +49 7 11 2 62 11 31
F +49 7 11 2 62 26 70
mail@synapsisdesign.com
www.synapsisdesign.com
Seite / Page 33, 51

Piotr Szpryngwald
Sophienblatt 48 A
D-24114 Kiel
M +49 1 76 35 52 09 35
piotr.s@gmx.de
Seite / Page 219

T
Hadi Teherani AG
Am Kaiserkai 26
D-20457 Hamburg
T +49 40 44 40 54 41
F +49 40 44 40 54 43
sj@haditeherani.de
www.haditeherani.de
Seite / Page 137

TOKII
Vordere Schmiedgasse 36-1
D-73525 Schwäbisch Gmünd
T +49 71 71 87 71 84
F +49 71 71 87 71 85
andreas.hess@white-id.com
www.tokii.de
Seite / Page 179

Tools Design
Henrik Holbæk, Claus Jensen
Rentemestervej 23 A
DK-2400 Kopenhagen NV
T +45 22 44 41 14
F +45 38 19 41 13
email@toolsdesign.dk
www.toolsdesign.dk
Seite / Page 91, 147, 157

Tupperware Belgium N. V.
Wijngaardveld 17
B-9300 Aalst
T +32 53 72 72 11
F +32 53 72 72 10
www.tupperware.com
Seite / Page 89

Werksdesign / In-house design
Tupperware
Worldwide Design & Engineering Team
Seite / Page 89

Tupperware Deutschland GmbH
Praunheimer Landstraße 70
D-60488 Frankfurt
T +49 69 76 80 20
F +49 69 76 80 22 99
marcscheifele@tupperware.de
www.tupperware.de
Seite / Page 89

U
United Navigation GmbH
Marco-Polo-Straße 1
D-73760 Ostfildern
T +49 7 11 4 50 20
F +49 7 11 4 50 23 20
m.kienle@united-navigation.com
www.united-navigation.com
Seite / Page 45

V
Vaude Sport
Vaudestraße
D-88069 Tett
T +49 75 42
F +49 75 42
info@vaude.
www.vaude.
Seite / Page

Werksdesign
Matthias Kim
Seite / Page

Werksdesign
Philipp Zieglｅ
Seite / Page

Viessmann W
Viessmanns
D-35108 Alle
T +49 64 52
F +49 64 52
scgm@viess
www.viessm
Seite / Page

Vistapark G
Philipp Meye
Bärenstraße
D-42117 Wu
T +49 2 02 2
F +49 2 02 2
office@vista
www.vistapa
Seite / Page

Volkswagen
Berliner Ring
D-38440 Wo
T +49 53 61
F +49 53 61
ruediger.folt
www.volksw
Seite / Page

Volkswagen
Volkswagen
Berliner Ring
D-38440 Wo
T +49 53 61
F +49 53 61
ruediger.folt
Seite / Page

Vorwerk & Co. Teppichwerke
Kuhlmannstraße 11
D-31785 Hameln
T +49 51 51 10 35 26
F +49 51 51 1 03 65 26
stefan.peetz@vorwerk-teppich.de
www.vorwerk-teppich.de
Seite / Page 137

Vottelerdesign
Matthias Votteler
Hohes Feld 27
D-30966 Hemmingen
T +49 1 77 8 34 85 89
F +49 51 01 92 53 97
matthias@vottelerdesign.de
www.vottelerdesign.de
Seite / Page 127

W
Wagner System GmbH
Tullastraße 19
D-77933 Lahr
T +49 78 21 9 47 70
F +49 78 21 9 47 76 0
info@wagner-system.de
www.wagner-system.de
Seite / Page 119

Werksdesign / In-house design
Roland Wagner
Seite / Page 119

Christina Weskott
Horbeller Straße 43
D-50858 Köln
T +49 22 34 27 10 60
F +49 22 34 27 10 66
atelier@christina-weskott.de
www.rheuma-ringe.de
Seite / Page 59

White-ID
Vordere Schmiedgasse 36-1
D-73525 Schwäbisch Gmünd
T +49 71 71 87 71 84
F +49 71 71 87 71 85
andreas.hess@white-id.com
www.white-id.de
Seite / Page 179

Windmühlenmesser
Robert Herder GmbH & Co. KG
Ellerstraße 16
D-42697 Solingen
T +49 2 12 26 70 50
F +49 2 12 7 53 27
info@windmuehlenmesser.de
www.windmuehlenmesser.de
Seite / Page 85

Werksdesign / In-house design
Giselheid Herder-Scholz,
Tomoyuki Takada
Seite / Page 85

WK Wohnen GmbH & Co.
Möbel Marketing KG
Im Gefierth 9a
D-63303 Dreieich
T +49 61 03 39 16 47
F +49 61 03 39 16 40
s.beikert@wkwohnen-de
www.wkwohnen.de
Seite / Page 107

WMF AG
Eberhardstraße
D-73312 Geislingen
T +49 73 31 25 88 80
F +49 73 31 25 89 51
info@wmf.de
www.wmf.de
Seite / Page 177

Vertrieb / Distributor
T +49 73 31 2 51
F +49 73 31 4 53 87
Seite / Page 177

Y
yellow design / yellow circle
Mühlstraße 7a
D-75172 Pforzheim
T +49 72 31 45 76 41 40
F +49 72 31 46 45 94
schlag@yellowdesign.com
www.yellowdesign.com
Seite / Page 45

Zhenwei You
c/o Wenqing Wei
Max-Horkheimer-Straße 10 / App. 3407
D-42119 Wuppertal
ivoyou@gmail.com
Seite / Page 221

Z
Carl Zeiss NTS GmbH
Carl-Zeiss-Straße 56
D-73447 Oberkochen
T +49 73 64 20 96 88
m.schweitzer@smt.zeiss.com
www.smt.zeiss.com
Seite / Page 29

Zweibrüder Optoelectronics GmbH
Kronenstraße 5-7
D-42699 Solingen
T +49 2 12 5 94 80
F +49 2 12 5 94 82 00
info@zweibrueder.com
www.zweibrueder.com
Seite / Page 167

Werksdesign / In-house design
Andre Kunzendorf, Erich Buhl, Xutao
Seite / Page 167

Namenregister
Index of names

Die fettgedruckten Seitenzahlen verweisen auf den Katalogteil, die mager gedruckten führen zum Adressenverzeichnis.

Page numbers in bold type refer to the catalogue section, while those in lightface type refer to the index of addresses.

A
ADS-Tec 25, 224
Altmann, Linda 81, 229
→ Stadtnomaden®
Armgardt, Jan 99, 224
Auerhahn 93, 224
Aydt, Manuel 173, 224
→ Crosscreative

B
Ballendat, Martin 187, 224
Baumann, Sarah 95, 228
→ Räder
Bene 123, 224
Bene Stuttgart 123, 224
Böhler, Christoph 29, 31 171, 224
Bohner, Matthias 25, 224
→ ADS-Tec
Borstelmann, Jens 93, 224
Bosch Hausgeräte 79, 224
Budde 201, 224
Buhl, Erich 167, 231
→ Zweibrüder

C
Citterio, Antonio 63, 224
Constructa-Neff 69, 71, 73, 77, 224
Cosentino Deutschland 197, 224
Cosentino SA 197, 224
Crosscreative 173, 224
Cullmann 173, 224

D
Daimler 203, 225
Demacker, Matthias 101, 225
Diakonisches Werk Baden 125, 225
Ding 3000 155, 225
DNS Designteam 151, 225
Dogtor Mia 153, 225
Dovo 57, 225
Dyson Deutschland 141, 225
Dyson Ltd. 141, 225
Dyson, James 141, 225

E
Eisfink Max Maier 75, 225
Emporia Telecom 49, 225
EOOS 103, 105, 225
Eva Solo 91, 157, 225

F
Festo 41, 225
Fett, Axel 25, 224
→ ADS-Tec
Fortis Peter Peter Team 149, 225
Fortis Uhren 149, 225

G
Gallus Druckmaschinen 27, 225
Gallus Ferd. Rüesch 27, 225
Grobleben, Ralf 71, 224
→ Constructa-Neff
Gustafsson, Nils 47, 226
→ Just Mobile

H
Häfen, Karoline von 41, 225
→ Festo
HAN Bürogeräte 143, 226
Hansgrohe 63, 226
Hansgrohe Deutschland Vertrieb 63, 226
Hauraton 195, 226
Helios Ventilatoren 193, 226
Herder-Scholz, Giselheid 85, 231
→ Windmühlenmesser
Herman Miller 131, 226
Herman Miller Deutschland 131, 226
HG Merz 199, 226
Hinderhofer, Jürgen 181, 229
→ Slogdesign
Höhler, Imke 215, 226
Hoffmann 31, 226
Holbæk, Henrik 91, 147, 157, 230
→ Tools Design
Huang, Erich 47, 226
→ Just Mobile
Huberle, Malou 153, 225
→ Dogtor Mia
Humanelektronik 53, 226

I
Innecken, B
Integra e.V.
→ Loony-De
IPDD 21, 22

J
Jensen, Cla
→ Tools Des
jp designs
Just Mobile

K
Kärcher 17
Kaiser 87, 2
Kind, Sonja
Keilbach 1
Keilbach, P
→ Keilbach
Kettnaker
Kimmerle,
→ Vaude
KLS Martin
Knöller, The
→ Construc
Knoll 103,
Krapf, Olive
→ Stadtnom
Kunzendorf
→ Zweibrüd

L
Langner, To
→ Räder
Leinmüller,
→ Construc
Lenz, Eberh
→ Ongo®
Leuwico 13
Liebherr 2
Loony-Des

M
Magazin 1
Mango Des
Martin 51,
Mercedes-
Merida & C
Meyer-Hay
Meyer, Phil
Molinari 10
Monoqool
MTD Produ

N
Nedo 35, 37, 227
Nimbus 161, 227
Nishimura 39, 227
Nüssler, Gerhard 69, 71, 73, 224
→ Constructa-Neff

O
Ongo® 133, 227
Ott, Thomas 79, 224
→ Bosch Hausgeräte

P
Paidi 187, 227
PearsonLloyd 123, 129, 228
Performa® 109, 228
Pfizenmayer, Julia 115, 226
→ jp designs
Phoenix Design 191, 228
Piltz Design 143, 228
Piltz, Henrich 143, 228
→ Piltz Design
Plewka, Michael 107, 228

R
Radschuweit, Thomas 147, 228
Räder 95, 145, 228
RDD Team 141, 225
→ Dyson
Recaro Aircraft Seating 207, 228
Reform Design Produkt 195, 228
Ricosta 185, 228
Rieck, Anne 145, 228
Rohde & Grahl 127, 228
Rudolph, Sven 155, 225
→ Ding 3000

S
Sachon, Robert 79, 224
→ Bosch Hausgeräte
Sattler Objektlicht 165, 228
Sattler, Ulrich 165, 228
Scala Design 35, 37, 29, 228
Schell 65, 228
Schelling, Carsten 155, 225
→ Ding 3000
Scherfdesign 185, 228
Schill, Udo 109, 228
Schlegel 23, 228
Schmidt, Stephan 125, 228
Schmidt, Tobias 77, 224
Schmidt Winterdienst und Kommunaltechnik 201, 228
Schmied, Alexander 117, 229
Schneider, Klaus 113, 229
Schreinerei Krapf 81, 229
→ Stadtnomaden®
Seefelder Möbelwerkstätten 99, 101, 229
Sick 33, 229
Sick Vertrieb 33, 229
Sickinger, Ute 87, 229
Signce Design 177, 229
Slawinski, Konstantin 155, 229
Slogdesign 181, 229
Spek Design 53, 229
Stadtnomaden® 81, 229
Steelcase 129, 229
Steelcase Werndl 129, 229
Steng, Andreas 163, 229
→ Steng Licht
Steng Licht 163, 229
Steng, Peter 163, 229
→ Steng Licht
Stotz-Design.com 57, 229
Strobel, Henning 217, 229
Studio 7.5 131, 229
SVG Medizinsysteme 55, 229
Synapsis Design 33, 51, 230
Szpryngwald, Piotr 219, 230

T
Takada, Tomoyuki 85, 231
→ Windmühlenmesser
Teherani, Hadi 137, 230
TOKII 179, 230
Tools Design 91, 147, 157, 230
Tupperware Belgium 89, 230
Tupperware Deutschland 89, 230
Tupperware Worldwide Design & Engineering Team 89, 230

U
United Navigation 45, 230

V
Vaude 175, 183, 230
Viessmann 191, 230
Vistapark 65, 230
Volkswagen 205, 230
Volkswagen Design 149, 205, 230
Vorwerk 137, 231
Vottelerdesign 127, 231
Votteler, Matthias 127, 231
→ Vottelerdesign

W
Wagner, Roland 119, 231
→ Wagner System
Wagner System 119, 231
Webermann, Ralf 155, 225
→ Ding 3000
Weskott, Christina 59, 231
White-ID 179, 231
Windmühlenmesser Robert Herder 85, 231
Wirsing, Michael 135, 227
→ Leuwico
WK Wohnen 107, 231
WMF 177, 231
Wolf-Garten 169, 227
→ MTD Products

Y
yellow design / yellow circle 45, 231
You, Zhenwei 221, 231

X
Xutao 167, 231
→ Zweibrüder

Z
Zeiss NTS 29, 231
Ziegler, Philipp 175, 230
→ Vaude
Zweibrüder 167, 231

**Fotonachweis
Photographs
(acknowledgements)**

soweit von den
Einreichern erwünscht

information provided by
competitors only:

Seite / Page 15
Michael Müller-Münker, Köln

Seite / Page 19
Mathias Ritzmann, Burg Halle

Seite / Page 124, 125
Udo Schönwald, Gersthofen

Seite / Page 198
Brigida González, Stuttgart

**Zäsurseiten der Goldpreisträger /
Pages preceding the Focus in Gold
award-winners**
Tom Philippi
Er lebt und arbeitet als freischaffender
Fotograf in Stuttgart.
www.tomphilippi.com

Tom Philippi
He lives and works as a freelance
photographer in Stuttgart.
www.tomphilippi.com

Umschlag / Cover
Robert Westrich
Er lebt und arbeitet als freischaffender
Fotograf in Stuttgart.
www.robertwestrich.com

Robert Westrich
He lives and works as a freelance
photographer in Stuttgart.
www.robertwestrich.com

Impressum
Publishing details

Internationaler
Designpreis
Baden-Württemberg
und
Mia Seeger Preis
2010

Baden-Württemberg
International
Design Award
and
Mia Seeger Prize
2010

Herausgeber / Editor
Design Center Stuttgart
Regierungspräsidium Stuttgart
Willi-Bleicher-Straße 19
D-70174 Stuttgart
Tel. +49 7 11 1 23 26 84
design@rps.bwl.de
www.design-center.de

Text und Redaktion /
Text and editorial supervision
Andrea Scholtz M.A.
büro wortgewandt, Stuttgart
www.wortgewandt.net

Übersetzung / Translation
Philip Mann, Marbach

Grafikdesign / Graphic design
stapelberg&fritz, Stuttgart
Roman Heinrich
www.stapelbergundfritz.com

Lithografie / Lithography
ctrl-s prepress GmbH, Stuttgart

Druck / Printing
Leibfarth + Schwarz GmbH + Co. KG
Dettingen / Erms
www.leibfarth-schwarz.de

Produktion / Production
Meike Pätzold, Stuttgart
www.grafikgilde.com

Papier / Paper
Juwel Offset,
PEFC zertifiziert / PEFC certified

Verlag und Vertrieb /
Publishing and distribution
avedition GmbH
Königsallee 57
D-71638 Ludwigsburg
T +49 71 41 1 47 73 91
kontakt@avedition.de
www.avedition.de

© 2010
avedition GmbH, Ludwigsburg, Design Center
Stuttgart und die Autoren / and the authors

Alle Rechte vorbehalten.
All rights reserved.

ISBN
978-3-89986-142-6

Printed in Germany

Die Publikation erscheint anlässlich
der Ausstellung
Focus Open 2010
Internationaler Designpreis
Baden-Württemberg
und Mia Seeger Preis 2010

16. Oktober bis 28. November 2010

This catalogue is published to accompany
the exhibition
Focus Open 2010
Baden-Württemberg
International Design Award
and Mia Seeger Prize 2010

16 October to 28 November 2010

Veranstalter
Design Center
Regierungsp
Willi-Bleiche
D-70174 Stu
Tel. +49 7 11

Projektleitu
Hildegard Hi

Organisatio
Michael Kerr

Ausstellung
Sandy Tsiris,
Stuttgart
www.sitibi.d

Inszenierun
Production
pulsmacher,
www.pulsma